Thank you
God Bless you in
All you do.

Fredy 2013

YEAR OF
PROMISE

Year of Promise

Rudolph Moseley Jr.

To order additional copies of this book, contact:
Xlibris Corporation
1-888-795-4274
www.Xlibris.com
Orders@Xlibris.com
89051

This book is dedicated to my wife Latoya and to our three sons Jaden, Jalen, and Jace. You all have been the fullfilment of God's precious promises to me. I love you.

CONTENTS

Introduction

Jeremiah 29:11

New International Version (NIV)

11 For I know the plans I have for you," declares the LORD, "plans to prosper you and not to harm you, plans to give you hope and a future.

You were born to be blessed. The blessings of the Lord are found in the house of the Living God. The scriptures are clear that all of God's many promises are YES and AMEN in Christ Jesus **2 Corinthians 1:20.** What that means is that God's promises never change and because He is the same yesterday today and forever we can stand today on these same promises. God has been making and keeping his promises to mankind from the very beginning. The key to your breakthrough and living a life of peace is to know what God says about you and the promises He has made to you. The Bible says consequently, your faith grows from hearing the message, and the message is heard through the word of Christ. **Romans 10:17**

The plans and promises of God have been guaranteed by the finished work of Jesus Christ on the Cross of Calvary. My prayer is that as you meditate on these promises during this year and the years to come, that your faith will grow. I pray that you will begin to see yourself the way God sees you. I pray that your perspective on life will change. I pray that you and your family will be blessed. My prayer for you and your family is taken from Deuteronomy 28:

¹ "If you fully obey the LORD your God and carefully keep all his commands that I am giving you today, the LORD your God will set you high above all the nations of the world. ² You will experience all these blessings if you obey the LORD your God:

³ Your towns and your fields will be blessed. ⁴ Your children and your crops will be blessed. The offspring of your herds and flocks will be blessed. ⁵ Your fruit baskets and breadboards will be blessed. ⁶ Wherever you go and whatever you do, you will be blessed.

⁷ "The LORD will conquer your enemies when they attack you. They will attack you from one direction, but they will scatter from you in seven!

⁸ "The LORD will guarantee a blessing on everything you do and will fill your storehouses with grain. The LORD your God will bless you in the land he is giving you.

⁹ "If you obey the commands of the LORD your God and walk in his ways, the LORD will establish you as his holy people as he swore he would do. ¹⁰ Then all the nations of the world will see that you are a people claimed by the LORD, and they will stand in awe of you.

[11] *"The LORD will give you prosperity in the land he swore to your ancestors to give you, blessing you with many children, numerous livestock, and abundant crops. [12] The LORD will send rain at the proper time from his rich treasury in the heavens and will bless all the work you do. You will lend to many nations, but you will never need to borrow from them. [13] If you listen to these commands of the LORD your God that I am giving you today, and if you carefully obey them, the LORD will make you the head and not the tail, and you will always be on top and never at the bottom. [14] You must not turn away from any of the commands I am giving you today, nor follow after other gods and worship them.* **Deuteronomy 28: 8-14 (NLT).***

Be blessed and receive the promises of God!!!!!!!!

God promises to love you with an unfailing love.

Psalm 145:8

New International Version

[8] The LORD is gracious and compassionate,
    slow to anger and rich in love.

New American Standard Bible

[8] The LORD is gracious and merciful;
    Slow to anger and great in lovingkindness.

The Message

[8] God is all mercy and grace—
    not quick to anger, is rich in love.

Amplified Bible

[8] The Lord is gracious and full of compassion,
slow to anger and abounding in mercy and
loving-kindness.

New Living Translation

[8] The Lord is merciful and compassionate,
    slow to get angry and filled with unfailing
    love.

Contemporary English Version

[8] You are merciful, LORD! You are kind and
patient and always loving.

New King James Version

[8] The LORD is gracious and full of
    compassion,
    Slow to anger and great in mercy.

Reflection

God promises to save your soul.

John 3:16

New International Version

[16] "For God so loved the world that he gave his one and only Son, that whoever believes in him shall not perish but have eternal life.

New American Standard Bible

[16] "For God so loved the world, that He gave His only begotten Son, that whoever believes in Him shall not perish, but have eternal life.

The Message

[16] This is how much God loved the world: He gave his Son, his one and only Son. And this is why: so that no one need be destroyed; by believing in him, anyone can have a whole and lasting life.

Amplified Bible

[16] For God so greatly loved and dearly prized the world that He [even] gave up His only begotten (unique) Son, so that whoever believes in (trusts in, clings to, relies on) Him shall not perish (come to destruction, be lost) but have eternal (everlasting) life.

New Living Translation

[16] "For God loved the world so much that he gave his one and only Son, so that everyone who believes in him will not perish but have eternal life.

Contemporary English Version

[16] God loved the people of this world so much that he gave his only Son, so that everyone who has faith in him will have eternal life and never really die.

New King James Version

[16] For God so loved the world that He gave His only begotten Son, that whoever believes in Him should not perish but have everlasting life.

Reflection

God promises to deliver you in times of trouble.

Psalm 41:1-2

New International Version

[1] Blessed is he who has regard for the weak; the LORD delivers him in times of trouble. [2] The LORD will protect him and preserve his life; he will bless him in the land and not surrender him to the desire of his foes.

New American Standard Bible

[1]How blessed is he who considers the helpless; The LORD will deliver him in a day of trouble. [2]The LORD will protect him and keep him alive, And he shall be called blessed upon the earth; And do not give him over to the desire of his enemies.

The Message

[1-2]Dignify those who are down on their luck; you'll feel good—that's what God does. God looks after us all, makes us robust with life— Lucky to be in the land, we're free from enemy worries.

Amplified Bible

[1]BLESSED (HAPPY, fortunate, to be envied) is he who considers the weak and the poor; the Lord will deliver him in the time of evil and trouble. [2]The Lord will protect him and keep him alive; he shall be called blessed in the land; and You will not deliver him to the will of his enemies.

New Living Translation

[1] Oh, the joys of those who are kind to the poor! The Lord rescues them when they are in trouble. [2] The Lord protects them and keeps them alive. He gives them prosperity in the land and rescues them from their enemies.

Reflection

Contemporary English Version

¹You, LORD God, bless everyone who cares for the poor, and you rescue those people in times of trouble. ²You protect them and keep them alive. You make them happy here in this land, and you don't hand them over to their enemies.

New King James Version

¹ Blessed is he who considers the poor; The LORD will deliver him in time of trouble. ² The LORD will preserve him and keep him alive, And he will be blessed on the earth; You will not deliver him to the will of his enemies.

RUDOLPH MOSELEY JR.

God promises to save your household.

Acts 16:31

New International Version

[31] They replied, "Believe in the Lord Jesus, and you will be saved—you and your household."

New American Standard Bible

[31] They said, "Believe in the Lord Jesus, and you will be saved, you and your household."

The Message

[31] They said, "Put your entire trust in the Master Jesus. Then you'll live as you were meant to live—and everyone in your house included!"

Amplified Bible

[31] And they answered, Believe in the Lord Jesus Christ [give yourself up to Him, take yourself out of your own keeping and entrust yourself into His keeping] and you will be saved, [and this applies both to] you and your household as well.

New Living Translation

[31] They replied, "Believe in the Lord Jesus and you will be saved, along with everyone in your household."

Contemporary English Version

[31] They replied, "Have faith in the Lord Jesus and you will be saved! This is also true for everyone who lives in your home."

New King James Version

[31] So they said, "Believe on the Lord Jesus Christ, and you will be saved, you and your household."

Reflection

God promises to give you long life.

Ephesians 6:1-3

New International Version

¹Children, obey your parents in the Lord, for this is right. ²"Honor your father and mother"—which is the first commandment with a promise—³"that it may go well with you and that you may enjoy long life on the earth."

New American Standard Bible

¹Children, obey your parents in the Lord, for this is right. ²HONOR YOUR FATHER AND MOTHER (which is the first commandment with a promise), ³SO THAT IT MAY BE WELL WITH YOU, AND THAT YOU MAY LIVE LONG ON THE EARTH.

The Message

¹⁻³ Children, do what your parents tell you. This is only right. "Honor your father and mother" is the first commandment that has a promise attached to it, namely, "so you will live well and have a long life."

Amplified Bible

¹CHILDREN, OBEY your parents in the Lord [as His representatives], for this is just and right. ²Honor (esteem and value as precious) your father and your mother—this is the first commandment with a promise—³That all may be well with you and that you may live long on the earth.

New Living Translation

¹ Children, obey your parents because you belong to the Lord, for this is the right thing to do. ² "Honor your father and mother." This is the first commandment with a promise: ³ If you honor your father and mother, "things will go well for you, and you will have a long life on the earth."

Reflection

Contemporary English Version

[1]Children, you belong to the Lord, and you do the right thing when you obey your parents. The first commandment with a promise says, [2]"Obey your father and your mother, [3]and you will have a long and happy life."

New King James Version

[1] Children, obey your parents in the Lord, for this is right. [2] "Honor your father and mother," which is the first commandment with promise: [3] "that it may be well with you and you may live long on the earth."

God promises to be with us during times of trouble.

Psalm 46:1-3

New International Version

¹ God is our refuge and strength, an ever-present help in trouble. ² Therefore we will not fear, though the earth give way and the mountains fall into the heart of the sea, ³ though its waters roar and foam and the mountains quake with their surging. Selah

New American Standard Bible

¹God is our refuge and strength, A very present help in trouble. ²Therefore we will not fear, though the earth should change And though the mountains slip into the heart of the sea; ³Though its waters roar and foam, Though the mountains quake at its swelling pride. Selah.

The Message

¹⁻³ God is a safe place to hide, ready to help when we need him. We stand fearless at the cliff-edge of doom, courageous in sea storm and earthquake, before the rush and roar of oceans, the tremors that shift mountains.

Amplified Bible

¹GOD IS our Refuge and Strength [mighty and impenetrable to temptation], a very present and well-proved help in trouble. ²Therefore we will not fear, though the earth should change and though the mountains be shaken into the midst of the seas, ³Though its waters roar and foam, though the mountains tremble at its swelling and tumult. Selah [pause, and calmly think of that]!

New Living Translation

¹ God is our refuge and strength, always ready to help in times of trouble. ² So we will not fear when earthquakes come and the mountains crumble into the sea. ³ Let the oceans roar and foam. Let the mountains tremble as the waters surge!

Reflection

Contemporary English Version

¹God is our mighty fortress, always ready to help in times of trouble. ²And so, we won't be afraid! Let the earth tremble and the mountains tumble into the deepest sea. ³Let the ocean roar and foam, and its raging waves shake the mountains.

(New King James Version)

¹ God is our refuge and strength, A very present help in trouble. ² Therefore we will not fear, Even though the earth be removed, And though the mountains be carried into the midst of the sea; ³ Though its waters roar and be trouble, Though the mountains shake with its swelling. Selah

God promises show His goodness to those who wait for Him.

Psalm 27:14

New International Version

14 Wait for the LORD; be strong and take heart and wait for the LORD.

New American Standard Bible

14 Wait for the LORD; Be strong and let your heart take courage; Yes, wait for the LORD.

The Message

13-14 I'm sure now I'll see God's goodness in the exuberant earth. Stay with God! Take heart. Don't quit. I'll say it again: Stay with God.

Amplified Bible

14 Wait and hope for and expect the Lord; be brave and of good courage and let your heart be stout and enduring. Yes, wait for and hope for and expect the Lord.

New Living Translation

14 Wait patiently for the Lord. Be brave and courageous. Yes, wait patiently for the Lord.

(Contemporary English Version)

14 Trust the LORD! Be brave and strong and trust the LORD.

(New King James Version)

14 Wait on the LORD; Be of good courage,
    And He shall strengthen your heart; Wait,
    I say, on the LORD!

Reflection

God promises to comfort, correct and protect you.

Psalm 23:4

New International Version

⁴ Even though I walk through the valley of the shadow of death, I will fear no evil, for you are with me; your rod and your staff, they comfort me.

New American Standard Bible

⁴ Even though I walk through the valley of the shadow of death, I fear no evil, for You are with me; Your rod and Your staff, they comfort me.

The Message

⁴ Even when the way goes through Death Valley, I'm not afraid when you walk at my side. Your trusty shepherd's crook makes me feel secure.

Amplified Bible

⁴Yes, though I walk through the [deep, sunless] valley of the shadow of death, I will fear or dread no evil, for You are with me; Your rod [to protect] and Your staff [to guide], they comfort me.

New Living Translation

⁴ Even when I walk through the darkest valley, I will not be afraid, for you are close beside me. Your rod and your staff protect and comfort me.

(Contemporary English Version)

⁴ I may walk through valleys as dark as death, but I won't be afraid. You are with me, and your shepherd's rod makes me feel safe.

(New King James Version)

⁴ Yea, though I walk through the valley of the shadow of death, I will fear no evil; For You are with me; Your rod and Your staff, they comfort me.

Reflection

God promises that no weapon formed against you will prevail.

Isaiah 54:17

New International Version

[17] no weapon forged against you will prevail, and you will refute every tongue that accuses you. This is the heritage of the servants of the LORD, and this is their vindication from me," declares the LORD.

New American Standard Bible

[17]"No weapon that is formed against you will prosper; And every tongue that accuses you in judgment you will condemn This is the heritage of the servants of the LORD, And their vindication is from Me," declares the LORD.

The Message

But no weapon that can hurt you has ever been forged. Any accuser who takes you to court will be dismissed as a liar. This is what God's servants can expect. I'll see to it that everything works out for the best." God's Decree.

Amplified Bible

[17]But no weapon that is formed against you shall prosper, and every tongue that shall rise against you in judgment you shall show to be in the wrong. This [peace, righteousness, security, triumph over opposition] is the heritage of the servants of the Lord [those in whom the ideal Servant of the Lord is reproduced]; this is the righteousness or the vindication which they obtain from Me [this is that which I impart to them as their justification], says the Lord.

Reflection

New Living Translation

[17] But in that coming day no weapon turned against you will succeed. You will silence every voice raised up to accuse you. These benefits are enjoyed by the servants of the Lord; their vindication will come from me. I, the Lord, have spoken!

(Contemporary English Version)

[17]Weapons made to attack you won't be successful; words spoken against you won't hurt at all. My servants, Jerusalem is yours! I, the LORD, promise to bless you with victory.

New King James Version

[17] No weapon formed against you shall prosper, And every tongue which rises against you in judgment You shall condemn. This is the heritage of the servants of the LORD, And their righteousness is from Me," Says the LORD.

God promises everlasting life to those who believe the Truth.

John 6:47

New International Version

⁴⁷I tell you the truth, he who believes has everlasting life.

New American Standard Bible

⁴⁷"Truly, truly, I say to you, he who believes has eternal life.

The Message

⁴⁷"I'm telling you the most solemn and sober truth now: Whoever believes in me has real life, eternal life.

Amplified Bible

⁴⁷I assure you, most solemnly I tell you, he who believes in Me [who adheres to, trusts in, relies on, and has faith in Me] has (now possesses) eternal life.

New Living Translation

⁴⁷ "I tell you the truth, anyone who believes has eternal life

(Contemporary English Version)

⁴⁷I tell you for certain that everyone who has faith in me has eternal life.

(New King James Version)

⁴⁷ Most assuredly, I say to you, he who believes in Me has everlasting life.

Reflection

God promises to reward those who diligently seek Him.

Hebrews 11:6

New International Version

⁶And without faith it is impossible to please God, because anyone who comes to him must believe that he exists and that he rewards those who earnestly seek him.

New American Standard Bible

⁶And without faith it is impossible to please Him, for he who comes to God must believe that He is and that He is a rewarder of those who seek Him.

The Message

⁶ It's impossible to please God apart from faith. And why? Because anyone who wants to approach God must believe both that he exists and that he cares enough to respond to those who seek him.

Amplified Bible

⁶But without faith it is impossible to please and be satisfactory to Him. For whoever would come near to God must [necessarily] believe that God exists and that He is the rewarder of those who earnestly and diligently seek Him [out].

New Living Translation

⁶ And it is impossible to please God without faith. Anyone who wants to come to him must believe that God exists and that he rewards those who sincerely seek him.

Contemporary English Version

⁶But without faith no one can please God. We must believe that God is real and that he rewards everyone who searches for him.

(New King James Version)

⁶ But without faith it is impossible to please Him, for he who comes to God must believe that He is, and that He is a rewarder of those who diligently seek Him.

Reflection

God promises to be faithful from generation to generation.

Deuteronomy 7:9

New International Version

⁹ Know therefore that the LORD your God is God; he is the faithful God, keeping his covenant of love to a thousand generations of those who love him and keep his commands.

New American Standard Bible

⁹"Know therefore that the LORD your God, He is God, the faithful God, who keeps His covenant and His lovingkindness to a thousandth generation with those who love Him and keep His commandments;

The Message

Know this: God, your God, is God indeed, a God you can depend upon. He keeps his covenant of loyal love with those who love him and observe his commandments for a thousand generations.

Amplified Bible

⁹Know, recognize, and understand therefore that the Lord your God, He is God, the faithful God, Who keeps covenant and steadfast love and mercy with those who love Him and keep His commandments, to a thousand generations,

New Living Translation

⁹ Understand, therefore, that the Lord your God is indeed God. He is the faithful God who keeps his covenant for a thousand generations and lavishes his unfailing love on those who love him and obey his commands.

Contemporary English Version

⁹You know that the LORD your God is the only true God. So love him and obey his commands, and he will faithfully keep his agreement with you and your descendants for a thousand generations.

Reflection

New King James Version

[9] "Therefore know that the LORD your God, He is God, the faithful God who keeps covenant and mercy for a thousand generations with those who love Him and keep His commandments;

God promises to be merciful.

Deuteronomy 4:31

New International Version

[31] For the LORD your God is a merciful God; he will not abandon or destroy you or forget the covenant with your forefathers, which he confirmed to them by oath.

New American Standard Bible

[31] "For the LORD your God is a compassionate God; He will not fail you nor destroy you nor forget the covenant with your fathers which He swore to them

The Message

God, your God, is above all a compassionate God. In the end he will not abandon you, he won't bring you to ruin, he won't forget the covenant with your ancestors which he swore to them.

Amplified Bible

[31] For the Lord your God is a merciful God; He will not fail you or destroy you or forget the covenant of your fathers, which He swore to them.

New Living Translation

[31] For the Lord your God is a merciful God; he will not abandon you or destroy you or forget the solemn covenant he made with your ancestors.

(Contemporary English Version)

[31] The LORD your God will have mercy—he won't destroy you or desert you. The LORD will remember his promise, and he will keep the agreement he made with your ancestors.

(New King James Version)

[31] (for the LORD your God is a merciful God), He will not forsake you nor destroy you, nor forget the covenant of your fathers which He swore to them.

Reflection

God promises to fulfill every one of His promises to you.

Numbers 23:19

New International Version

¹⁹ God is not a man, that he should lie, nor a son of man, that he should change his mind. Does he speak and then not act? Does he promise and not fulfill?

New American Standard Bible

¹⁹"God is not a man, that He should lie, Nor a son of man, that He should repent; Has He said, and will He not do it? Or has He spoken, and will He not make it good?

The Message

God is not man, one given to lies, and not a son of man changing his mind. Does he speak and not do what he says? Does he promise and not come through?

Amplified Bible

¹⁹God is not a man, that He should tell or act a lie, neither the son of man, that He should feel repentance or compunction [for what He has promised]. Has He said and shall He not do it? Or has He spoken and shall He not make it good?

New Living Translation

¹⁹ God is not a man, so he does not lie. He is not human, so he does not change his mind. Has he ever spoken and failed to act? Has he ever promised and not carried it through?

Contemporary English Version

¹⁹God is no mere human! He doesn't tell lies or change his mind.
   God always keeps his promises.

Reflection

New King James Version

[19] "God is not a man, that He should lie,
Nor a son of man, that He should repent.
Has He said, and will He not do?
Or has He spoken, and will He not make it good?

RUDOLPH MOSELEY JR.

God promises to help you.

Isaiah 41:13

New International Version

[13] For I am the LORD, your God,
who takes hold of your right hand
and says to you, Do not fear;
I will help you.

New American Standard Bible

[13]"For I am the LORD your God, who
upholds your right hand,
Who says to you, 'Do not fear, I will help
you.'

The Message

Because I, your God,
have a firm grip on you and I'm not
letting go.
I'm telling you, 'Don't panic.
I'm right here to help you.'

Amplified Bible

[13]For I the Lord your God hold your right
hand; I am the Lord, Who says to you, Fear
not; I will help you!

New Living Translation

[13] For I hold you by your right hand—
I, the Lord your God.
And I say to you,
'Don't be afraid. I am here to help you.

(Contemporary English Version)

[13]I am the LORD your God. I am holding
your hand, so don't be afraid. I am here to help
you.

(New King James Version)

[13] For I, the LORD your God, will hold your right hand,
Saying to you, 'Fear not, I will help you.'

Reflection

God promises that His people will never be put to shame.

Joel 2:26

New International Version

²⁶ You will have plenty to eat, until you are full,
and you will praise the name of the LORD your God,
who has worked wonders for you;
never again will my people be shamed.

New American Standard Bible

²⁶"You will have plenty to eat and be satisfied
And praise the name of the LORD your God,
Who has dealt wondrously with you;
Then My people will never be put to shame.

The Message

You'll eat your fill of good food.
You'll be full of praises to your God,
The God who has set you back on your heels in wonder.
Never again will my people be despised.

Amplified Bible

²⁶And you shall eat in plenty and be satisfied and praise the name of the Lord, your God, Who has dealt wondrously with you. And My people shall never be put to shame.

New Living Translation

²⁶ Once again you will have all the food you want,
and you will praise the Lord your God,
who does these miracles for you.
Never again will my people be disgraced.

(Contemporary English Version)

²⁶My people, you will eat until you are satisfied. Then you will praise me for the wonderful things I have done. Never again will you be put to shame.

Reflection

(New King James Version)

[26] You shall eat in plenty and be satisfied,
And praise the name of the LORD your God,
Who has dealt wondrously with you;
And My people shall never be put to shame.

God promises to forgive us after we have forgiven others.

Mark 11:25-26

New International Version

25And when you stand praying, if you hold anything against anyone, forgive him, so that your Father in heaven may forgive you your sins."

New American Standard Bible

25"Whenever you stand praying, forgive, if you have anything against anyone, so that your Father who is in heaven will also forgive you your transgressions. 26["But if you do not forgive, neither will your Father who is in heaven forgive your transgressions."]

The Message

And when you assume the posture of prayer, remember that it's not all asking. If you have anything against someone, forgive—only then will your heavenly Father be inclined to also wipe your slate clean of sins."

Amplified Bible

25And whenever you stand praying, if you have anything against anyone, forgive him and let it drop (leave it, let it go), in order that your Father Who is in heaven may also forgive you your [own] failings and shortcomings and let them drop. 26But if you do not forgive, neither will your Father in heaven forgive your failings and shortcomings.

New Living Translation

25 But when you are praying, first forgive anyone you are holding a grudge against, so that your Father in heaven will forgive your sins, too."

Contemporary English Version

25-26Whenever you stand up to pray, you must forgive what others have done to you. Then your Father in heaven will forgive your sins.

Reflection

(New King James Version)

[25] "And whenever you stand praying, if you have anything against anyone, forgive him, that your Father in heaven may also forgive you your trespasses. [26] But if you do not forgive, neither will your Father in heaven forgive your trespasses."

God promises that you will bear fruit.

John 15:5

New International Version

⁵"I am the vine; you are the branches. If a man remains in me and I in him, he will bear much fruit; apart from me you can do nothing.

New American Standard Bible

⁵"I am the vine, you are the branches; he who abides in Me and I in him, he bears much fruit, for apart from Me you can do nothing.

The Message

⁵⁻⁸"I am the Vine, you are the branches. When you're joined with me and I with you, the relation intimate and organic, the harvest is sure to be abundant. Separated, you can't produce a thing.

Amplified Bible

⁵I am the Vine; you are the branches. Whoever lives in Me and I in him bears much (abundant) fruit. However, apart from Me [cut off from vital union with Me] you can do nothing.

New Living Translation

⁵ "Yes, I am the vine; you are the branches. Those who remain in me, and I in them, will produce much fruit. For apart from me you can do nothing.

(Contemporary English Version)

⁵I am the vine, and you are the branches. If you stay joined to me, and I stay joined to you, then you will produce lots of fruit. But you cannot do anything without me.

(New King James Version)

⁵ "I am the vine, you are the branches. He who abides in Me, and I in him, bears much fruit; for without Me you can do nothing.

Reflection

God promises that His love will endure forever.

Psalm 138:8

New International Version

[8] The LORD will fulfill his purpose for me;
    your love, O LORD, endures forever—
    do not abandon the works of your hands.

New American Standard Bible

[8]The LORD will accomplish what concerns
    me;
    Your lovingkindness, O LORD, is
    everlasting;
    Do not forsake the ⸢works of Your hands.

The Message

Finish what you started in me, God.
    Your love is eternal—don't quit on me
now.

Amplified Bible

[8]The Lord will perfect that which concerns
me; Your mercy and loving-kindness, O Lord,
endure forever—forsake not the works of Your
own hands.

New Living Translation

[8] The Lord will work out his plans for my
    life—
    for your faithful love, O Lord, endures
    forever.
    Don't abandon me, for you made me.

(Contemporary English Version)

[8]You, LORD, will always treat me with
kindness. Your love never fails. You have made
us what we are. Don't give up on us now!

New King James Version

[8] The LORD will perfect that which concerns me;
    Your mercy, O LORD, endures forever;
    Do not forsake the works of Your hands.

Reflection

God promises to lead and to guide you.

Isaiah 30:21

New International Version

²¹ Whether you turn to the right or to the left, your ears will hear a voice behind you, saying, "This is the way; walk in it."

New American Standard Bible

²¹Your ears will hear a word behind you, "This is the way, walk in it," whenever you turn to the right or to the left

The Message

The moment he hears, he'll answer. Just as the Master kept you alive during the hard times, he'll keep your teacher alive and present among you. Your teacher will be right there, local and on the job, urging you on whenever you wander left or right: "This is the right road. Walk down this road."

Amplified Bible

²¹ And your ears will hear a word behind you, saying, This is the way; walk in it, when you turn to the right hand and when you turn to the left.

New Living Translation

²¹ Your own ears will hear him.
Right behind you a voice will say,
"This is the way you should go,"
whether to the right or to the left.

Contemporary English Version

²¹Whether you turn to the right or to the left, you will hear a voice saying, "This is the road! Now follow it."

New King James Version

²¹ Your ears shall hear a word behind you, saying,
"This is the way, walk in it,"
Whenever you turn to the right hand
Or whenever you turn to the left.

Reflection

God promises to forgive us of our sins.

1 John 1:9

New International Version

⁹If we confess our sins, he is faithful and just and will forgive us our sins and purify us from all unrighteousness.

New American Standard Bible

⁹If we confess our sins, He is faithful and righteous to forgive us our sins and to cleanse us from all unrighteousness

The Message

⁸⁻¹⁰If we claim that we're free of sin, we're only fooling ourselves. A claim like that is errant nonsense. On the other hand, if we admit our sins—make a clean breast of them—he won't let us down; he'll be true to himself. He'll forgive our sins and purge us of all wrongdoing. If we claim that we've never sinned, we out-and-out contradict God—make a liar out of him. A claim like that only shows off our ignorance of God.

Amplified Bible

⁹If we [freely] admit that we have sinned and confess our sins, He is faithful and just (true to His own nature and promises) and will forgive our sins [dismiss our lawlessness] and [continuously] cleanse us from all unrighteousness [everything not in conformity to His will in purpose, thought, and action].

New Living Translation

⁹ But if we confess our sins to him, he is faithful and just to forgive us our sins and to cleanse us from all wickedness.

Reflection

(Contemporary English Version)

[9]But if we confess our sins to God, he can always be trusted to forgive us and take our sins away.

(New King James Version)

[9] If we confess our sins, He is faithful and just to forgive us our sins and to cleanse us from all unrighteousness.

God promises to never to remember our sin.

Isaiah 43:25

New International Version)

25 "I, even I, am he who blots out your transgressions, for my own sake, and remembers your sins no more.

New American Standard Bible

25"I, even I, am the one who wipes out your transgressions for My own sake, And I will not remember your sins.

The Message

25"But I, yes I, am the one
    who takes care of your sins—that's what I do.
    I don't keep a list of your sins.

Amplified Bible

25I, even I, am He Who blots out and cancels your transgressions, for My own sake, and I will not remember your sins.

New Living Translation

25 "I—yes, I alone—will blot out your sins for
    my own sake
    and will never think of them again.

(Contemporary English Version)

25But I wipe away your sins because of who I am.
    And so, I will forget the wrongs you have done.

(New King James Version)

25 "I, even I, am He who blots out your transgressions for My own sake; And I will not remember your sins.

Reflection

God promises to keep us safe when we run to Him.

Psalm 37:39

New International Version

[39] The salvation of the righteous comes from
   the LORD;
      he is their stronghold in time of trouble.

New American Standard Bible

[39]But the salvation of the righteous is from the
   LORD;
      He is their strength in time of trouble.

The Message

[39-40] The spacious, free life is from God,
      it's also protected and safe.
God-strengthened, we're delivered from evil—
      when we run to him, he saves us.

Amplified Bible

[39]But the salvation of the [consistently]
righteous is of the Lord; He is their Refuge and
secure Stronghold in the time of trouble.

New Living Translation

[39] The Lord rescues the godly;
      he is their fortress in times of trouble.

Contemporary English Version

[39]The LORD protects his people, and they
      can come to him
      in times of trouble.

(New King James Version)

[39] But the salvation of the righteous is from
   the LORD;
      He is their strength in the time of
trouble.

Reflection

God promises to raise the heads of the fallen.

Psalm 146:8

New International Version

8 the LORD gives sight to the blind,
the LORD lifts up those who are bowed down,
the LORD loves the righteous.

New American Standard Bible

8The LORD opens the eyes of the blind;
The LORD raises up those who are bowed
down;
The LORD loves the righteous;

The Message

God frees prisoners—
he gives sight to the blind,
he lifts up the fallen.
God loves good people, protects strangers,
takes the side of orphans and widows,
but makes short work of the wicked.

Amplified Bible

8The Lord opens the eyes of the blind, the Lord
lifts up those who are bowed down, the Lord
loves the [uncompromisingly] righteous (those
upright in heart and in right standing with Him).

New Living Translation

8 The Lord opens the eyes of the blind.
The Lord lifts up those who are weighed down.
The Lord loves the godly.

(Contemporary English Version)

8and heals blind eyes. He gives a helping hand
to everyone who falls. The LORD loves good
people

(New King James Version)

8 The LORD opens the eyes of the blind;
The LORD raises those who are bowed down;
The LORD loves the righteous.

Reflection

God promises to make His thoughts known to us.

Proverbs 1:23

New International Version

²³ If you had responded to my rebuke,
  I would have poured out my heart to you
  and made my thoughts known to you.

New American Standard Bible

²³"Turn to my reproof,
  Behold, I will pour out my spirit on you;
  I will make my words known to you.

The Message

²³ About face! I can revise your life.
  Look, I'm ready to pour out my spirit on you;
  I'm ready to tell you all I know.

Amplified Bible

²³If you will turn (repent) and give heed to my reproof, behold, I [Wisdom] will pour out my spirit upon you, I will make my words known to you.

New Living Translation

²³ Come and listen to my counsel.
  I'll share my heart with you
  and make you wise.

(Contemporary English Version)

²³Listen as I correct you and tell you what I think.

New King James Version

²³ Turn at my rebuke;
  Surely I will pour out my spirit on you;
  I will make my words known to you.

Reflection

God promises to lift our spirits when we praise Him.

Psalm 42:11

New International Version

¹¹ Why are you downcast, O my soul?
   Why so disturbed within me?
   Put your hope in God,
   for I will yet praise him,
   my Savior and my God.

New American Standard Bible

¹¹Why are you in despair, O my soul?
   And why have you become disturbed
   within me?
   Hope in God, for I shall yet praise Him,
      The help of my countenance and my
God.

The Message

¹¹ Why are you down in the dumps, dear soul?
Why are you crying the blues? Fix my eyes on
God—soon I'll be praising again. He puts a
smile on my face. He's my God.

Amplified Bible

¹¹Why are you cast down, O my inner self?
And why should you moan over me and be
disquieted within me? Hope in God and wait
expectantly for Him, for I shall yet praise Him,
Who is the help of my countenance, and my
God.

New Living Translation

¹¹ Why am I discouraged? Why is my heart so
sad? I will put my hope in God! I will praise
him again— my Savior and my God!

(Contemporary English Version)

¹¹Why am I discouraged? Why am I restless? I trust you! And I will praise you again
because you help me, and you are my God.

Reflection

New King James Version

[11] Why are you cast down, O my soul?
   And why are you disquieted within me?
   Hope in God;
   For I shall yet praise Him,
    The help of my countenance and my God.

RUDOLPH MOSELEY JR.

God promises deliverance to those who put their hope in Him.

Psalm 31:24

New International Version

²⁴ Be strong and take heart,
all you who hope in the LORD.

New American Standard Bible

²⁴Be strong and let your heart take courage,
All you who hope in the LORD.

The Message

²⁴ Be brave. Be strong. Don't give up.
Expect God to get here soon.

Amplified Bible

²⁴Be strong and let your heart take courage, all
you who wait for and hope for and expect the
Lord!

New Living Translation

²⁴ So be strong and courageous,
all you who put your hope in the Lord!

Contemporary English Version

²⁴All who trust the LORD,
be cheerful and strong.

New King James Version

²⁴ Be of good courage,
And He shall strengthen your heart,
All you who hope in the LORD.

Reflection

God promises to give wisdom.

Proverbs 15:33

New International Version

[33] The fear of the LORD teaches a man
wisdom,
    and humility comes before honor.

New American Standard Bible

[33]The fear of the LORD is the instruction for
wisdom,
    And before honor comes humility.

The Message

[33] Fear-of-God is a school in skilled living—
    first you learn humility, then you
experience glory.

Amplified Bible

[33]The reverent and worshipful fear of the Lord
brings instruction in Wisdom, and humility
comes before honor.

New Living Translation

[33] Fear of the Lord teaches wisdom;
    humility precedes honor.

(Contemporary English Version)

[33]Showing respect to the LORD will make
    you wise,
    and being humble will bring honor to you.

(New King James Version)

[33] The fear of the LORD is the instruction of
wisdom,
    And before honor is humility.

Reflection

God promises joy for those who weep.

Psalm 126:5-6

New International Version

[5] Those who sow in tears will reap with songs of joy. [6] He who goes out weeping, carrying seed to sow, will return with songs of joy, carrying sheaves with him.

New American Standard Bible

[5] Those who sow in tears shall reap with joyful shouting. [6] He who goes to and fro weeping, carrying his bag of seed, Shall indeed come again with a shout of joy, bringing his sheaves with him.

The Message

So those who planted their crops in despair will shout hurrahs at the harvest, So those who went off with heavy hearts will come home laughing, with armloads of blessing.

Amplified Bible

[5] They who sow in tears shall reap in joy and singing. [6] He who goes forth bearing seed and weeping [at needing his precious supply of grain for sowing] shall doubtless come again with rejoicing, bringing his sheaves with him.

New Living Translation

[5] Those who plant in tears will harvest with shouts of joy. [6] They weep as they go to plant their seed, but they sing as they return with the harvest.

(Contemporary English Version)

[5] We cried as we went out to plant our seeds. Now let us celebrate as we bring in the crops.
[6] We cried on the way to plant our seeds, but we will celebrate and shout as we bring in the crops.

Reflection

(New King James Version)

[5] Those who sow in tears Shall reap in joy.[6] He who continually goes forth weeping, Bearing seed for sowing, Shall doubtless come again with rejoicing, Bringing his sheaves with him.

God promises joy for obedience.

John 15:10-11

New International Version

[10]If you obey my commands, you will remain in my love, just as I have obeyed my Father's commands and remain in his love. [11]I have told you this so that my joy may be in you and that your joy may be complete.

New American Standard Bible

[10]"If you keep My commandments, you will abide in My love; just as I have kept My Father's commandments and abide in His love. [11]"These things I have spoken to you so that My joy may be in you, and that your joy may be made full.

The Message

If you keep my commands, you'll remain intimately at home in my love. That's what I've done—kept my Father's commands and made myself at home in his love. [11-15]"I've told you these things for a purpose: that my joy might be your joy, and your joy wholly mature. This is my command: Love one another the way I loved you.

Amplified Bible

[10]If you keep My commandments [if you continue to obey My instructions], you will abide in My love and live on in it, just as I have obeyed My Father's commandments and live on in His love. [11]I have told you these things, that My joy and delight may be in you, and that your joy and gladness may be of full measure and complete and overflowing.

New Living Translation

[10] When you obey my commandments, you remain in my love, just as I obey my Father's commandments and remain in his love. [11] I have told you these things so that you will be filled with my joy. Yes, your joy will overflow!

Reflection

Contemporary English Version

[10]If you obey me, I will keep loving you, just as my Father keeps loving me, because I have obeyed him. [11]I have told you this to make you as completely happy as I am.

(New King James Version)

[10] If you keep My commandments, you will abide in My love, just as I have kept My Father's commandments and abide in His love. [11] "These things I have spoken to you, that My joy may remain in you, and that your joy may be full.

God promises prosperity and long life.

Proverbs 3:1-2

New International Version

¹ My son, do not forget my teaching,
    but keep my commands in your heart,
² for they will prolong your life many years
    and bring you prosperity.

New American Standard Bible

¹My son, do not forget my teaching,
    But let your heart keep my
    commandments;
²For length of days and years of life
    And peace they will add to you.

The Message

¹⁻² Good friend, don't forget all I've taught you;
take to heart my commands. They'll help you
live a long, long time, a long life lived full and
well.

Amplified Bible

¹MY SON, forget not my law or teaching, but
let your heart keep my commandments; ²For
length of days and years of a life [worth living]
and tranquility [inward and outward and
continuing through old age till death], these
shall they add to you.

New Living Translation

¹ My child, never forget the things I have taught
you. Store my commands in your heart. ² If
you do this, you will live many years, and your
life will be satisfying.

(Contemporary English Version)

¹My child, remember my teachings and
instructions and obey them completely. ²They will help you live a long and
prosperous life.

Reflection

New King James Version

[1] My son, do not forget my law, But let your heart keep my commands;
[2] For length of days and long life
And peace they will add to you.

RUDOLPH MOSELEY JR.

God promises to save all who believe in Him.

John 3:16

New International Version

16"For God so loved the world that he gave his one and only Son, that whoever believes in him shall not perish but have eternal life.

New American Standard Bible

16"For God so loved the world, that He gave His only begotten Son, that whoever believes in Him shall not perish, but have eternal life.

The Message

16"This is how much God loved the world: He gave his Son, his one and only Son. And this is why: so that no one need be destroyed; by believing in him, anyone can have a whole and lasting life

Amplified Bible

16For God so greatly loved and dearly prized the world that He [even] gave up His only begotten ([a]unique) Son, so that whoever believes in (trusts in, clings to, relies on) Him shall not perish (come to destruction, be lost) but have eternal (everlasting) life.

New Living Translation

16 "For God loved the world so much that he gave his one and only Son, so that everyone who believes in him will not perish but have eternal life.

(Contemporary English Version)

16God loved the people of this world so much that he gave his only Son, so that everyone who has faith in him will have eternal life and never really die.

Reflection

(New King James Version)

16 For God so loved the world that He gave His only begotten Son, that whoever believes in Him should not perish but have everlasting life.

God promises to open the eyes of the blind.

Psalm 146:8

New International Version

8 the LORD gives sight to the blind,
  the LORD lifts up those who are bowed
  down,
    the LORD loves the righteous

New American Standard Bible

8The LORD opens the eyes of the blind;
  The LORD raises up those who are bowed
  down;
    The LORD loves the righteous;

The Message

God frees prisoners he gives sight to the blind,
  he lifts up the fallen.
    God loves good people,

Amplified Bible

8The Lord opens the eyes of the blind, the
Lord lifts up those who are bowed down, the
Lord loves the [uncompromisingly] righteous
(those upright in heart and in right standing
with Him).

New Living Translation

8 The Lord opens the eyes of the blind.
The Lord lifts up those who are weighed
    down.
The Lord loves the godly.

Contemporary English Version

8and heals blind eyes. He gives a helping hand
to everyone who falls. The LORD loves good
people

(New King James Version)

8 The LORD opens the eyes of the blind;
  The LORD raises those who are bowed down;
    The LORD loves the righteous.

Reflection

God promises to bless those satisfied with life.

Matthew 5:5

New International Version

⁵Blessed are the meek,
for they will inherit the earth.

New American Standard Bible

⁵"Blessed are the gentle,
for they shall inherit the earth.

The Message

⁵"You're blessed when you're content with just who you are—no more, no less. That's the moment you find yourselves proud owners of everything that can't be bought.

Amplified Bible

⁵Blessed (happy, blithesome, joyous, spiritually prosperous—with life-joy and satisfaction in God's favor and salvation, regardless of their outward conditions) are the meek (the mild, patient, long-suffering), for they shall inherit the earth!

New Living Translation

⁵ God blesses those who are humble,
for they will inherit the whole earth.

Contemporary English Version

⁵God blesses those people
who are humble.
The earth will belong
to them!

(New King James Version)

⁵ Blessed are the meek,
For they shall inherit the earth.

Reflection

God promises to give you the ability to create wealth.

Deuteronomy 8:18

New International Version

[18] But remember the LORD your God, for it is he who gives you the ability to produce wealth, and so confirms his covenant, which he swore to your forefathers, as it is today.

New American Standard Bible

[18]"But you shall remember the LORD your God, for it is He who is giving you power to make wealth, that He may confirm His covenant which He swore to your fathers, as it is this day.

The Message

Remember that God, your God, gave you the strength to produce all this wealth so as to confirm the covenant that he promised to your ancestors—as it is today.

Amplified Bible

[18]But you shall [earnestly] remember the Lord your God, for it is He Who gives you power to get wealth, that He may establish His covenant which He swore to your fathers, as it is this day.

New Living Translation

[18] Remember the Lord your God. He is the one who gives you power to be successful, in order to fulfill the covenant he confirmed to your ancestors with an oath.

(Contemporary English Version)

[18]Instead, remember that the LORD your God gives you the strength to make a living. That's how he keeps the promise he made to your ancestors.

(New King James Version)

[18] "And you shall remember the LORD your God, for it is He who gives you power to get wealth, that He may establish His covenant which He swore to your fathers, as it is this day.

Reflection

God promises to bless those who follow His ways.

Deuteronomy 6:18

New International Version

[18] Do what is right and good in the LORD's sight, so that it may go well with you and you may go in and take over the good land that the LORD promised on oath to your forefathers,

New American Standard Bible

[18]"You shall do what is right and good in the sight of the LORD, that it may be well with you and that you may go in and possess the good land which the LORD swore to give your fathers,

The Message

Carefully keep the commands of God, your God, all the requirements and regulations he gave you. Do what is right; do what is good in God's sight so you'll live a good life and be able to march in and take this pleasant land that God so solemnly promised through your ancestors,

Amplified Bible

[18]And you shall do what is right and good in the sight of the Lord, that it may go well with you and that you may go in and possess the good land which the Lord swore to give to your fathers,

New Living Translation

[18] Do what is right and good in the Lord's sight, so all will go well with you. Then you will enter and occupy the good land that the Lord swore to give your ancestors.

(Contemporary English Version)

[18-19]and live in a way that pleases him. Then you will be able to go in and take this good land from your enemies, just as he promised your ancestors.

Reflection

(New King James Version)

18 And you shall do what is right and good in the sight of the LORD, that it may be well with you, and that you may go in and possess the good land of which the LORD swore to your fathers,

---

God promises to bless those who are faithful.

Galatians 6:9

New International Version

⁹Let us not become weary in doing good, for at the proper time we will reap a harvest if we do not give up.

New American Standard Bible

⁹Let us not lose heart in doing good, for in due time we will reap if we do not grow weary

The Message

⁹⁻¹⁰So let's not allow ourselves to get fatigued doing good. At the right time we will harvest a good crop if we don't give up, or quit. Right now, therefore, every time we get the chance, let us work for the benefit of all, starting with the people closest to us in the community of faith.

Amplified Bible

⁹And let us not lose heart and grow weary and faint in acting nobly and doing right, for in due time and at the appointed season we shall reap, if we do not loosen and relax our courage and faint.

New Living Translation

⁹ So let's not get tired of doing what is good. At just the right time we will reap a harvest of blessing if we don't give up.

(Contemporary English Version)

⁹Don't get tired of helping others. You will be rewarded when the time is right, if you don't give up.

(New King James Version)

⁹ And let us not grow weary while doing good, for in due season we shall reap if we do not lose heart.

Reflection

God promises to give you peace when you pray.

Philippians 4:6-7

New International Version

Reflection

[6]Do not be anxious about anything, but in everything, by prayer and petition, with thanksgiving, present your requests to God. [7]And the peace of God, which transcends all understanding, will guard your hearts and your minds in Christ Jesus.

New American Standard Bible

[6]Be anxious for nothing, but in everything by prayer and supplication with thanksgiving let your requests be made known to God. [7]And the peace of God, which surpasses all comprehension, will guard your hearts and your minds in Christ Jesus.

The Message

[6-7]Don't fret or worry. Instead of worrying, pray. Let petitions and praises shape your worries into prayers, letting God know your concerns. Before you know it, a sense of God's wholeness, everything coming together for good, will come and settle you down. It's wonderful what happens when Christ displaces worry at the center of your life.

Amplified Bible

[6]Do not fret or have any anxiety about anything, but in every circumstance and in everything, by prayer and petition (definite requests), with thanksgiving, continue to make your wants known to God.

[7]And God's peace [shall be yours, that tranquil state of a soul assured of its salvation through Christ, and so fearing nothing from God and being content with its earthly lot of whatever sort that is, that peace] which transcends all understanding shall garrison and mount guard over your hearts and minds in Christ Jesus.

New Living Translation

[6] Don't worry about anything; instead, pray about everything. Tell God what you need, and thank him for all he has done. [7] Then you will experience God's peace, which exceeds anything we can understand. His peace will guard your hearts and minds as you live in Christ Jesus.

(Contemporary English Version)

[6]Don't worry about anything, but pray about everything. With thankful hearts offer up your prayers and requests to God. [7]Then, because you belong to Christ Jesus, God will bless you with peace that no one can completely understand. And this peace will control the way you think and feel.

(New King James Version)

[6] Be anxious for nothing, but in everything by prayer and supplication, with thanksgiving, let your requests be made known to God; [7] and the peace of God, which surpasses all understanding, will guard your hearts and minds through Christ Jesus.

God promises to give answers when we seek Him.

Matthew 7:7-8

New International Version

Ask, Seek, Knock

[7]"Ask and it will be given to you; seek and you will find; knock and the door will be opened to you. [8]For everyone who asks receives; he who seeks finds; and to him who knocks, the door will be opened.

New American Standard Bible

Prayer and the Golden Rule

[7]"Ask, and it will be given to you; seek, and you will find; knock, and it will be opened to you. [8]"For everyone who asks receives, and he who seeks finds, and to him who knocks it will be opened.

The Message

[7-11]"Don't bargain with God. Be direct. Ask for what you need. This isn't a cat-and-mouse, hide-and-seek game we're in. If your child asks for bread, do you trick him with sawdust? If he asks for fish, do you scare him with a live snake on his plate? As bad as you are, you wouldn't think of such a thing. You're at least decent to your own children. So don't you think the God who conceived you in love will be even better?

Amplified Bible

[7]Keep on asking and it will be given you; keep on seeking and you will find; keep on knocking [reverently] and [the door] will be opened to you. [8]For everyone who keeps on asking receives; and he who keeps on seeking finds; and to him who keeps on knocking, [the door] will be opened.

Reflection

New Living Translation

[7] "Keep on asking, and you will receive what you ask for. Keep on seeking, and you will find. Keep on knocking, and the door will be opened to you. [8] For everyone who asks, receives. Everyone who seeks, finds. And to everyone who knocks, the door will be opened.

(Contemporary English Version)

[7] Ask, and you will receive. Search, and you will find. Knock, and the door will be opened for you. [8] Everyone who asks will receive. Everyone who searches will find. And the door will be opened for everyone who knocks.

(New King James Version)

[7] "Ask, and it will be given to you; seek, and you will find; knock, and it will be opened to you. [8] For everyone who asks receives, and he who seeks finds, and to him who knocks it will be opened.

God promises to answer prayer when we have believe Him.

Matthew 21:22

New International Version

²²If you believe, you will receive whatever you ask for in prayer."

New American Standard Bible

²²"And all things you ask in prayer, believing, you will receive."

The Message

²¹⁻²²But Jesus was matter-of-fact: "Yes—and if you embrace this kingdom life and don't doubt God, you'll not only do minor feats like I did to the fig tree, but also triumph over huge obstacles. This mountain, for instance, you'll tell, 'Go jump in the lake,' and it will jump. Absolutely everything, ranging from small to large, as you make it a part of your believing prayer, gets included as you lay hold of God."

Amplified Bible

²²And whatever you ask for in prayer, having faith and [really] believing, you will receive.

New Living Translation

²² You can pray for anything, and if you have faith, you will receive it."

(Contemporary English Version)

²²If you have faith when you pray, you will be given whatever you ask for."

(New King James Version)

²² And whatever things you ask in prayer, believing, you will receive."

Reflection

God promises that His name will bring protection.

Proverbs 18:10

New International Version

[10] The name of the LORD is a strong tower;
the righteous run to it and are safe.

New American Standard Bible

[10]The name of the LORD is a strong tower;
The righteous runs into it and is safe.

The Message

[10] God's name is a place of protection—
good people can run there and be safe.

Amplified Bible

[10]The name of the Lord is a strong tower; the
[consistently] righteous man [upright and in
right standing with God] runs into it and is
safe, high [above evil] and strong.

New Living Translation

[10] The name of the Lord is a strong fortress;
the godly run to him and are safe.

(Contemporary English Version)

[10]The LORD is a mighty tower
where his people can run
for safety—

(New King James Version)

[10] The name of the LORD is a strong tower;
The righteous run to it and are safe.

Reflection

God promises to make you new.

2 Corinthians 5:17

New International Version

¹⁷Therefore, if anyone is in Christ, he is a new creation; the old has gone, the new has come!

New American Standard Bible

¹⁷Therefore if anyone is in Christ, he is a new creature; the old things passed away; behold, new things have come.

The Message

Now we look inside, and what we see is that anyone united with the Messiah gets a fresh start, is created new. The old life is gone; a new life burgeons! Look at it!

Amplified Bible

¹⁷Therefore if any person is [ingrafted] in Christ (the Messiah) he is a new creation (a new creature altogether); the old [previous moral and spiritual condition] has passed away. Behold, the fresh and new has come!

New Living Translation

¹⁷ This means that anyone who belongs to Christ has become a new person. The old life is gone; a new life has begun!

(Contemporary English Version)

¹⁷Anyone who belongs to Christ is a new person. The past is forgotten, and everything is new.

(New King James Version)

¹⁷ Therefore, if anyone is in Christ, he is a new creation; old things have passed away; behold, all things have become new.

Reflection

God promises to restore us when we are truly sorry about sin.

Psalm 34:18

New International Version

[18] The LORD is close to the brokenhearted
and saves those who are crushed in spirit.

New American Standard Bible

[18] The LORD is near to the brokenhearted
And saves those who are crushed in spirit.

The Message

[18] If your heart is broken, you'll find God
right there;
if you're kicked in the gut, he'll help you
catch your breath.

Amplified Bible

[18] The Lord is close to those who are of a
broken heart and saves such as are crushed with
sorrow for sin and are humbly and thoroughly
penitent.

New Living Translation

[18] The Lord is close to the brokenhearted;
he rescues those whose spirits are crushed

Contemporary English Version

[18] The LORD is there to rescue all who are
discouraged and have given up hope

New King James Version

[18] The LORD is near to those who have a
broken heart,
And saves such as have a contrite spirit.

Reflection

God promises that Jesus paid the price for all sin.

1 John 2:1-2

New International Version

¹My dear children, I write this to you so that you will not sin. But if anybody does sin, we have one who speaks to the Father in our defense—Jesus Christ, the Righteous One. ²He is the atoning sacrifice for our sins, and not only for ours but also for the sins of the whole world.

New American Standard Bible

¹My little children, I am writing these things to you so that you may not sin And if anyone sins, we have an Advocate with the Father, Jesus Christ the righteous; ²and He Himself is the propitiation for our sins; and not for ours only, but also for those of the whole world.

The Message

¹⁻²I write this, dear children, to guide you out of sin. But if anyone does sin, we have a Priest-Friend in the presence of the Father: Jesus Christ, righteous Jesus. When he served as a sacrifice for our sins, he solved the sin problem for good—not only ours, but the whole world's.

Amplified Bible

¹MY LITTLE children, I write you these things so that you may not violate God's law and sin. But if anyone should sin, we have an Advocate (One Who will intercede for us) with the Father—[it is] Jesus Christ [the all] righteous [upright, just, Who conforms to the Father's will in every purpose, thought, and action]. ²And He [that same Jesus Himself] is the propitiation (the atoning sacrifice) for our sins, and not for ours alone but also for [the sins of] the whole world.

Reflection

New Living Translation

[1] My dear children, I am writing this to you so that you will not sin. But if anyone does sin, we have an advocate who pleads our case before the Father. He is Jesus Christ, the one who is truly righteous. [2] He himself is the sacrifice that atones for our sins—and not only our sins but the sins of all the world.

(Contemporary English Version)

[1] My children, I am writing this so that you won't sin. But if you do sin, Jesus Christ always does the right thing, and he will speak to the Father for us. [2] Christ is the sacrifice that takes away our sins and the sins of all the world's people.

(New King James Version)

[1] My little children, these things I write to you, so that you may not sin. And if anyone sins, we have an Advocate with the Father, Jesus Christ the righteous. [2] And He Himself is the propitiation for our sins, and not for ours only but also for the whole world.

God promises to rain righteousness on you.

Hosea 10:12

New International Version

¹² Sow for yourselves righteousness, reap the
fruit of unfailing love,
and break up your unplowed ground;
for it is time to seek the LORD,
until he comes
and showers righteousness on you.

New American Standard Bible

¹²Sow with a view to righteousness, Reap in
accordance with kindness;
Break up your fallow ground,
For it is time to seek the LORD
Until He comes to rain righteousness on you.

The Message

Sow righteousness, reap love. It's time to till the
ready earth, it's time to dig in with God, Until
he arrives with righteousness ripe for harvest.

Amplified Bible

¹²Sow for yourselves according to righteousness
(uprightness and right standing with God);
reap according to mercy and loving-kindness.
Break up your uncultivated ground, for it is
time to seek the Lord, to inquire for and of
Him, and to require His favor, till He comes
and teaches you righteousness and rains His
righteous gift of salvation upon you.

New Living Translation

¹² I said, 'Plant the good seeds of
righteousness, and you will harvest a crop
of love. Plow up the hard ground of your
hearts, for now is the time to seek the Lord,
that he may come and shower righteousness upon you.'

Reflection

Contemporary English Version

[12]Plow your fields, scatter seeds of justice, and harvest faithfulness. Worship me, the LORD, and I will send my saving power down like rain.

New King James Version

[12] Sow for yourselves righteousness;
    Reap in mercy;
    Break up your fallow ground,
    For it is time to seek the LORD,
     Till He comes and rains righteousness on you.

God promises to reward those who seek Him.

Hebrews 11:6

New International Version

⁶And without faith it is impossible to please God, because anyone who comes to him must believe that he exists and that he rewards those who earnestly seek him.

New American Standard Bible

⁶And without faith it is impossible to please Him, for he who comes to God must believe that He is and that He is a rewarder of those who seek Him.

The Message

⁵⁻⁶By an act of faith, Enoch skipped death completely. "They looked all over and couldn't find him because God had taken him." We know on the basis of reliable testimony that before he was taken "he pleased God." It's impossible to please God apart from faith. And why? Because anyone who wants to approach God must believe both that he exists and that he cares enough to respond to those who seek him.

Amplified Bible

⁶But without faith it is impossible to please and be satisfactory to Him. For whoever would come near to God must [necessarily] believe that God exists and that He is the rewarder of those who earnestly and diligently seek Him [out].

New Living Translation

⁶ And it is impossible to please God without faith. Anyone who wants to come to him must believe that God exists and that he rewards those who sincerely seek him.

Reflection

Contemporary English Version

[6]But without faith no one can please God. We must believe that God is real and that he rewards everyone who searches for him.

New King James Version

[6] But without faith it is impossible to please Him, for he who comes to God must believe that He is, and that He is a rewarder of those who diligently seek Him.

God promises to reward you in this life.

Luke 18:29-30

New International Version

[29]"I tell you the truth," Jesus said to them, "no one who has left home or wife or brothers or parents or children for the sake of the kingdom of God [30]will fail to receive many times as much in this age and, in the age to come, eternal life."

New American Standard Bible

[29]And He said to them, "Truly I say to you, there is no one who has left house or wife or brothers or parents or children, for the sake of the kingdom of God, [30]who will not receive many times as much at this time and in the age to come, eternal life."

The Message

[29-30]"Yes," said Jesus, "and you won't regret it. No one who has sacrificed home, spouse, brothers and sisters, parents, children—whatever—will lose out. It will all come back multiplied many times over in your lifetime. And then the bonus of eternal life!"

Amplified Bible

[29]And He said to them, I say to you truly, there is no one who has left house or wife or brothers or parents or children for the sake of the kingdom of God [30]Who will not receive in return many times more in this world and, in the coming age, eternal life.

New Living Translation

[29] "Yes," Jesus replied, "and I assure you that everyone who has given up house or wife or brothers or parents or children, for the sake of the Kingdom of God, [30] will be repaid many times over in this life, and will have eternal life in the world to come."

Reflection

Contemporary English Version

[29]Jesus answered, "You can be sure that anyone who gives up home or wife or brothers or family or children because of God's kingdom [30]will be given much more in this life. And in the future world they will have eternal life."

New King James Version

[29] So He said to them, "Assuredly, I say to you, there is no one who has left house or parents or brothers or wife or children, for the sake of the kingdom of God, [30] who shall not receive many times more in this present time, and in the age to come eternal life."

God promises to heal our broken lives.

Jeremiah 17:14

New International Version

[14] Heal me, O LORD, and I will be healed;
   save me and I will be saved,
      for you are the one I praise.

New American Standard Bible

[14]Heal me, O LORD, and I will be healed;
   Save me and I will be saved,
      For You are my praise.

The Message

[14-18]God, pick up the pieces.
   Put me back together again.
      You are my praise!

Amplified Bible

[14]Heal me, O Lord, and I shall be healed;
save me, and I shall be saved, for You are my
praise.

New Living Translation

[14] O Lord, if you heal me, I will be truly healed;
if you save me, I will be truly saved. My praises
are for you alone!

Contemporary English Version

[14]You, LORD, are the one I praise. So heal me
   and rescue me!
Then I will be completely well and perfectly
safe.

New King James Version

[14] Heal me, O LORD, and I shall be healed;
   Save me, and I shall be saved,
      For You are my praise.

Reflection

God promises that Jesus will save His people from their sins.

Matthew 1:21

New International Version

²¹She will give birth to a son, and you are to give him the name Jesus, because he will save his people from their sins."

New American Standard Bible

²¹"She will bear a Son; and you shall call His name Jesus, for He will save His people from their sins."

The Message

²¹She will bring a son to birth, and when she does, you, Joseph, will name him Jesus—'God saves'—because he will save his people from their sins."

Amplified Bible

²¹She will bear a Son, and you shall call His name Jesus [the Greek form of the Hebrew Joshua, which means Savior], for He will save His people from their sins [that is, prevent them from failing and missing the true end and scope of life, which is God].

New Living Translation

²¹ And she will have a son, and you are to name him Jesus, for he will save his people from their sins."

Contemporary English Version

²¹Then after her baby is born, name him Jesus, because he will save his people from their sins."

New King James Version

²¹ And she will bring forth a Son, and you shall call His name JESUS, for He will save His people from their sins."

Reflection

God promise that Jesus takes away all sin.

1 John 3:5

New International Version

⁵But you know that he appeared so that he might take away our sins. And in him is no sin.

New American Standard Bible

⁵You know that He appeared in order to take away sins; and in Him there is no sin.

The Message

Surely you know that Christ showed up in order to get rid of sin. There is no sin in him, and sin is not part of his program. No one who lives deeply in Christ makes a practice of sin. None of those who do practice sin have taken a good look at Christ. They've got him all backward.

Amplified Bible

⁵You know that He appeared in visible form and became Man to take away [upon Himself] sins, and in Him there is no sin [essentially and forever].

New Living Translation

⁵ And you know that Jesus came to take away our sins, and there is no sin in him.

Contemporary English Version

⁵You know that Christ came to take away sins. He isn't sinful,

New King James Version

⁵ And you know that He was manifested to take away our sins, and in Him there is no sin.

Reflection

God promises to forgive sins through his covenant.

Matthew 26:28

New International Version

28This is my blood of the covenant, which is poured out for many for the forgiveness of sins.

New American Standard Bible

28for this is My blood of the covenant, which is poured out for many for forgiveness of sins.

The Message

Drink this, all of you. This is my blood, God's new covenant poured out for many people for the forgiveness of sins.

Amplified Bible

28For this is My blood of the new covenant, which [ratifies the agreement and] is being poured out for many for the forgiveness of sins.

New Living Translation

28 for this is my blood, which confirms the covenant between God and his people. It is poured out as a sacrifice to forgive the sins of many.

Contemporary English Version

28This is my blood, and with it God makes his agreement with you. It will be poured out, so that many people will have their sins forgiven.

New King James Version

28 For this is my blood of the new covenant, which is shed for many for the remission of sins.

Reflection

God promises to prosper all the work of your hands and more.

Deuteronomy 30:9

New International Version

⁹ Then the LORD your God will make you most prosperous in all the work of your hands and in the fruit of your womb, the young of your livestock and the crops of your land. The LORD will again delight in you and make you prosperous, just as he delighted in your fathers,

New American Standard Bible

⁹"Then the LORD your God will prosper you abundantly in all the work of your hand, in the offspring of your body and in the offspring of your cattle and in the produce of your ground, for the LORD will again rejoice over you for good, just as He rejoiced over your fathers;

The Message

⁹ God, your God, will outdo himself in making things go well for you: you'll have babies, get calves, grow crops, and enjoy an all-around good life. Yes, God will start enjoying you again, making things go well for you just as he enjoyed doing it for your ancestors.

Amplified Bible

⁹And the Lord your God will make you abundantly prosperous in every work of your hand, in the fruit of your body, of your cattle, of your land, for good; for the Lord will again delight in prospering you, as He took delight in your fathers

New Living Translation

⁹ "The Lord your God will then make you successful in everything you do. He will give you many children and numerous livestock, and he will cause your fields to produce abundant harvests, for the Lord will again delight in being good to you as he was to your ancestors.

Reflection

Contemporary English Version

⁹and he will bless you with many children, large herds and flocks, and abundant crops. The LORD will be happy to do good things for you, just as he did for your ancestors.

New King James Version

⁹ The LORD your God will make you abound in all the work of your hand, in the fruit of your body, in the increase of your livestock, and in the produce of your land for good. For the LORD will again rejoice over you for good as He rejoiced over your fathers,

God promises to be our refuge and strength.

Psalm 46:1-2

New International Version

[1] God is our refuge and strength, an ever-present help in trouble. [2] Therefore we will not fear, though the earth give way and the mountains fall into the heart of the sea

New American Standard Bible

[1] God is our refuge and strength, A very present help in trouble. [2] Therefore we will not fear, though the earth should change And though the mountains slip into the heart of the sea;

The Message

[1-3] God is a safe place to hide, ready to help when we need him. We stand fearless at the cliff-edge of doom, courageous in seastorm and earthquake, Before the rush and roar of oceans, the tremors that shift mountains.

Amplified Bible

[1] GOD IS our Refuge and Strength [mighty and impenetrable to temptation], a very present and well-proved help in trouble. [2] Therefore we will not fear, though the earth should change and though the mountains be shaken into the midst of the seas,

New Living Translation

[1] God is our refuge and strength, always ready to help in times of trouble. [2] So we will not fear when earthquakes come and the mountains crumble into the sea.

Contemporary English Version

[1] God is our mighty fortress, always ready to help in times of trouble. [2] And so, we won't be afraid! Let the earth tremble and the mountains tumble into the deepest sea.

Reflection

New King James Version

[1] God is our refuge and strength, A very present help in trouble. [2] Therefore we will not fear, Even though the earth be removed, And though the mountains be carried into the midst of the sea;

God promises to give you wisdom.

James 1:5

New International Version

⁵If any of you lacks wisdom, he should ask God, who gives generously to all without finding fault, and it will be given to him.

New American Standard Bible

⁵But if any of you lacks wisdom, let him ask of God, who gives to all generously and without reproach, and it will be given to him.

The Message

⁵If you don't know what you're doing, pray to the Father. He loves to help. You'll get his help, and won't be condescended to when you ask for it.

New Living Translation

⁵ If you need wisdom, ask our generous God, and he will give it to you. He will not rebuke you for asking.

Contemporary English Version

⁵If any of you need wisdom, you should ask God, and it will be given to you. God is generous and won't correct you for asking.

New King James Version

⁵ If any of you lacks wisdom, let him ask of God, who gives to all liberally and without reproach, and it will be given to him.

Reflection

God promises that there is wisdom in His word.

Psalm 119:130

New International Version

[130] The unfolding of your words gives light;
it gives understanding to the simple.

New American Standard Bible

[130] The unfolding of Your words gives light;
It gives understanding to the simple.

The Message

[130] Break open your words, let the light shine
out, let ordinary people see the meaning.

Amplified Bible

[130] The entrance and unfolding of Your words
give light; their unfolding gives understanding
(discernment and comprehension) to the
simple.

New Living Translation

[130] The teaching of your word gives light, so
even the simple can understand.

Contemporary English Version

[130] Understanding your word brings light to the
minds

New King James Version

[130] The entrance of Your words gives light;
It gives understanding to the simple.
of ordinary people.

Reflection

God promises that if He builds the house your labour will not be in vain.

Psalm 127:1

New International Version

[1] Unless the LORD builds the house, its builders labor in vain. Unless the LORD watches over the city, the watchmen stand guard in vain.

New American Standard Bible

[1] Unless the LORD builds the house, They labor in vain who build it; Unless the LORD guards the city, The watchman keeps awake in vain.

The Message

[1] If God doesn't build the house, the builders only build shacks. If God doesn't guard the city, the night watchman might as well nap.

Amplified Bible

[1] EXCEPT THE Lord builds the house, they labor in vain who build it; except the Lord keeps the city, the watchman wakes but in vain.

New Living Translation

[1] Unless the Lord builds a house, the work of the builders is wasted. Unless the Lord protects a city, guarding it with sentries will do no good.

Contemporary English Version

Only the LORD Can Bless a Home [1] Without the help of the LORD it is useless to build a home or to guard a city.

New King James Version

[1] Unless the LORD builds the house, They labor in vain who build it; Unless the LORD guards the city, The watchman stays awake in vain.

Reflection

God promises to meet all of your needs

Philippians 4:19

New International Version

¹⁹And my God will meet all your needs according to his glorious riches in Christ Jesus.

New American Standard Bible

¹⁹And my God will supply all your needs according to His riches in glory in Christ Jesus.

The Message

¹⁹You can be sure that God will take care of everything you need, his generosity exceeding even yours in the glory that pours from Jesus.

Amplified Bible

¹⁹And my God will liberally supply (fill to the full) your every need according to His riches in glory in Christ Jesus.

New Living Translation

¹⁹ And this same God who takes care of me will supply all your needs from his glorious riches, which have been given to us in Christ Jesus.

Contemporary English Version

¹⁹I pray that God will take care of all your needs with the wonderful blessings that come from Christ Jesus!

New King James Version

¹⁹ And my God shall supply all your need according to His riches in glory by Christ Jesus.

Reflection

God promises to bring glory to His name.

Psalm 86:9

New International Version

⁹ All the nations you have made
  will come and worship before you, O
  Lord;
    they will bring glory to your name.

New American Standard Bible

⁹All nations whom You have made shall come
and worship before You, O Lord, And they
shall glorify Your name.

The Message

⁹All the nations you made are on their way,
    ready to give honor to you, O Lord,
Ready to put your beauty on display,
    parading your greatness,
And the great things you do—

Amplified Bible

⁹All nations whom You have made shall come
and fall down before You, O Lord; and they
shall glorify Your name.

New Living Translation

⁹ All the nations you made will come and bow
before you, Lord; they will praise your holy
name.

Contemporary English Version

⁹You created each nation, and they will all bow
down to worship and honor you.

(New King James Version)

⁹ All nations whom You have made Shall come
and worship before you, O Lord, And shall
glorify Your name.

Reflection

God promises to take care of your enemies.

Romans 12:19-21

New International Version

[19]Do not take revenge, my friends, but leave room for God's wrath, for it is written: "It is mine to avenge; I will repay, "says the Lord. [20]On the contrary: "If your enemy is hungry, feed him; if he is thirsty, give him something to drink. In doing this, you will heap burning coals on his head." [21]Do not be overcome by evil, but overcome evil with good.

New American Standard Bible

[19]Never take your own revenge, beloved, but leave room for the wrath of God, for it is written, "VENGEANCE IS MINE, I WILL REPAY," says the Lord. [20]"BUT IF YOUR ENEMY IS HUNGRY, FEED HIM, AND IF HE IS THIRSTY, GIVE HIM A DRINK; FOR IN SO DOING YOU WILL HEAP BURNING COALS ON HIS HEAD." [21]Do not be overcome by evil, but overcome evil with good.

The Message

[17-19]Don't hit back; discover beauty in everyone. If you've got it in you, get along with everybody. Don't insist on getting even; that's not for you to do. "I'll do the judging," says God. "I'll take care of it." [20-21]Our Scriptures tell us that if you see your enemy hungry, go buy that person lunch, or if he's thirsty, get him a drink. Your generosity will surprise him with goodness. Don't let evil get the best of you; get the best of evil by doing good.

Amplified Bible

[19]Beloved, never avenge yourselves, but leave the way open for [God's] wrath; for it is written, Vengeance is Mine, I will repay (requite), says the Lord.[20]But if your enemy is hungry, feed him; if he is thirsty, give him drink; for by so doing you will

Reflection

heap burning coals upon his head. [21]Do not let yourself be overcome by evil, but overcome (master) evil with good.

New Living Translation

[19] Dear friends, never take revenge. Leave that to the righteous anger of God. For the Scriptures say, "I will take revenge; I will pay them back," says the Lord. [20] Instead, "If your enemies are hungry, feed them. If they are thirsty, give them something to drink. In doing this, you will heap burning coals of shame on their heads. [21] Don't let evil conquer you, but conquer evil by doing good.

Contemporary English Version

[19]Dear friends, don't try to get even. Let God take revenge. In the Scriptures the Lord says "I am the one to take revenge and pay them back." [20]The Scriptures also say, "If your enemies are hungry, give them something to eat. And if they are thirsty, give them something to drink. This will be the same as piling burning coals on their heads." [21]Don't let evil defeat you, but defeat evil with good.

New King James Version

[19] Beloved, do not avenge yourselves, but rather give place to wrath; for it is written, "Vengeance is Mine, I will repay," says the Lord. [20] Therefore "If your enemy is hungry, feed him ;If he is thirsty, give him a drink; For in so doing you will heap coals of fire on his head." [21] Do not be overcome by evil, but overcome evil with good.

God promises that all things are possible to them that believe.

Mark 9:23

New International Version

23 "'If you can'?" said Jesus. "Everything is possible for him who believes."

New American Standard Bible

23And Jesus said to him, "If You can?' All things are possible to him who believes."

The Message

23Jesus said, "If? There are no 'ifs' among believers. Anything can happen."

Amplified Bible

23And Jesus said, [You say to Me], If You can do anything? [Why,] all things can be (are possible) to him who believes!

New Living Translation

23 "What do you mean, 'If I can'?" Jesus asked. "Anything is possible if a person believes."

Contemporary English Version

23Jesus replied, "Why do you say `if you can'? Anything is possible for someone who has faith!"

New King James Version

23 Jesus said to him, "If you can believe, all things are possible to him who believes."

Reflection

God promises to bless those who are a blessing to others.

Luke 14:13-14

New International Version

[13]But when you give a banquet, invite the poor, the crippled, the lame, the blind, [14]and you will be blessed. Although they cannot repay you, you will be repaid at the resurrection of the righteous."

New American Standard Bible

[13]"But when you give a reception, invite the poor, the crippled, the lame, the blind, [14]and you will be blessed, since they do not have the means to repay you; for you will be repaid at the resurrection of the righteous."

The Message

[13]Invite some people who never get invited out, the misfits from the wrong side of the tracks. You'll be—and experience—a blessing. They won't be able to return the favor, but the favor will be returned—oh, how it will be returned!—at the resurrection of God's people."

Amplified Bible

[13]But when you give a banquet or a reception, invite the poor, the disabled, the lame, and the blind. [14]Then you will be blessed (happy, fortunate, and to be envied), because they have no way of repaying you, and you will be recompensed at the resurrection of the just (upright).

New Living Translation

[13] Instead, invite the poor, the crippled, the lame, and the blind. [14] Then at the resurrection of the righteous, God will reward you for inviting those who could not repay you."

Reflection

Contemporary English Version

[13]When you give a feast, invite the poor, the crippled, the lame, and the blind. [14]They cannot pay you back. But God will bless you and reward you when his people rise from death.

New King James Version

[13] But when you give a feast, invite the poor, the maimed, the lame, the blind. [14] And you will be blessed, because they cannot repay you; for you shall be repaid at the resurrection of the just."

God promises that when He is the mentor for your children they will be blessed.

Isaiah 54:13

New International Version

¹³ All your sons will be taught by the LORD, and great will be your children's peace.

New American Standard Bible

¹³"All your sons will be taught of the LORD; And the well-being of your sons will be great.

The Message

¹³All your children will have God for their teacher—what a mentor for your children! You'll be built solid, grounded in righteousness, far from any trouble—nothing to fear! far from terror—it won't even come close!

Amplified Bible

¹³And all your [spiritual] children shall be disciples [taught by the Lord and obedient to His will], and great shall be the peace and undisturbed composure of your children.

New Living Translation

¹³ I will teach all your children, and they will enjoy great peace.

Contemporary English Version

¹³I will teach your children, and make them successful.

New King James Version

¹³ All your children shall be taught by the LORD, And great shall be the peace of your children.

Reflection

God promises to preserve your life.

Psalm 138:7

New International Version

⁷ Though I walk in the midst of trouble,
   you preserve my life;
   you stretch out your hand against the
   anger of my foes,
      with your right hand you save me.

New American Standard Bible

⁷Though I walk in the midst of trouble, You
   will revive me;
   You will stretch forth Your hand against
   the wrath of my enemies,
      And Your right hand will save me.

The Message

⁷When I walk into the thick of trouble,
   keep me alive in the angry turmoil.
With one hand
   strike my foes,
With your other hand save me.

Amplified Bible

⁷Though I walk in the midst of trouble, You
will revive me; You will stretch forth Your hand
against the wrath of my enemies, and Your
right hand will save me.

New Living Translation

⁷ Though I am surrounded by troubles,
   you will protect me from the anger of my
   enemies.
You reach out your hand,
   and the power of your right hand saves
me.

Contemporary English Version

⁷I am surrounded by trouble, but you protect me against my angry enemies. With
your own powerful arm you keep me safe.

Reflection

New King James Version

[7] Though I walk in the midst of trouble, You will revive me; You will stretch out Your hand Against the wrath of my enemies, And Your right hand will save me.

God promises to be your shield.

Psalm 18:2

New International Version)

² The LORD is my rock, my fortress and my deliverer; my God is my rock, in whom I take refuge. He is my shield and the horn of my salvation, my stronghold.

New American Standard Bible

²The LORD is my rock and my fortress and my deliverer, My God, my rock, in whom I take refuge; My shield and the horn of my salvation, my stronghold.

The Message

²God is bedrock under my feet, the castle in which I live, my rescuing knight. My God—the high crag where I run for dear life, hiding behind the boulders, safe in the granite hideout.

Amplified Bible

²The Lord is my Rock, my Fortress, and my Deliverer; my God, my keen and firm Strength in Whom I will trust and take refuge, my Shield, and the Horn of my salvation, my High Tower.

New Living Translation

² The Lord is my rock, my fortress, and my savior; my God is my rock, in whom I find protection. He is my shield, the power that saves me, and my place of safety.

Contemporary English Version

²You are my mighty rock, my fortress, my protector, the rock where I am safe, my shield, my powerful weapon, and my place of shelter.

New King James Version

² The LORD is my rock and my fortress and my deliverer; My God, my strength, in whom I will trust; My shield and the horn of my salvation, my stronghold.

Reflection

God promises not to forsake the faithful.

Psalm 37:28

New International Version

[28] For the LORD loves the just
and will not forsake his faithful ones.
They will be protected forever,
but the offspring of the wicked will be cut o

New American Standard Bible

[28]For the LORD loves justice
And does not forsake His godly ones;
They are preserved forever,
But the descendants of the wicked will be
cut off.

The Message

[28] Turn your back on evil, work for the good
and don't quit.
God loves this kind of thing, never turns
away from his friends.
Live this way and you've got it made, but
bad eggs will be tossed out.

Amplified Bible

[28]For the Lord delights in justice and forsakes
not His saints; they are preserved forever, but
the offspring of the wicked [in time] shall be
cut off.

New Living Translation

[28] For the Lord loves justice, and he will never
abandon the godly. He will keep them safe
forever, but the children of the wicked will die.

Contemporary English Version

[28]The LORD loves justice, and he won't ever
desert his faithful people. He always protects
them, but destroys the children of the wicked.

New King James Version

[28] For the LORD loves justice, And does not forsake His saints; They are
preserved forever, But the descendants of the wicked shall be cut off.

Reflection

God promises to give you peace with your enemies.

Proverbs 16:7

New International Version

⁷ When a man's ways are pleasing to the
LORD,
 he makes even his enemies live at peace
with him.

New American Standard Bible

⁷When a man's ways are pleasing to the
LORD,
 He makes even his enemies to be at peace
with him.

The Message

⁷ When God approves of your life,
 even your enemies will end up shaking
your hand.

Amplified Bible

⁷When a man's ways please the Lord, He makes
even his enemies to be at peace with him.

New Living Translation

⁷ When people's lives please the Lord,
 even their enemies are at peace with
them.

Contemporary English Version

⁷When we please the LORD, even our
enemies make friends with us.

New King James Version

⁷ When a man's ways please the LORD,
 He makes even his enemies to be at peace
with him.

Reflection

God promises that salvation is His gift to you.

Ephesians 2:8

New International Version

[8]For it is by grace you have been saved, through faith—and this not from yourselves, it is the gift of God—

New American Standard Bible

[8]For by grace you have been saved through faith; and that not of yourselves, it is the gift of God;

The Message

[7-8] Now God has us where he wants us, with all the time in this world and the next to shower grace and kindness upon us in Christ Jesus. Saving is all his idea, and all his work. All we do is trust him enough to let him do it. It's God's gift from start to finish!

Amplified Bible

[8]For it is by free grace (God's unmerited favor) that you are saved (delivered from judgment and made partakers of Christ's salvation) through [your] faith. And this [salvation] is not of yourselves [of your own doing, it came not through your own striving], but it is the gift of God;

New Living Translation

[8] God saved you by his grace when you believed. And you can't take credit for this; it is a gift from God.

Contemporary English Version

[8]You were saved by faith in God, who treats us much better than we deserve. This is God's gift to you, and not anything you have done on your own.

New King James Version

[8] For by grace you have been saved through faith, and that not of yourselves; it is the gift of God.

Reflection

God promises to give you the power to control yourself.

2 Timothy 1:7

New International Version

⁷For God did not give us a spirit of timidity, but a spirit of power, of love and of self-discipline.

New American Standard Bible

⁷For God has not given us a spirit of timidity, but of power and love and discipline.

The Message

⁷ God doesn't want us to be shy with his gifts, but bold and loving and sensible.

Amplified Bible

⁷For God did not give us a spirit of timidity (of cowardice, of craven and cringing and fawning fear), but [He has given us a spirit] of power and of love and of calm and well-balanced mind and discipline and self-control.

New Living Translation

⁷ For God has not given us a spirit of fear and timidity, but of power, love, and self-discipline.

Contemporary English Version

⁷God's Spirit doesn't make cowards out of us. The Spirit gives us power, love, and self-control.

New King James Version

⁷ For God has not given us a spirit of fear, but of power and of love and of a sound mind.

Reflection

God promises to bring satisfaction to those who seek to do good.

Proverbs 13:25

New International Version

[25] The righteous eat to their hearts' content,
   but the stomach of the wicked goes hungry.

New American Standard Bible

[25] The righteous has enough to satisfy his
   appetite,
   But the stomach of the wicked is in need.

The Message

[25] An appetite for good brings much
   satisfaction,
   but the belly of the wicked always wants
more.

Amplified Bible

[25] The [uncompromisingly] righteous eats to
his own satisfaction, but the stomach of the
wicked is in want.

New Living Translation

[25] The godly eat to their hearts' content,
   but the belly of the wicked goes hungry.

Contemporary English Version

[25] If you live right, you will have plenty to eat; if
you don't live right, you will go away empty.

New King James Version

[25] The righteous eats to the satisfying of his
   soul,
   But the stomach of the wicked shall be in
want.

Reflection

God promises to forgive you when we forgive others.

Matthew 6:14

New International Version

[14]For if you forgive men when they sin against you, your heavenly Father will also forgive you.

New American Standard Bible

[14]"For if you forgive others for their transgressions, your heavenly Father will also forgive you.

The Message

[14-15]"In prayer there is a connection between what God does and what you do. You can't get forgiveness from God, for instance, without also forgiving others. If you refuse to do your part, you cut yourself off from God's part.

Amplified Bible

[14]For if you forgive people their trespasses [their reckless and willful sins, leaving them, letting them go, and giving up resentment], your heavenly Father will also forgive you.

New Living Translation

[14] "If you forgive those who sin against you, your heavenly Father will forgive you.

Contemporary English Version

[14]If you forgive others for the wrongs they do to you, your Father in heaven will forgive you.

New King James Version

[14] "For if you forgive men their trespasses, your heavenly Father will also forgive you.

Reflection

God promises that you will bear fruit in your old age.

Psalm 92:14

New International Version

¹⁴ They will still bear fruit in old age,
they will stay fresh and green,

New American Standard Bible

¹⁴They will still yield fruit in old age;
They shall be full of sap and very green,

The Message

¹⁴They'll grow tall in the presence of God,
lithe and green, virile still in old age."

Amplified Bible

¹⁴[Growing in grace] they shall still bring forth
fruit in old age; they shall be full of sap [of
spiritual vitality] and [rich in the] verdure [of
trust, love, and contentment].

New Living Translation

¹⁴ Even in old age they will still produce fruit;
they will remain vital and green.

Contemporary English Version

¹⁴They will be like trees that stay healthy and
fruitful, even when they are old.

New King James Version

¹⁴ They shall still bear fruit in old age;
They shall be fresh and flourishing,

Reflection

God promises to be our guide to the very end.

Psalm 48:14

New International Version

¹⁴ For this God is our God forever and ever;
he will be our guide even to the end.

New American Standard Bible

¹⁴For such is God, Our God forever and ever;
He will guide us until death

The Message

¹⁴Our God forever, who guides us till the end
of time.

Amplified Bible

¹⁴For this God is our God forever and ever; He
will be our guide [even] until death.

New Living Translation

¹⁴ For that is what God is like. He is our God
forever and ever,
and he will guide us until we die.

Contemporary English Version

¹⁴"Our God is like this forever and will always
guide us."

New King James Version

¹⁴ For this is God, Our God forever and ever;
He will be our guide, Even to death.

Reflection

God promises to order your steps.

Proverbs 16:9

New International Version

9 In his heart a man plans his course,
but the LORD determines his steps.

New American Standard Bible

9The mind of man plans his way,
But the LORD directs his steps.

The Message

9 We plan the way we want to live,
but only God makes us able to live it.

Amplified Bible

9A man's mind plans his way, but the Lord
directs his steps and makes them sure.

New Living Translation

9 We can make our plans,
but the Lord determines our steps.

Contemporary English Version

9We make our own plans, but the LORD
decides where we will go.

New King James Version

9 A man's heart plans his way,
But the LORD directs his steps.

Reflection

God promises to direct the steps of the godly.

Psalm 37:23

New International Version

23 If the LORD delights in a man's way,
he makes his steps firm;

New American Standard Bible

23The steps of a man are established by the
LORD,
And He delights in his way.

The Message

23-24 Stalwart walks in step with God;
his path blazed by God, he's happy.

Amplified Bible

23The steps of a [good] man are directed and
established by the Lord when He delights in
his way [and He busies Himself with his every
step].

New Living Translation

23 The Lord directs the steps of the godly.
He delights in every detail of their lives.

Contemporary English Version

23If you do what the LORD wants, he will
make certain each step you take is sure.

New King James Version

23 The steps of a good man are ordered by the
LORD,
And He delights in his way.

Reflection

God promises to be your teacher.

Isaiah 28:26

New International Version

26 His God instructs him
   and teaches him the right way.

New American Standard Bible

26For his God instructs and teaches him properly.

The Message

26They know exactly what to do and when to
   do it.
      Their God is their teacher.

Amplified Bible

26[And he trains each of them correctly] for his God instructs him correctly and teaches him.

New Living Translation

26 The farmer knows just what to do,
   for God has given him understanding.

Contemporary English Version

26They learn this from their God.

New King James Version

26 For He instructs him in right judgment,
   His God teaches him.

Reflection

God promises to keep you on track.

Proverbs 3:6

New International Version

⁶ in all your ways acknowledge him,
  and he will make your paths straight.

New American Standard Bible

⁶In all your ways acknowledge Him,
  And He will make your paths straight.

The Message

⁶ Listen for God's voice in everything you do,
  everywhere you go;
    he's the one who will keep you on track.

Amplified Bible

⁶In all your ways know, recognize, and acknowledge Him, and He will direct and make straight and plain your paths.

New Living Translation

⁶ Seek his will in all you do,
  and he will show you which path to take.

Contemporary English Version

⁶Always let him lead you, and he will clear the road for you to follow.

New King James Version

⁶ In all your ways acknowledge Him, And He shall direct your paths.

Reflection

God promises to have mercy when we turn to Him.

Isaiah 55:7

New International Version

[7] Let the wicked forsake his way and the evil man his thoughts. Let him turn to the LORD, and he will have mercy on him, and to our God, for he will freely pardon.

New American Standard Bible

[7]Let the wicked forsake his way
   And the unrighteous man his thoughts;
   And let him return to the LORD,
   And He will have compassion on him,
   And to our God,
      For He will abundantly pardon.

The Message

[7]Let the wicked abandon their way of life and the evil their way of thinking. Let them come back to God, who is merciful, come back to our God, who is lavish with forgiveness

Amplified Bible

[7]Let the wicked forsake his way and the unrighteous man his thoughts; and let him return to the Lord, and He will have love, pity, and mercy for him, and to our God, for He will multiply to him His abundant pardon.

New Living Translation

[7] Let the wicked change their ways and banish the very thought of doing wrong. Let them turn to the Lord that he may have mercy on them. Yes, turn to our God, for he will forgive generously.

Reflection

Contemporary English Version

[7]Give up your crooked ways and your evil thoughts. Return to the LORD our God. He will be merciful and forgive your sins.

New King James Version

[7] Let the wicked forsake his way, And the unrighteous man his thoughts; Let him return to the LORD, And He will have mercy on him; And to our God, For He will abundantly pardon.

God promises to show compassion to those who run to Him.

2 Chronicles 30:9

New International Version

⁹ If you return to the LORD, then your brothers and your children will be shown compassion by their captors and will come back to this land, for the LORD your God is gracious and compassionate. He will not turn his face from you if you return to him."

New American Standard Bible

⁹"For if you return to the LORD, your brothers and your sons will find compassion before those who led them captive and will return to this land For the LORD your God is gracious and compassionate, and will not turn His face away from you if you return to Him."

The Message

⁹ If you come back to God, your captive relatives and children will be treated compassionately and allowed to come home. Your God is gracious and kind and won't snub you—come back and he'll welcome you with open arms.

Amplified Bible

⁹For if you return to the Lord, your brethren and your children shall find compassion with their captors and return to this land. For the Lord your God is gracious and merciful, and He will not turn away His face from you if you return to Him.

New Living Translation

⁹ "For if you return to the Lord, your relatives and your children will be treated mercifully by their captors, and they will be able to return to this land. For the Lord your God is gracious and merciful. If you return to him, he will not continue to turn his face from you."

Reflection

Contemporary English Version

[9]and the enemies that have captured your families will show pity and send them back home. The LORD God is kind and merciful, and if you turn back to him, he will no longer turn his back on you.

New King James Version

[9] For if you return to the LORD, your brethren and your children will be treated with compassion by those who lead them captive, so that they may come back to this land; for the LORD your God is gracious and merciful, and will not turn His face from you if you return to Him."

God promises to remove our sin from us.

Psalm 103:12

New International Version

[12] as far as the east is from the west, so far has he removed our transgressions from us.

New American Standard Bible

[12]As far as the east is from the west, So far has He removed our transgressions from us.

The Message

[12]And as far as sunrise is from sunset,
    he has separated us from our sins.

Amplified Bible

[12]As far as the east is from the west, so far has He removed our transgressions from us.

New Living Translation

[12] He has removed our sins as far from us
    as the east is from the west.

Contemporary English Version

[12]How far has the LORD taken our sins from us? Farther than the distance from east to west!

New King James Version

[12] As far as the east is from the west,
    So far has He removed our transgressions from us.

Reflection

God promises to give peace when we are anxious.

1 John 3:20

New International Version

[20]whenever our hearts condemn us. For God is greater than our hearts, and he knows everything.

New American Standard Bible

[20]in whatever our heart condemns us; for God is greater than our heart and knows all things.

The Message

[20] For God is greater than our worried hearts and knows more about us than we do ourselves.

Amplified Bible

[20]Whenever our hearts in [tormenting] self-accusation make us feel guilty and condemn us. [For we are in God's hands.] For He is above and greater than our consciences (our hearts), and He knows (perceives and understands) everything [nothing is hidden from Him].

New Living Translation

[20] Even if we feel guilty, God is greater than our feelings, and he knows everything.

Contemporary English Version

[20]But even if we don't feel at ease, God is greater than our feelings, and he knows everything.

New King James Version

[20] For if our heart condemns us, God is greater than our heart, and knows all things.

Reflection

God promises to wipe our slate clean when we repent.

Hebrews 8:12

New International Version

¹²For I will forgive their wickedness
   and will remember their sins no more."

New American Standard Bible

¹²"FOR I WILL BE MERCIFUL TO THEIR INIQUITIES, AND I WILL REMEMBER THEIR SINS NO MORE."

The Message

¹² They'll get to know me by being kindly
      forgiven,
      with the slate of their sins forever wiped
clean.

Hebrews 8:12 Amplified Bible

¹²For I will be merciful and gracious toward their sins and I will remember their deeds of unrighteousness no more.

New Living Translation

¹² And I will forgive their wickedness,
      and I will never again remember their
sins."

Contemporary English Version

¹²I will treat them with kindness, even though
      they are wicked.
      I will forget their sins."

New King James Version

¹² For I will be merciful to their unrighteousness,
and their sins and their lawless deeds I will
remember no more."

Reflection

God promises that we are a new creation in Him.

2 Corinthians 5:17

New International Version

¹⁷Therefore, if anyone is in Christ, he is a new creation; the old has gone, the new has come!

New American Standard Bible

¹⁷Therefore if anyone is in Christ, he is a new creature; the old things passed away; behold, new things have come.

The Message

¹⁷Now we look inside, and what we see is that anyone united with the Messiah gets a fresh start, is created new. The old life is gone; a new life burgeons! Look at it!

Amplified Bible

¹⁷Therefore if any person is [ingrafted] in Christ (the Messiah) he is a new creation (a new creature altogether); the old [previous moral and spiritual condition] has passed away. Behold, the fresh and new has come!

New Living Translation

¹⁷ This means that anyone who belongs to Christ has become a new person. The old life is gone; a new life has begun!

Contemporary English Version

¹⁷Anyone who belongs to Christ is a new person. The past is forgotten, and everything is new.

New King James Version

¹⁷ Therefore, if anyone is in Christ, he is a new creation; old things have passed away; behold, all things have become new.

Reflection

God promises to forgive our wicked acts.

Jeremiah 31:34

New International Version

³⁴ No longer will a man teach his neighbor, or a man his brother, saying, 'Know the LORD,' because they will all know me, from the least of them to the greatest," declares the LORD. "For I will forgive their wickedness and will remember their sins no more."

New American Standard Bible

³⁴"They will not teach again, each man his neighbor and each man his brother, saying, 'Know the LORD,' for they will all know Me, from the least of them to the greatest of them," declares the LORD, "for I will forgive their iniquity, and their sin I will remember no more."

The Message

³⁴ They will no longer go around setting up schools to teach each other about God. They'll know me firsthand, the dull and the bright, the smart and the slow. I'll wipe the slate clean for each of them. I'll forget they ever sinned! God's Decree.

Amplified Bible

³⁴And they will no more teach each man his neighbor and each man his brother, saying, Know the Lord, for they will all know Me [recognize, understand, and be acquainted with Me], from the least of them to the greatest, says the Lord. For I will forgive their iniquity, and I will [seriously] remember their sin no more.

New Living Translation

³⁴ And they will not need to teach their neighbors, nor will they need to teach their relatives, saying, 'You should know the Lord.' For everyone, from the least to the greatest, will know me already," says the Lord. "And I will forgive their wickedness, and I will never again remember their sins."

Reflection

Contemporary English Version

[34]"No longer will they have to teach one another to obey me. I, the LORD, promise that all of them will obey me, ordinary people and rulers alike. I will forgive their sins and forget the evil things they have done."

New King James Version

[34] No more shall every man teach his neighbor, and every man his brother, saying, 'Know the LORD,' for they all shall know Me, from the least of them to the greatest of them, says the LORD. For I will forgive their iniquity, and their sin I will remember no more."

God promises that the blood of Jesus cleanses us from all sin.

1 John 1:7

New International Version

⁷But if we walk in the light, as he is in the light, we have fellowship with one another, and the blood of Jesus, his Son, purifies us from all sin.

New American Standard Bible

⁷but if we walk in the Light as He Himself is in the Light, we have fellowship with one another, and the blood of Jesus His Son cleanses us from all sin.

The Message

⁷But if we walk in the light, God himself being the light, we also experience a shared life with one another, as the sacrificed blood of Jesus, God's Son, purges all our sin.

Amplified Bible

⁷But if we [really] are living and walking in the Light, as He [Himself] is in the Light, we have [true, unbroken] fellowship with one another, and the blood of Jesus Christ His Son cleanses (removes) us from all sin and guilt [keeps us cleansed from sin in all its forms and manifestations].

New Living Translation

⁷ But if we are living in the light, as God is in the light, then we have fellowship with each other, and the blood of Jesus, his Son, cleanses us from all sin.

Contemporary English Version

⁷But if we live in the light, as God does, we share in life with each other. And the blood of his Son Jesus washes all our sins away.

New King James Version

⁷ But if we walk in the light as He is in the light, we have fellowship with one another, and the blood of Jesus Christ His Son cleanses us from all sin.

Reflection

God promises to hold us up.

Psalm 37:24

New International Version

²⁴ though he stumble, he will not fall,
   for the LORD upholds him with his hand.

New American Standard Bible

²⁴When he falls, he will not be hurled headlong,
   Because the LORD is the One who holds his hand.

The Message

²⁴If he stumbles, he's not down for long;
   God has a grip on his hand.

Amplified Bible

²⁴Though he falls, he shall not be utterly cast down, for the Lord grasps his hand in support and upholds him.

New Living Translation

²⁴ Though they stumble, they will never fall,
   for the Lord holds them by the hand.

Contemporary English Version

²⁴ The LORD will hold your hand, and if you stumble, you still won't fall.

New King James Version

²⁴ Though he fall, he shall not be utterly cast down;
   For the LORD upholds him with His hand.

Reflection

God promises to be our hiding place.

Psalm 32:7

New International Version

⁷ You are my hiding place; you will protect me from trouble and surround e with songs of deliverance. Selah

New American Standard Bible

⁷You are my hiding place; You preserve me from trouble;

The Message

⁷ God's my island hideaway,
    keeps danger far from the shore,
        throws garlands of hosannas around my neck.

You surround me with songs of deliverance. Selah.

Amplified Bible

⁷You are a hiding place for me; You, Lord, preserve me from trouble, You surround me with songs and shouts of deliverance. Selah [pause, and calmly think of that]!

New Living Translation

⁷ For you are my hiding place;
    you protect me from trouble.
        You surround me with songs of victory.

Contemporary English Version

⁷You are my hiding place! You protect me from trouble, and you put songs in my heart because you have saved me.

New King James Version

⁷ You are my hiding place;
    You shall preserve me from trouble;
        You shall surround me with songs of deliverance. Selah

Reflection

God promises to put a smile on our face when we put our trust in Him.

Psalm 42:11

New International Version

¹¹ Why are you downcast, O my soul? Why so disturbed within me? Put your hope in God, for I will yet praise him, my Savior and my God.

New American Standard Bible

¹¹Why are you in despair, O my soul? And why have you become disturbed within me? Hope in God, for I shall yet praise Him, The help of my countenance and my God.

The Message

¹¹ Why are you down in the dumps, dear soul?
    Why are you crying the blues?
Fix my eyes on God—
    soon I'll be praising again.
He puts a smile on my face.
    He's my God.

Amplified Bible

¹¹Why are you cast down, O my inner self? And why should you moan over me and be disquieted within me? Hope in God and wait expectantly for Him, for I shall yet praise Him, Who is the help of my countenance, and my God.

New Living Translation

¹¹ Why am I discouraged? Why is my heart so sad?
    I will put my hope in God! I will praise him again—
    my Savior and my God!

Contemporary English Version

¹¹Why am I discouraged? Why am I restless?

I trust you! And I will praise you again because you help me, and you are my God.

Reflection

New King James Version

[11] Why are you cast down, O my soul? And why are you disquieted within me?

Hope in God; For I shall yet praise Him,
The help of my countenance and my God.

God promises to send angels to guard us.

Psalm 91:10-11

New International Version

[10] then no harm will befall you, no disaster will come near your tent. [11] For he will command his angels concerning you to guard you in all your ways;

New American Standard Bible

[10]No evil will befall you,
Nor will any plague come near your tent.
[11]For He will give His angels charge concerning you,
To guard you in all your ways.

The Message

Yes, because God's your refuge, the High God your very own home,
Evil can't get close to you, harm can't get through the door.
He ordered his angels to guard you wherever you go.
If you stumble, they'll catch you; their job is to keep you from falling.

Amplified Bible

[10]There shall no evil befall you, nor any plague or calamity come near your tent. [11]For He will give His angels [especial] charge over you to accompany and defend and preserve you in all your ways [of obedience and service].

New Living Translation

[10] no evil will conquer you;
no plague will come near your home.
[11] For he will order his angels
to protect you wherever you go.

Contemporary English Version

[10]and no terrible disasters will strike you or your home. [11]God will command his angels to protect you wherever you go.

Reflection

New King James Version

[10] No evil shall befall you,
   Nor shall any plague come near your dwelling;
[11] For He shall give His angels charge over you,
   To keep you in all your ways.

RUDOLPH MOSELEY JR.

God promises to preserve the faithful.

Psalm 31:23

New International Version

²³ Love the LORD, all his saints!
  The LORD preserves the faithful,
    but the proud he pays back in full

New American Standard Bible

²³O love the LORD, all you His godly ones!
  The LORD preserves the faithful
  And fully recompenses the proud doer.

The Message

²³ Love God, all you saints;
  God takes care of all who stay close to
  him,
But he pays back in full
    those arrogant enough to go it alone.

Amplified Bible

²³O love the Lord, all you His saints! The Lord
preserves the faithful, and plentifully pays back
him who deals haughtily.

New Living Translation

²³ Love the Lord, all you godly ones!
  For the Lord protects those who are loyal
  to him,
    but he harshly punishes the arrogant.

Contemporary English Version

²³All who belong to the LORD, show how you
love him. The LORD protects the faithful, but
he severely punishes everyone who is proud.

New King James Version

²³ Oh, love the LORD, all you His saints!
  For the LORD preserves the faithful,
  And fully repays the proud person.

Reflection

God promises to save by His mighty right hand.

Psalm 138:7

New International Version

⁷ Though I walk in the midst of trouble,
  you preserve my life;
  you stretch out your hand against the
  anger of my foes,
  with your right hand you save me.

New American Standard Bible

⁷Though I walk in the midst of trouble, You
  will revive me;
  You will stretch forth Your hand against
  the wrath of my enemies,
  And Your right hand will save me.

The Message

⁷When I walk into the thick of trouble,
  keep me alive in the angry turmoil.
With one hand strike my foes, With your
  other hand
    save me.

Amplified Bible

⁷Though I walk in the midst of trouble, You
will revive me; You will stretch forth Your hand
against the wrath of my enemies, and Your
right hand will save me.

New Living Translation

⁷ Though I am surrounded by troubles,
  you will protect me from the anger of my
  enemies.
You reach out your hand,
    and the power of your right hand saves
me.

Contemporary English Version

⁷I am surrounded by trouble, but you protect me against my angry enemies. With
your own powerful arm you keep me safe.

Reflection

New King James Version

[7] Though I walk in the midst of trouble, You will revive me;
You will stretch out Your hand
Against the wrath of my enemies,
And Your right hand will save me.

God promises to deliver from all troubles.

Psalm 34:19

New International Version

¹⁹ A righteous man may have many troubles,
but the LORD delivers him from them all;

New American Standard Bible

¹⁹Many are the afflictions of the righteous,
But the LORD delivers him out of them all.

The Message

¹⁹ Disciples so often get into trouble;
still, God is there every time.

Amplified Bible

¹⁹Many evils confront the [consistently] righteous, but the Lord delivers him out of them all.

New Living Translation

¹⁹ The righteous person faces many troubles,
but the Lord comes to the rescue each time.

Contemporary English Version

¹⁹The LORD's people may suffer a lot, but he will always bring them safely through.

New King James Version

¹⁹ Many are the afflictions of the righteous,
But the LORD delivers him out of them all

Reflection

God promises to be your rock.

Psalm 18:2

New International Version

² The LORD is my rock, my fortress and my
   deliverer;
   my God is my rock, in whom I take
   refuge.
   He is my shield and the horn of my
salvation, my stronghold.

New American Standard Bible

²The LORD is my rock and my fortress and
   my deliverer,
   My God, my rock, in whom I take refuge;
   My shield and the horn of my salvation,
my stronghold.

The Message

²My God—the high crag where I run for dear
life, hiding behind the boulders, safe in the
granite hideout.

Amplified Bible

²The Lord is my Rock, my Fortress, and my
Deliverer; my God, my keen and firm Strength
in Whom I will trust and take refuge, my
Shield, and the Horn of my salvation, my
High Tower.

New Living Translation

² The Lord is my rock, my fortress, and my
   savior;
   my God is my rock, in whom I find
   protection.
He is my shield, the power that saves me,
   and my place of safety.

Contemporary English Version

²You are my mighty rock, my fortress, my protector, the rock where I am safe, my
shield, my powerful weapon, and my place of shelter.

Reflection

New King James Version

[2] The LORD is my rock and my fortress and my deliverer;
  My God, my strength, in whom I will trust;
    My shield and the horn of my salvation, my stronghold.

God promises to give you peace because He has overcome the world.

John 16:33

New International Version

[33]"I have told you these things, so that in me you may have peace. In this world you will have trouble. But take heart! I have overcome the world."

New American Standard Bible

[33]"These things I have spoken to you, so that in Me you may have peace In the world you have tribulation, but take courage; I have overcome the world."

The Message

[33]I've told you all this so that trusting me, you will be unshakable and assured, deeply at peace. In this godless world you will continue to experience difficulties. But take heart! I've conquered the world."

Amplified Bible

[33]I have told you these things, so that in Me you may have [perfect] peace and confidence. In the world you have tribulation and trials and distress and frustration; but be of good cheer [take courage; be confident, certain, undaunted]! For I have overcome the world. [I have deprived it of power to harm you and have conquered it for you.]

New Living Translation

[33] I have told you all this so that you may have peace in me. Here on earth you will have many trials and sorrows. But take heart, because I have overcome the world."

Reflection

Contemporary English Version

[33]I have told you this, so that you might have peace in your hearts because of me. While you are in the world, you will have to suffer. But cheer up! I have defeated the world. [a]

New King James Version

[33] These things I have spoken to you, that in Me you may have peace. In the world you will[a] have tribulation; but be of good cheer, I have overcome the world."

God promises to give you the Holy Spirit.

John 14:16-17

(New International Version, ©2011)

[16] And I will ask the Father, and he will give you another advocate to help you and be with you forever—[17] the Spirit of truth. The world cannot accept him, because it neither sees him nor knows him. But you know him, for he lives with you and will be in you.

New American Standard Bible

[16]"I will ask the Father, and He will give you another Helper, that He may be with you forever; [17]that is the Spirit of truth, whom the world cannot receive, because it does not see Him or know Him, but you know Him because He abides with you and will be in you.

The Message

[16-17] I will talk to the Father, and he'll provide you another Friend so that you will always have someone with you. This Friend is the Spirit of Truth. The godless world can't take him in because it doesn't have eyes to see him, doesn't know what to look for. But you know him already because he has been staying with you, and will even be in you!

Amplified Bible

[16]And I will ask the Father, and He will give you another Comforter (Counselor, Helper, Intercessor, Advocate, Strengthener, and Standby), that He may remain with you forever—[17]The Spirit of Truth, Whom the world cannot receive (welcome, take to its heart), because it does not see Him or know and recognize Him. But you know and recognize Him, for He lives with you [constantly] and will be in you.

Reflection

New Living Translation

[16] And I will ask the Father, and he will give you another Advocate, who will never leave you. [17] He is the Holy Spirit, who leads into all truth. The world cannot receive him, because it isn't looking for him and doesn't recognize him. But you know him, because he lives with you now and later will be in you.

Contemporary English Version

[16]Then I will ask the Father to send you the Holy Spirit who will help you and always be with you. [17]The Spirit will show you what is true. The people of this world cannot accept the Spirit, because they don't see or know him. But you know the Spirit, who is with you and will keep on living in you.

New King James Version

[16] And I will pray the Father, and He will give you another Helper, that He may abide with you forever—[17] the Spirit of truth, whom the world cannot receive, because it neither sees Him nor knows Him; but you know Him, for He dwells with you and will be in you.

God promises to bless those who bless you.

Mark 9:41

(New International Version, ©2011)

⁴¹ Truly I tell you, anyone who gives you a cup of water in my name because you belong to the Messiah will certainly not lose their reward.

New American Standard Bible

⁴¹"For whoever gives you a cup of water to drink because of your name as followers of Christ, truly I say to you, he will not lose his reward.

The Message

³⁹⁻⁴¹Jesus wasn't pleased. "Don't stop him. No one can use my name to do something good and powerful, and in the next breath cut me down. If he's not an enemy, he's an ally. Why, anyone by just giving you a cup of water in my name is on our side. Count on it that God will notice.

Amplified Bible

⁴¹For I tell you truly, whoever gives you a cup of water to drink because you belong to and bear the name of Christ will by no means fail to get his reward.

New Living Translation

⁴¹ If anyone gives you even a cup of water because you belong to the Messiah, I tell you the truth, that person will surely be rewarded.

Contemporary English Version

⁴¹And anyone who gives you a cup of water in my name, just because you belong to me, will surely be rewarded.

New King James Version

⁴¹ For whoever gives you a cup of water to drink in My name, because you belong to Christ, assuredly, I say to you, he will by no means lose his reward.

Reflection

God promises to promote the humble.

1 Peter 5:6

(New International Version, ©2011)

⁶ Humble yourselves, therefore, under God's mighty hand, that he may lift you up in due time.

New American Standard Bible

⁶Therefore humble yourselves under the mighty hand of God, that He may exalt you at the proper time,

The Message

⁶⁻⁷So be content with who you are, and don't put on airs. God's strong hand is on you; he'll promote you at the right time. Live carefree before God; he is most careful with you.

Amplified Bible

⁶Therefore humble yourselves [demote, lower yourselves in your own estimation] under the mighty hand of God, that in due time He may exalt you,

New Living Translation

⁶ So humble yourselves under the mighty power of God, and at the right time he will lift you up in honor.

Contemporary English Version

⁶Be humble in the presence of God's mighty power, and he will honor you when the time comes.

New King James Version

⁶ Therefore humble yourselves under the mighty hand of God, that He may exalt you in due time,

Reflection

God promises that you will be overcome with joy.

Isaiah 51:11

(New International Version, ©2011)

¹¹ Those the LORD has rescued will return. They will enter Zion with singing; everlasting joy will crown their heads. Gladness and joy will overtake them, and sorrow and sighing will flee away

New American Standard Bible

¹¹So the ransomed of the LORD will return and come with joyful shouting to Zion, And everlasting joy will be on their heads. They will obtain gladness and joy, And sorrow and sighing will flee away.

The Message

¹¹In the same way God's ransomed will come back, come back to Zion cheering, shouting, Joy eternal wreathing their heads, exuberant ecstasies transporting them—and not a sign of moans or groans.

Amplified Bible

¹¹[The Lord God says] And the redeemed of the Lord shall return and come with singing to Zion; everlasting joy shall be upon their heads. They shall obtain joy and gladness, and sorrow and sighing shall flee away.

New Living Translation

¹¹ Those who have been ransomed by the
    Lord will return.
       They will enter Jerusalemsinging, crowned
       with everlasting joy.
Sorrow and mourning will disappear, and they
will be filled with joy and gladness

Reflection

Contemporary English Version

¹¹Now those you have rescued will return to Jerusalem, singing on their way. They will be crowned with great happiness, never again to be burdened with sadness and sorrow.

New King James Version

¹¹ So the ransomed of the LORD shall return, And come to Zion with singing, With everlasting joy on their heads. They shall obtain joy and gladness; Sorrow and sighing shall flee away.

God promises to prolong your life.

Deuteronomy 6:2

(New International Version, ©2011)

² so that you, your children and their children after them may fear the LORD your God as long as you live by keeping all his decrees and commands that I give you, and so that you may enjoy long life.

New American Standard Bible

²so that you and your son and your grandson might fear the LORD your God, to keep all His statutes and His commandments which I command you, all the days of your life, and that your days may be prolonged.

The Message

¹⁻² This is the commandment, the rules and regulations, that God, your God, commanded me to teach you to live out in the land you're about to cross into to possess. This is so that you'll live in deep reverence before God lifelong, observing all his rules and regulations that I'm commanding you, you and your children and your grandchildren, living good long lives.

Amplified Bible

²That you may [reverently] fear the Lord your God, you and your son and your son's son, and keep all His statutes and His commandments which I command you all the days of your life, and that your days may be prolonged.

New Living Translation

² and you and your children and grandchildren must fear the Lord your God as long as you live. If you obey all his decrees and commands, you will enjoy a long life.

Reflection

Contemporary English Version

[2]And if you and your descendants want to live a long time, you must always worship the LORD and obey his laws.

New King James Version

[2] that you may fear the LORD your God, to keep all His statutes and His commandments which I command you, you and your son and your grandson, all the days of your life, and that your days may be prolonged.

God promises that His love for us came first.

1 John 4:10

(New International Version, ©2011)

¹⁰ This is love: not that we loved God, but he loved us and sent his Son as an atoning sacrifice for our sins.

New American Standard Bible

¹⁰In this is love, not that we loved God, but that He loved us and sent His Son to be the propitiation for our sins.

The Message

¹⁰ This is the kind of love we are talking about—not that we once upon a time loved God, but that he loved us and sent his Son as a sacrifice to clear away our sins and the damage they've done to our relationship with God.

Amplified Bible

¹⁰In this is love: not that we loved God, but that He loved us and sent His Son to be the propitiation (the atoning sacrifice) for our sins.

New Living Translation

¹⁰ This is real love—not that we loved God, but that he loved us and sent his Son as a sacrifice to take away our sins.

Contemporary English Version

¹⁰Real love isn't our love for God, but his love for us. God sent his Son to be the sacrifice by which our sins are forgiven.

New King James Version

¹⁰ In this is love, not that we loved God, but that He loved us and sent His Son to be the propitiation for our sins.

Reflection

God promises to love us.

1 John 4:19

(New International Version, ©2011)

[19] We love because he first loved us.

New American Standard Bible

[19](We love, because He first loved us.

The Message

[19]We, though, are going to love—love and be loved. First we were loved, now we love. He loved us first.

Amplified Bible

[19]We love Him, because He first loved us.

New Living Translation

[19] We love each other because he loved us first.

Contemporary English Version

[19]We love because God loved us first.

New King James Version

[19] We love Him because He first loved us.

Reflection

God promises to judge with righteousness.

Isaiah 11:4

(New International Version, ©2011)

⁴ but with righteousness he will judge the needy,
with justice he will give decisions for the poor of the earth.
He will strike the earth with the rod of his mouth;
with the breath of his lips he will slay the wicked.

New American Standard Bible)

⁴But with righteousness He will judge the poor,
And decide with fairness for the afflicted of the earth;
And He will strike the earth with the rod of His mouth,
And with the breath of His lips He will slay the wicked.

The Message

⁴ He'll judge the needy by what is right, render decisions on earth's poor with justice His words will bring everyone to awed attention. A mere breath from his lips will topple the wicked.

Amplified Bible

⁴But with righteousness and justice shall He judge the poor and decide with fairness for the meek, the poor, and the downtrodden of the earth; and He shall smite the earth and the oppressor with the rod of His mouth, and with the breath of His lips He shall slay the wicked.

New Living Translation

⁴ He will give justice to the poor and make fair decisions for the exploited. The earth will shake at the force of his word, and one breath from his mouth will destroy the wicked.

Reflection

Contemporary English Version

[4]The poor and the needy will be treated with fairness and with justice. His word will be law everywhere in the land, and criminals will be put to death.

(New King James Version)

[4] But with righteousness He shall judge the poor,
    And decide with equity for the meek of the earth;
    He shall strike the earth with the rod of His mouth,
    And with the breath of His lips He shall slay the wicked.

God promises to bless those who look out for the less fortunate.

Psalm 41:1

(New International Version, ©2011)

[1] Blessed are those who have regard for the
weak;
the LORD delivers them in times of trouble.

New American Standard Bible

[1]How blessed is he who considers the helpless;
The LORD will deliver him in a day of
trouble

The Message

A David Psalm

[1]Dignify those who are down on their luck;
you'll feel good—that's what God does. God
looks after us all, makes us robust with life—

Amplified Bible

[1]BLESSED (HAPPY, fortunate, to be envied)
is he who considers the weak and the poor; the
Lord will deliver him in the time of evil and
trouble.

New Living Translation

[1] Oh, the joys of those who are kind to the poor!
The Lord rescues them when they are in trouble.

Contemporary English Version

[1]You, LORD God, bless everyone who cares
for the poor, and you rescue those people in
times of trouble.

New King James Version

[1] Blessed is he who considers the poor;
The LORD will deliver him in time of
trouble.

Reflection

God promises to be with you.

Philippians 4:9

(New International Version, ©2011)

⁹ Whatever you have learned or received or heard from me, or seen in me—put it into practice. And the God of peace will be with you.

New American Standard Bible

⁹The things you have learned and received and heard and seen in me, practice these things, and the God of peace will be with you.

The Message

⁹ Put into practice what you learned from me, what you heard and saw and realized. Do that, and God, who makes everything work together, will work you into his most excellent harmonies.

Amplified Bible

⁹Practice what you have learned and received and heard and seen in me, and model your way of living on it, and the God of peace (of untroubled, undisturbed well-being) will be with you.

New Living Translation

⁹ Keep putting into practice all you learned and received from me—everything you heard from me and saw me doing. Then the God of peace will be with you.

Contemporary English Version

⁹You know the teachings I gave you, and you know what you heard me say and saw me do. So follow my example. And God, who gives peace, will be with you.

Reflection

New King James Version

⁹ The things which you learned and received and heard and saw in me, these do, and the God of peace will be with you.

God promises that our trials will make us stronger.

Romans 5:3-4

(New International Version, ©2011)

[3] Not only so, but we also glory in our sufferings, because we know that suffering produces perseverance; [4] perseverance, character; and character, hope.

New American Standard Bible

[3] And not only this, but we also exult in our tribulations, knowing that tribulation brings about perseverance; [4] and perseverance, proven character; and proven character, hope;

The Message

[3-5] There's more to come: We continue to shout our praise even when we're hemmed in with troubles, because we know how troubles can develop passionate patience in us, and how that patience in turn forges the tempered steel of virtue, keeping us alert for whatever God will do next. In alert expectancy such as this, we're never left feeling shortchanged. Quite the contrary—we can't round up enough containers to hold everything God generously pours into our lives through the Holy Spirit!

Amplified Bible

[3] Moreover [let us also be full of joy now!] let us exult and triumph in our troubles and rejoice in our sufferings, knowing that pressure and affliction and hardship produce patient and unswerving endurance. [4] And endurance (fortitude) develops maturity of character (approved faith and tried integrity). And character [of this sort] produces [the habit of] joyful and confident hope of eternal salvation.

Reflection

New Living Translation

[3] We can rejoice, too, when we run into problems and trials, for we know that they help us develop endurance. [4] And endurance develops strength of character, and character strengthens our confident hope of salvation.

Contemporary English Version

[3] But that's not all! We gladly suffer, [a] because we know that suffering helps us to endure. [4] And endurance builds character, which gives us a hope

New King James Version

[3] And not only that, but we also glory in tribulations, knowing that tribulation produces perseverance; [4] and perseverance, character; and character, hope.

God promises that His peace is not like the worlds peace.

John 14:27

(New International Version, ©2011)

[27] Peace I leave with you; my peace I give you. I do not give to you as the world gives. Do not let your hearts be troubled and do not be afraid.

New American Standard Bible

[27]"Peace I leave with you; My peace I give to you; not as the world gives do I give to you Do not let your heart be troubled, nor let it be fearful.

The Message

[27]Peace. I don't leave you the way you're used to being left—feeling abandoned, bereft. So don't be upset. Don't be distraught.

Amplified Bible

[27]Peace I leave with you; My [own] peace I now give and bequeath to you. Not as the world gives do I give to you. Do not let your hearts be troubled, neither let them be afraid. [Stop allowing yourselves to be agitated and disturbed; and do not permit yourselves to be fearful and intimidated and cowardly and unsettled.]

New Living Translation

[27] "I am leaving you with a gift—peace of mind and heart. And the peace I give is a gift the world cannot give. So don't be troubled or afraid.

Contemporary English Version

[27]I give you peace, the kind of peace that only I can give. It isn't like the peace that this world can give. So don't be worried or afraid.

New King James Version

[27] Peace I leave with you, My peace I give to you; not as the world gives do I give to you. Let not your heart be troubled, neither let it be afraid.

Reflection

God promises to listen to us when we seek Him.

Jeremiah 29:12

(New International Version, ©2011)

[12] Then you will call on me and come and pray to me, and I will listen to you.

New American Standard Bible

[12]'Then you will call upon Me and come and pray to Me, and I will listen to you.

The Message

[12]"When you call on me, when you come and pray to me, I'll listen.

Amplified Bible

[12]Then you will call upon Me, and you will come and pray to Me, and I will hear and heed you.

New Living Translation

[12] In those days when you pray, I will listen.

Contemporary English Version

[12]You will turn back to me and ask for help, and I will answer your prayers.

New King James Version

[12] Then you will call upon Me and go and pray to Me, and I will listen to you.

Reflection

God promises that He hears us when we pray.

Isaiah 65:24

(New International Version, ©2011)

24 Before they call I will answer;
    while they are still speaking I will hear.

New American Standard Bible

24"It will also come to pass that before they call, I will (A)answer; and while they are still speaking, I will hear.

The Message

Before they call out, I'll answer.
    Before they've finished speaking, I'll have heard.

Amplified Bible

24And it shall be that before they call I will answer; and while they are yet speaking I will hear.(A)

New Living Translation

24 I will answer them before they even call to me.
    While they are still talking about their needs,
    I will go ahead and answer their prayers!

Contemporary English Version

24I will answer their prayers before they finish praying.

New King James Version

24 "It shall come to pass
    That before they call, I will answer;
    And while they are still speaking, I will hear.

Reflection

God promises to give sweet sleep.

Proverbs 3:24

(New International Version, ©2011)

24 When you lie down, you will not be afraid;
when you lie down, your sleep will be sweet.

New American Standard Bible

24When you lie down, you will not be afraid;
When you lie down, your sleep will be sweet.

The Message

24 You'll take afternoon naps without a worry,
you'll enjoy a good night's sleep.

Amplified Bible

24When you lie down, you shall not be afraid;
yes, you shall lie down, and your sleep shall be sweet.

New Living Translation

24 You can go to bed without fear;
you will lie down and sleep soundly.

Contemporary English Version

24you will rest without a worry and sleep soundly.

New King James Version

24 When you lie down, you will not be afraid;
Yes, you will lie down and your sleep will be sweet

Reflection

God promises to be our light and our salvation.

Psalm 27:1

(New International Version, ©2011)

¹ The LORD is my light and my salvation—
 whom shall I fear?
The LORD is the stronghold of my life—
 of whom shall I be afraid?

New American Standard Bible

A Psalm of David.

¹The LORD is my light and my salvation;
 Whom shall I fear?
The LORD is the defense of my life;
 Whom shall I dread?

The Message

¹ Light, space, zest—that's God!
 So, with him on my side I'm fearless,
 afraid of no one and nothing.

Amplified Bible

¹THE LORD is my Light and my
Salvation—whom shall I fear or dread? The
Lord is the Refuge and Stronghold of my
life—of whom shall I be afraid?

New Living Translation

¹ The Lord is my light and my salvation—
 so why should I be afraid?
The Lord is my fortress, protecting me from
 danger,
 so why should I tremble?

Contemporary English Version

¹You, LORD, are the light that keeps me safe.
I am not afraid of anyone. You protect me, and
I have no fears.

Reflection

New King James Version

[1] The LORD is my light and my salvation;
  Whom shall I fear?
The LORD is the strength of my life;
  Of whom shall I be afraid?

RUDOLPH MOSELEY JR.

God promises to bind up the wounds of the brokenhearted.

Psalm 147:3

New International Version

³ He heals the brokenhearted
and binds up their wounds.

New American Standard Bible

³He heals the brokenhearted
And binds up their wounds.

The Message

³He heals the heartbroken
and bandages their wounds.

Amplified Bible

³He heals the brokenhearted and binds up their wounds [curing their pains and their sorrows].

New Living Translation

³ He heals the brokenhearted and bandages their wounds.

Contemporary English Version

³He renews our hopes and heals our bodies.

New King James Version

³ He heals the brokenhearted
And binds up their wounds

Reflection

God promises to reward the righteous with good things.

Proverbs 13:21

New International Version

[21] Trouble pursues the sinner,
  but the righteous are rewarded with good things.

New American Standard Bible

[21] Adversity pursues sinners,
  But the righteous will be rewarded with prosperity.

The Message

[21] Disaster entraps sinners,
  but God-loyal people get a good life.

Amplified Bible

[21] Evil pursues sinners, but the consistently upright and in right standing with God is recompensed with good.

New Living Translation

[21] Trouble chases sinners,
  while blessings reward the righteous.

Contemporary English Version

[21] You are in for trouble if you sin, but you will be rewarded if you live right.

New King James Version

[21] Evil pursues sinners,
  But to the righteous, good shall be repaid.

Reflection

God promises to make us the righteousness of God.

2 Corinthians 5:21

New International Version

[21] God made him who had no sin to be sin for us, so that in him we might become the righteousness of God.

New American Standard Bible

[21]He made Him who knew no sin to be sin on our behalf, so that we might become the righteousness of God in Him.

The Message

[21]How? you ask. In Christ. God put the wrong on him who never did anything wrong, so we could be put right with God

Amplified Bible

[21]For our sake He made Christ [virtually] to be sin Who knew no sin, so that in and through Him we might become [endued with, viewed as being in, and examples of] the righteousness of God [what we ought to be, approved and acceptable and in right relationship with Him, by His goodness].

New Living Translation

[21] For God made Christ, who never sinned, to be the offering for our sin, so that we could be made right with God through Christ.

Contemporary English Version

[21]Christ never sinned! But God treated him as a sinner, so that Christ could make us acceptable to God.

New King James Version

[21] For He made Him who knew no sin to be sin for us, that we might become the righteousness of God in Him.

Reflection

God promises to be found when we seek Him with all our heart.

Jeremiah 29:13

New International Version

¹³ You will seek me and find me when you seek me with all your heart.

New American Standard Bible

¹³'You will seek Me and find Me when you search for Me with all your heart.

The Message

¹³⁻¹⁴"When you come looking for me, you'll find me. "Yes, when you get serious about finding me and want it more than anything else, I'll make sure you won't be disappointed." God's Decree.

Amplified Bible

¹³Then you will seek Me, inquire for, and require Me [as a vital necessity] and find Me when you search for Me with all your heart.

New Living Translation

¹³ If you look for me wholeheartedly, you will find me.

Contemporary English Version

¹³You will worship me with all your heart, and I will be with you

New King James Version

¹³ And you will seek Me and find Me, when you search for Me with all your heart.

Reflection

God promises to heal us.

Peter 2:24

New International Version

²⁴ "He himself bore our sins" in his body on the cross, so that we might die to sins and live for righteousness; "by his wounds you have been healed."

New American Standard Bible

²⁴and He Himself bore our sins in His body on the cross, so that we might die to sin and live to righteousness; for by His wounds you were healed.

The Message

²⁴ He used his servant body to carry our sins to the Cross so we could be rid of sin, free to live the right way. His wounds became your healing.

Amplified Bible

²⁴He personally bore our sins in His [own] body on the tree [as on an altar and offered Himself on it], that we might die (cease to exist) to sin and live to righteousness. By His wounds you have been healed.

New Living Translation

²⁴ He personally carried our sins in his body on the cross so that we can be dead to sin and live for what is right. By his wounds you are healed.

Contemporary English Version

²⁴Christ carried the burden of our sins. He was nailed to the cross, so that we would stop sinning and start living right. By his cuts and bruises you are healed.

New King James Version

²⁴ who Himself bore our sins in His own body on the tree, that we, having died to sins, might live for righteousness—by whose stripes you were healed.

Reflection

God promises that sin does not have power over you anymore.

Romans 6:14

New International Version

¹⁴ For sin shall no longer be your master, because you are not under the law, but under grace.

New American Standard Bible

¹⁴ For sin shall not be master over you, for you are not under law but under grace.

The Message

¹⁴ Sin can't tell you how to live. After all, you're not living under that old tyranny any longer. You're living in the freedom of God.

Amplified Bible

¹⁴ For sin shall not [any longer] exert dominion over you, since now you are not under Law [as slaves], but under grace [as subjects of God's favor and mercy].

New Living Translation

¹⁴ Sin is no longer your master, for you no longer live under the requirements of the law. Instead, you live under the freedom of God's grace.

Contemporary English Version

¹⁴ Don't let sin keep ruling your lives. You are ruled by God's kindness and not by the Law.

New King James Version

¹⁴ For sin shall not have dominion over you, for you are not under law but under grace.

Reflection

God promises that Jesus got the punishment that we deserved.

Isaiah 53:6

New International Version

⁶ We all, like sheep, have gone astray,
    each of us has turned to our own way;
and the LORD has laid on him
    the iniquity of us all.

New American Standard Bible

⁶All of us like sheep have gone astray,
    Each of us has turned to his own way;
    But the LORD has caused the iniquity of
    us all
    To fall on Him.

The Message

⁶ We've all done our own thing, gone our own
    way.
    And God has piled all our sins, everything
    we've done wrong,
    on him, on him.

Amplified Bible

⁶All we like sheep have gone astray, we have
turned everyone to his own way; and the Lord
has made to light upon Him the guilt and
iniquity of us all.

New Living Translation

⁶ All of us, like sheep, have strayed away. We
have left God's paths to follow our own. Yet the
Lord laid on him the sins of us all.

Contemporary English Version

⁶All of us were like sheep that had wandered off.
We had each gone our own way, but the LORD
gave him the punishment we deserved.

New King James Version

⁶ All we like sheep have gone astray;
    We have turned, every one, to his own way;
    And the LORD has laid on Him the iniquity of us all.

Reflection

God promises that you are healed.

Isaiah 53:5

New International Version

⁵ But he was pierced for our transgressions,
   he was crushed for our iniquities;
the punishment that brought us peace was on
   him,
   and by his wounds we are healed.

New American Standard Bible

⁵But He was pierced through for our
   transgressions,
   He was crushed for our iniquities;
   The chastening for our well-being fell
   upon Him,
   And by His scourging we are healed.

The Message

⁶But it was our sins that did that to him,
   that ripped and tore and crushed
   him—our sins!
He took the punishment, and that made us
   whole.
   Through his bruises we get healed.

Amplified Bible

⁵But He was wounded for our transgressions,
He was bruised for our guilt and iniquities;
the chastisement [needful to obtain] peace and
well-being for us was upon Him, and with the
stripes [that wounded] Him we are healed and
made whole.

Contemporary English Version

⁵He was wounded and crushed because of our
sins; by taking our punishment, he made us
completely well.

New King James Version

⁵ But He was wounded for our transgressions, He was bruised for our iniquities;
The chastisement for our peace was upon Him, And by His stripes we are healed.

Reflection

God promises that His favor will shine on you always.

Job 22:28

New International Version

²⁸ What you decide on will be done,
    and light will shine on your ways.

New American Standard Bible

²⁸"You will also decree a thing, and it will be
    established for you;
    And light will shine on your ways.

The Message

²⁸You'll decide what you want and it will
    happen;
    your life will be bathed in light.

Amplified Bible

²⁸You shall also decide and decree a thing, and
it shall be established for you; and the light [of
God's favor] shall shine upon your ways.

New Living Translation

²⁸ You will succeed in whatever you choose to
    do,
    and light will shine on the road ahead of
you.

Contemporary English Version

²⁸He will do whatever you ask, and life will be
bright.

Reflection

God promises to give you the desires of your heart.

Psalm 37:3-5

New International Version

³ Trust in the LORD and do good; dwell in the land and enjoy safe pasture. ⁴ Take delight in the LORD, and he will give you the desires of your heart. ⁵ Commit your way to the LORD; trust in him and he will do this:

New American Standard Bible

³Trust in the LORD and do good; Dwell in the land and cultivate faithfulness. ⁴Delight yourself in the LORD; And He will give you the desires of your heart. ⁵Commit your way to the LORD, Trust also in Him, and He will do it.

The Message

³⁻⁴ Get insurance with God and do a good deed, settle down and stick to your last. Keep company with God, get in on the best. ⁵⁻⁶ Open up before God, keep nothing back; he'll do whatever needs to be done:

Amplified Bible

³Trust (lean on, rely on, and be confident) in the Lord and do good; so shall you dwell in the land and feed surely on His faithfulness, and truly you shall be fed. ⁴Delight yourself also in the Lord, and He will give you the desires and secret petitions of your heart. ⁵Commit your way to the Lord [roll and repose each care of your load on Him]; trust (lean on, rely on, and be confident) also in Him and He will bring it to pass.

Reflection

Contemporary English Version

³Trust the LORD and live right! The land will be yours, and you will be safe. ⁴Do what the LORD wants, and he will give you your heart's desire. ⁵Let the LORD lead you and trust him to help.

New King James Version

³ Trust in the LORD, and do good; Dwell in the land, and feed on His faithfulness ⁴ Delight yourself also in the LORD, And He shall give you the desires of your heart. ⁵ Commit your way to the LORD, Trust also in Him, And He shall bring it to pass.

God promises to bless the people who trust in Him.

Psalm 84:11-12

New International Version

[11] For the LORD God is a sun and shield; the LORD bestows favor and honor; no good thing does he withhold from those whose walk is blameless. [12] LORD Almighty, blessed is the one who trusts in you.

New American Standard Bible

[11] For the LORD God is a sun and shield; The LORD gives grace and glory; No good thing does He withhold from those who walk uprightly. [12] O LORD of hosts, How blessed is the man who trusts in You!

The Message

[11] All sunshine and sovereign is God, generous in gifts and glory. He doesn't scrimp with his traveling companions. It's smooth sailing all the way with God-of-the-Angel-Armies.

Amplified Bible

[11] For the Lord God is a Sun and Shield; the Lord bestows [present] grace and favor and [future] glory (honor, splendor, and heavenly bliss)! No good thing will He withhold from those who walk uprightly. [12] O Lord of hosts, blessed (happy, fortunate, to be envied) is the man who trusts in You [leaning and believing on You, committing all and confidently looking to You, and that without fear or misgiving]!

New Living Translation

[11] For the Lord God is our sun and our shield. He gives us grace and glory. The Lord will withhold no good thing from those who do what is right. [12] O Lord of Heaven's Armies, what joy for those who trust in you.

Reflection

Contemporary English Version

[11]Our LORD and our God, you are like the sun and also like a shield. You treat us with kindness and with honor, never denying any good thing to those who live right. [12]LORD God All-Powerful, you bless everyone who trusts you.

God promises to make your path straight when you trust Him.

Proverbs 3:5-6

New International Version

[5] Trust in the LORD with all your heart and lean not on your own understanding; [6] in all your ways submit to him, and he will make your paths straight.

New American Standard Bible

[5] Trust in the LORD with all your heart And do not lean on your own understanding. [6] In all your ways acknowledge Him, And He will make your paths straight.

The Message

[5-11] Trust God from the bottom of your heart; don't try to figure out everything on your own. Listen for God's voice in everything you do, everywhere you go; he's the one who will keep you on track.

Amplified Bible

[5] Lean on, trust in, and be confident in the Lord with all your heart and mind and do not rely on your own insight or understanding. [6] In all your ways know, recognize, and acknowledge Him, and He will direct and make straight and plain your paths.

New Living Translation

[5] Trust in the Lord with all your heart; do not depend on your own understanding. [6] Seek his will in all you do, and he will show you which path to take.

Contemporary English Version

[5] With all your heart you must trust the LORD and not your own judgment. [6] Always let him lead you, and he will clear the road for you to follow.

Reflection

God promises to give you wisdom.

Ecclesiastes 2:26

New International Version

²⁶ To the person who pleases him, God gives wisdom, knowledge and happiness, but to the sinner he gives the task of gathering and storing up wealth to hand it over to the one who pleases God. This too is meaningless, a chasing after the wind.

New American Standard Bible

²⁶For to a person who is good in His sight He has given wisdom and knowledge and joy, while to the sinner He has given the task of gathering and collecting so that he may give to one who is good in God's sight This too is vanity and striving after wind.

The Message

²⁶ God may give wisdom and knowledge and joy to his favorites, but sinners are assigned a life of hard labor, and end up turning their wages over to God's favorites. Nothing but smoke—and spitting into the wind.

Amplified Bible

²⁶For to the person who pleases Him God gives wisdom and knowledge and joy; but to the sinner He gives the work of gathering and heaping up, that he may give to one who pleases God. This also is vanity and a striving after the wind and a feeding on it.

New Living Translation

²⁶ God gives wisdom, knowledge, and joy to those who please him. But if a sinner becomes wealthy, God takes the wealth away and gives it to those who please him. This, too, is meaningless—like chasing the wind.

Reflection

Contemporary English Version

[26]If we please God, he will make us wise, understanding, and happy. But if we sin, God will make us struggle for a living, then he will give all we own to someone who pleases him. This makes no more sense than chasing the wind.

New King James Version

[26] For God gives wisdom and knowledge and joy to a man who is good in His sight; but to the sinner He gives the work of gathering and collecting, that he may give to him who is good before God. This also is vanity and grasping for the wind.

God promises that His teaching will bring light to your path.

Proverbs 6:23

New International Version

23 For this command is a lamp, this teaching is a light, and correction and instruction are the way to life,

New American Standard Bible

23For the commandment is a lamp and the teaching is light;
And reproofs for discipline are the way of life

The Message

23For sound advice is a beacon,
good teaching is a light,
moral discipline is a life path.

Amplified Bible

23For the commandment is a lamp, and the whole teaching [of the law] is light, and reproofs of discipline are the way of life,

New Living Translation

23 For their command is a lamp and their instruction a light; their corrective discipline is the way to life.

Contemporary English Version

23The Law of the Lord is a lamp, and its teachings shine brightly. Correction and self-control will lead you through life.

New King James Version

23 For the commandment is a lamp, And the law a light; Reproofs of instruction are the way of life.

Reflection

God promises that His word brings direction.

Psalm 119:105

New International Version

[105] Your word is a lamp for my feet,
a light on my path.

New American Standard Bible

[105]Your word is a lamp to my feet And a light to my path.

The Message

[105]By your words I can see where I'm going; they throw a beam of light on my dark path.

Amplified Bible

[105]Your word is a lamp to my feet and a light to my path.

New Living Translation

[105] Your word is a lamp to guide my feet and a light for my path.

Contemporary English Version

[105]Your word is a lamp that gives light wherever I walk.

New King James Version

[105] Your word is a lamp to my feet

Reflection

God promises to give rest to the weary.

Matthew 11:28

New International Version

²⁸ "Come to me, all you who are weary and burdened, and I will give you rest.

New American Standard Bible

²⁸"Come to Me, all who are weary and heavy-laden, and I will give you rest.

The Message

²⁸ Come to me. Get away with me and you'll recover your life. I'll show you how to take a real rest.

Amplified Bible

²⁸Come to Me, all you who labor and are heavy-laden and overburdened, and I will cause you to rest. [I will ease and relieve and refresh your souls.]

New Living Translation

²⁸ Then Jesus said, "Come to me, all of you who are weary and carry heavy burdens, and I will give you rest.

Contemporary English Version

²⁸If you are tired from carrying heavy burdens, come to me and I will give you rest.

New King James Version

²⁸ Come to Me, all you who labor and are heavy laden, and I will give you rest.

Reflection

God promises to be help when you need Him.

Psalm 46:1-2

New International Version

[1] God is our refuge and strength, an ever-present help in trouble. [2] Therefore we will not fear, though the earth give way and the mountains fall into the heart of the sea,

New American Standard Bible

[1] God is our refuge and strength, A very present help in trouble. [2] Therefore we will not fear, though the earth should change And though the mountains slip into the heart of the sea;

The Message

[1-2] God is a safe place to hide, ready to help when we need him. We stand fearless at the cliff-edge of doom, courageous in sea storm and earthquake, Before the rush and roar of oceans, the tremors that shift mountains.

Amplified Bible

[1] GOD IS our Refuge and Strength [mighty and impenetrable to temptation], a very present and well-proved help in trouble. [2] Therefore we will not fear, though the earth should change and though the mountains be shaken into the midst of the seas,

New Living Translation

[1] God is our refuge and strength, always ready to help in times of trouble. [2] So we will not fear when earthquakes come and the mountains crumble into the sea.

Contemporary English Version

[1] God is our mighty fortress, always ready to help in times of trouble. [2] And so, we won't be afraid! Let the earth tremble and the mountains tumble into the deepest sea.

Reflection

New King James Version

¹ God is our refuge and strength, A very present help in trouble ² Therefore we will not fear, Even though the earth be removed, And though the mountains be carried into the midst of the sea;

God promises to bless and sustain those who trust in Him.

Jeremiah 17:8

New International Version

⁸ They will be like a tree planted by the water that sends out its roots by the stream. It does not fear when heat comes; its leaves are always green. It has no worries in a year of drought and never fails to bear fruit."

New American Standard Bible

⁸"For he will be like a tree planted by the water, That extends its roots by a stream And will not fear when the heat comes; But its leaves will be green, And it will not be anxious in a year of drought Nor cease to yield fruit.

The Message

⁷⁻⁸"But blessed is the man who trusts me, God, the woman who sticks with God. They're like trees replanted in Eden, putting down roots near the rivers—Never a worry through the hottest of summers, never dropping a leaf Serene and calm through droughts, bearing fresh fruit every season.

Amplified Bible

⁸For he shall be like a tree planted by the waters that spreads out its roots by the river; and it shall not see and fear when heat comes; but its leaf shall be green. It shall not be anxious and full of care in the year of drought, nor shall it cease yielding fruit.

Reflection

God promises to be a safe-house for the oppressed.

Psalm 9:9-10

New International Version

⁹ The LORD is a refuge for the oppressed, a stronghold in times of trouble. ¹⁰ Those who know your name trust in you, for you, LORD, have never forsaken those who seek you.

New American Standard Bible

⁹The LORD also will be a stronghold for the oppressed, A stronghold in times of trouble; ¹⁰And those who know Your name will put their trust in You, For You, O LORD, have not forsaken those who seek You.

The Message

⁹⁻¹⁰ God's a safe-house for the battered, a sanctuary during bad times. The moment you arrive, you relax; you're never sorry you knocked.

Amplified Bible

⁹The Lord also will be a refuge and a high tower for the oppressed, a refuge and a stronghold in times of trouble (high cost, destitution, and desperation). ¹⁰And they who know Your name [who have experience and acquaintance with Your mercy] will lean on and confidently put their trust in You, for You, Lord, have not forsaken those who seek (inquire of and for) You [on the authority of God's Word and the right of their necessity].

New Living Translation

⁹ The Lord is a shelter for the oppressed, a refuge in times of trouble. ¹⁰ Those who know your name trust in you, for you, O Lord, do not abandon those who search for you.

Reflection

Contemporary English Version

⁹The poor can run to you because you are a fortress in times of trouble. ¹⁰Everyone who honors your name can trust you, because you are faithful to all who depend on you.

New King James Version

⁹ The LORD also will be a refuge for the oppressed, A refuge in times of trouble. ¹⁰ And those who know Your name will put their trust in You; For You, LORD, have not forsaken those who seek You.

God promises to be present when we worship Him in truth.

John 4:24

New International Version

24 God is spirit, and his worshipers must worship in the Spirit and in truth."

New American Standard Bible

24"God is spirit, and those who worship Him must worship in spirit and truth."

The Message

24 God is sheer being itself—Spirit. Those who worship him must do it out of their very being, their spirits, their true selves, in adoration."

Amplified Bible

24God is a Spirit (a spiritual Being) and those who worship Him must worship Him in spirit and in truth (reality).

New Living Translation

24 For God is Spirit, so those who worship him must worship in spirit and in truth."

Contemporary English Version

24God is Spirit, and those who worship God must be led by the Spirit to worship him according to the truth.

New King James Version

24 God is Spirit, and those who worship Him must worship in spirit and truth."

Reflection

God promises to give a reward when we bless our enemies.

Proverbs 25:21-22

New International Version

[21] If your enemy is hungry, give him food to eat; if he is thirsty, give him water to drink. [22] In doing this, you will heap burning coals on his head, and the LORD will reward you.

New American Standard Bible

[21]If your enemy is hungry, give him food to eat; And if he is thirsty, give him water to drink; [22]For you will heap burning coals on his head, And the LORD will reward you.

The Message

[21-22] If you see your enemy hungry, go buy him lunch; if he's thirsty, bring him a drink. Your generosity will surprise him with goodness, and God will look after you.

Amplified Bible

[21]If your enemy is hungry, give him bread to eat; and if he is thirsty, give him water to drink; [22]For in doing so, you will heap coals of fire upon his head, and the Lord will reward you.

New Living Translation

[21] If your enemies are hungry, give them food to eat. If they are thirsty, give them water to drink. [22] You will heap burning coals of shame on their heads, and the Lord will reward you.

Contemporary English Version

[21]If your enemies are hungry, give them something to eat. And if they are thirsty, give them something to drink. [22]This will be the same as piling burning coals on their heads. And the LORD will reward you.

Reflection

New King James Version

[21] If your enemy is hungry, give him bread to eat; And if he is thirsty, give him water to drink; [22] For so you will heap coals of fire on his head, And the LORD will reward you.

God promises to save our household.

Acts 16:31

New International Version

³¹ They replied, "Believe in the Lord Jesus, and you will be saved—you and your household."

New American Standard Bible

³¹They said, "Believe in the Lord Jesus, and you will be saved, you and your household."

The Message

³¹ "Sirs, what do I have to do to be saved, to really live?" They said, "Put your entire trust in the Master Jesus. Then you'll live as you were meant to live—and everyone in your house included!"

Amplified Bible

³¹And they answered, Believe in the Lord Jesus Christ [give yourself up to Him, take yourself out of your own keeping and entrust yourself into His keeping] and you will be saved, [and this applies both to] you and your household as well.

New Living Translation

³¹ They replied, "Believe in the Lord Jesus and you will be saved, along with everyone in your household

Contemporary English Version

³¹They replied, "Have faith in the Lord Jesus and you will be saved! This is also true for everyone who lives in your home."

New King James Version

³¹ So they said, "Believe on the Lord Jesus Christ, and you will be saved, you and your household."

Reflection

God promises to not leave you in darkness.

John 12:46

New International Version

⁴⁶ I have come into the world as a light, so that no one who believes in me should stay in darkness.

New American Standard Bible

⁴⁶"I have come as Light into the world, so that everyone who believes in Me will not remain in darkness.

The Message

⁴⁶ I am Light that has come into the world so that all who believe in me won't have to stay any longer in the dark.

Amplified Bible

⁴⁶I have come as a Light into the world, so that whoever believes in Me [whoever cleaves to and trusts in and relies on Me] may not continue to live in darkness.

New Living Translation

⁴⁶ I have come as a light to shine in this dark world, so that all who put their trust in me will no longer remain in the dark.

Contemporary English Version

⁴⁶I am the light that has come into the world. No one who has faith in me will stay in the dark.

New King James Version

⁴⁶ I have come as a light into the world, that whoever believes in Me should not abide in darkness.

Reflection

God promises that you will never go hungry or thirsty.

John 6:35

New International Version

35 Then Jesus declared, "I am the bread of life. Whoever comes to me will never go hungry, and whoever believes in me will never be thirsty.

New American Standard Bible

35 Jesus said to them, "I am the bread of life; he who comes to Me will not hunger, and he who believes in Me will never thirst.

The Message

35 Jesus said, "I am the Bread of Life. The person who aligns with me hungers no more and thirsts no more, ever.

Amplified Bible

35 Jesus replied, I am the Bread of Life. He who comes to Me will never be hungry, and he who believes in and cleaves to and trusts in and relies on Me will never thirst any more (at any time).

New Living Translation

35 Jesus replied, "I am the bread of life. Whoever comes to me will never be hungry again. Whoever believes in me will never be thirsty.

Contemporary English Version

35 Jesus replied: I am the bread that gives life! No one who comes to me will ever be hungry. No one who has faith in me will ever be thirsty.

New King James Version

35 And Jesus said to them, "I am the bread of life. He who comes to Me shall never hunger, and he who believes in Me shall never thirst.

Reflection

God promises that you will never be put to shame.

Romans 9:33

New International Version

33 As it is written: "See, I lay in Zion a stone that causes people to stumble and a rock that makes them fall, and the one who believes in him will never be put to shame."

New American Standard Bible

33just as it is written, "BEHOLD, I LAY IN ZION A STONE OF STUMBLING AND A ROCK OF OFFENSE, AND HE WHO BELIEVES IN HIM WILL NOT BE DISAPPOINTED."

The Message

33 Careful! I've put a huge stone on the road to Mount Zion, a stone you can't get around. But the stone is me! If you're looking for me, you'll find me on the way, not in the way.

Amplified Bible

33As it is written, Behold I am laying in Zion a Stone that will make men stumble, a Rock that will make them fall; but he who believes in Him [who adheres to, trusts in, and relies on Him] shall not be put to shame nor be disappointed in his expectations.

New Living Translation

33 God warned them of this in the Scriptures when he said, "I am placing a stone in Jerusalem[a] that makes people stumble, a rock that makes them fall. But anyone who trusts in him will never be disgraced."

Reflection

Contemporary English Version

33just as God says in the Scriptures, "Look! I am placing in Zion a stone to make people stumble and fall. But those who have faith in that one will never be disappointed."

New King James Version

[33] As it is written: "Behold, I lay in Zion a stumbling stone and rock of offense, And whoever believes on Him will not be put to shame."

RUDOLPH MOSELEY JR.

God promises that if you give to the poor you will have treasure in heaven.

Luke 12:33

New International Version

³³ Sell your possessions and give to the poor. Provide purses for yourselves that will not wear out, a treasure in heaven that will never fail, where no thief comes near and no moth destroys.

New American Standard Bible

³³ "Sell your possessions and give to charity; make yourselves money belts which do not wear out, an unfailing treasure in heaven, where no thief comes near nor moth destroys.

The Message

³³⁻³⁴"Be generous. Give to the poor. Get yourselves a bank that can't go bankrupt, a bank in heaven far from bankrobbers, safe from embezzlers, a bank you can bank on. It's obvious, isn't it? The place where your treasure is, is the place you will most want to be, and end up being.

Amplified Bible

³³Sell what you possess and give donations to the poor; provide yourselves with purses and handbags that do not grow old, an unfailing and inexhaustible treasure in the heavens, where no thief comes near and no moth destroys.

New Living Translation

³³ "Sell your possessions and give to those in need. This will store up treasure for you in heaven! And the purses of heaven never get old or develop holes. Your treasure will be safe; no thief can steal it and no moth can destroy it.

Reflection

Contemporary English Version

[33]Sell what you have and give the money to the poor. Make yourselves moneybags that never wear out. Make sure your treasure is safe in heaven, where thieves cannot steal it and moths cannot destroy it.

New King James Version

[33] Sell what you have and give alms; provide yourselves money bags which do not grow old, a treasure in the heavens that does not fail, where no thief approaches nor moth destroys.

God promises to give you a return for hard work.

Ecclesiastes 11:1

New International Version

¹ Ship your grain across the sea;
    after many days you may receive a return.

New American Standard Bible

¹Cast your bread on the surface of the waters, for you will find it after many days.

The Message

Be generous: Invest in acts of charity. Charity yields high returns.

Amplified Bible

¹ CAST YOUR bread upon the waters, for you will find it after many days.

New Living Translation

¹ Send your grain across the seas,
    and in time, profits will flow back to you.

Contemporary English Version

It Pays To Work Hard ¹Be generous, and someday you will be rewarded.

New King James Version

Cast your bread upon the waters,
    For you will find it after many days.

Reflection

God promises to bless the children of the generous.

Psalm 37:26

New International Version

²⁶ They are always generous and lend freely;
their children will be a blessing.

New American Standard Bible

²⁶All day long he is gracious and lends,
And his descendants are a blessing.

The Message

²⁵⁻²⁶ I once was young, now I'm a graybeard—not
once have I seen an abandoned believer, or his
kids out roaming the streets. Every day he's out
giving and lending, his children making him
proud.

Amplified Bible

²⁶All day long they are merciful and deal
graciously; they lend, and their offspring are
blessed.

New Living Translation

²⁶ The godly always give generous loans to
others,
and their children are a blessing.

Contemporary English Version

²⁶They gladly give and lend, and their children
turn out good.

New King James Version

²⁶ He is ever merciful, and lends;
And his descendants are blessed.

Reflection

God promises that the needs of the righteous will always be met.

Psalm 37:25

New International Version

²⁵ I was young and now I am old, yet I have never seen the righteous forsaken or their children begging bread.

New American Standard Bible

²⁵I have been young and now I am old. Yet I have not seen the righteous forsaken Or his descendants begging bread.

The Message

²⁵ I once was young, now I'm a graybeard—not once have I seen an abandoned believer,

Amplified Bible

²⁵I have been young and now am old, yet have I not seen the [uncompromisingly] righteous forsaken or their seed begging bread.

New Living Translation

²⁵ Once I was young, and now I am old. Yet I have never seen the godly abandoned or their children begging for bread.

Contemporary English Version

²⁵As long as I can remember, good people have never been left helpless, and their children have never gone begging for food.

New King James Version

²⁵ I have been young, and now am old; Yet I have not seen the righteous forsaken, Nor his descendants begging bread.

Reflection

God promises to bless you when you give.

Luke 6:38

New International Version

³⁸ Give, and it will be given to you. A good measure, pressed down, shaken together and running over, will be poured into your lap. For with the measure you use, it will be measured to you."

New American Standard Bible

³⁸"Give, and it will be given to you. They will pour into your lap a good measure—pressed down, shaken together, and running over. For by your standard of measure it will be measured to you in return."

The Message

³⁸ Give away your life; you'll find life given back, but not merely given back—given back with bonus and blessing. Giving, not getting, is the way. Generosity begets generosity."

Amplified Bible

³⁸Give, and [gifts] will be given to you; good measure, pressed down, shaken together, and running over, will they pour into [the pouch formed by] the bosom [of your robe and used as a bag]. For with the measure you deal out [with the measure you use when you confer benefits on others], it will be measured back to you.

New Living Translation

³⁸ Give, and you will receive. Your gift will return to you in full—pressed down, shaken together to make room for more, running over, and poured into your lap. The amount you give will determine the amount you get back."

Reflection

Contemporary English Version

³⁸ If you give to others, you will be given a full amount in return. It will be packed down, shaken together, and spilling over into your lap. The way you treat others is the way you will be treated.

New King James Version

³⁸ Give, and it will be given to you: good measure, pressed down, shaken together, and running over will be put into your bosom. For with the same measure that you use, it will be measured back to you."

God promises to bless those who believe in Jesus.

John 20:29

New International Version

²⁹ Then Jesus told him, "Because you have seen me, you have believed; blessed are those who have not seen and yet have believed."

New American Standard Bible

²⁹Jesus said to him, "Because you have seen Me, have you believed? Blessed are they who did not see, and yet believed."

The Message

²⁹Jesus said, "So, you believe because you've seen with your own eyes. Even better blessings are in store for those who believe without seeing."

Amplified Bible

²⁹Jesus said to him, Because you have seen Me, Thomas, do you now believe (trust, have faith)? Blessed and happy and to be envied are those who have never seen Me and yet have believed and adhered to and trusted and relied on Me.

New Living Translation

²⁹ Then Jesus told him, "You believe because you have seen me. Blessed are those who believe without seeing me."

Contemporary English Version

²⁹Jesus said, "Thomas, do you have faith because you have seen me? The people who have faith in me without seeing me are the ones who are really blessed!"

New King James Version

²⁹ Jesus said to him, "Thomas, because you have seen Me, you have believed. Blessed are those who have not seen and yet have believed."

Reflection

God promises eternal life to those who believe in Jesus.

John 6:47

New International Version

47 Very truly I tell you, the one who believes has eternal life.

New American Standard Bible

47"Truly, truly, I say to you, he who believes has eternal life.

The Message

47"I'm telling you the most solemn and sober truth now: Whoever believes in me has real life, eternal life.

Amplified Bible

47I assure you, most solemnly I tell you, he who believes in Me [who adheres to, trusts in, relies on, and has faith in Me] has (now possesses) eternal life.

New Living Translation

47 "I tell you the truth, anyone who believes has eternal life.

Contemporary English Version

47I tell you for certain that everyone who has faith in me has eternal life.

New King James Version

47 Most assuredly, I say to you, he who believes in Me[a] has everlasting life.

Reflection

God promises that if you give to the poor you will never go hungry.

Proverbs 28:27

New International Version

[27] Those who give to the poor will lack nothing, but those who close their eyes to them receive many curses.

New American Standard Bible

[27] He who gives to the poor will never want, But he who shuts his eyes will have many curses.

The Message

[27] Be generous to the poor—you'll never go hungry; shut your eyes to their needs, and run a gauntlet of curses.

Amplified Bible

[27] He who gives to the poor will not want, but he who hides his eyes [from their want] will have many a curse.

New Living Translation

[27] Whoever gives to the poor will lack
   nothing,
   but those who close their eyes to poverty
will be cursed.

Contemporary English Version

[27] Giving to the poor will keep you from poverty, but if you close your eyes to their needs, everyone will curse you.

New King James Version

[27] He who gives to the poor will not lack,
   But he who hides his eyes will have many
curses.

Reflection

God promises to bless the cheerful giver.

---

2 Corinthians 9:7

New International Version

⁷ Each of you should give what you have decided in your heart to give, not reluctantly or under compulsion, for God loves a cheerful giver.

New American Standard Bible

⁷ Each one must do just as he has purposed in his heart, not grudgingly or under compulsion, for (God loves a cheerful giver.

The Message

⁶⁻⁷Remember: A stingy planter gets a stingy crop; a lavish planter gets a lavish crop. I want each of you to take plenty of time to think it over, and make up your own mind what you will give. That will protect you against sob stories and arm-twisting. God loves it when the giver delights in the giving.

Amplified Bible

⁷Let each one [give] as he has made up his own mind and purposed in his heart, not reluctantly or sorrowfully or under compulsion, for God loves (He takes pleasure in, prizes above other things, and is unwilling to abandon or to do without) a cheerful (joyous, "prompt to do it") giver [whose heart is in his giving].

New Living Translation

⁷ You must each decide in your heart how much to give. And don't give reluctantly or in response to pressure. "For God loves a person who gives cheerfully

Reflection

Contemporary English Version

[7]Each of you must make up your own mind about how much to give. But don't feel sorry that you must give and don't feel that you are forced to give. God loves people who love to give.

New King James Version

[7] So let each one give as he purposes in his heart, not grudgingly or of necessity; for God loves a cheerful giver

God promises to acquit anyone who trusts in Him.

John 3:18

New International Version

¹⁸ Whoever believes in him is not condemned, but whoever does not believe stands condemned already because they have not believed in the name of God's one and only Son.

New American Standard Bible

¹⁸"He who believes in Him is not judged; he who does not believe has been judged already, because he has not believed in the name of the only begotten Son of God.

The Message

¹⁸Anyone who trusts in him is acquitted; anyone who refuses to trust him has long since been under the death sentence without knowing it. And why? Because of that person's failure to believe in the one-of-a-kind Son of God when introduced to him.

Amplified Bible

¹⁸He who believes in Him [who clings to, trusts in, relies on Him] is not judged [he who trusts in Him never comes up for judgment; for him there is no rejection, no condemnation—he incurs no damnation]; but he who does not believe (cleave to, rely on, trust in Him) is judged already [he has already been convicted and has already received his sentence] because he has not believed in and trusted in the name of the only begotten Son of God. [He is condemned for refusing to let his trust rest in Christ's name.]

Reflection

New Living Translation

¹⁸ "There is no judgment against anyone who believes in him. But anyone who does not believe in him has already been judged for not believing in God's one and only Son.

Contemporary English Version

[18]No one who has faith in God's Son will be condemned. But everyone who doesn't have faith in him has already been condemned for not having faith in God's only Son.

New King James Version

[18] "He who believes in Him is not condemned; but he who does not believe is condemned already, because he has not believed in the name of the only begotten Son of God.

God promises that those who believe in Jesus have eternal life.

John 3:36

New International Version

36 Whoever believes in the Son has eternal life, but whoever rejects the Son will not see life, for God's wrath remains on them.

New American Standard Bible

36"He who believes in the Son has eternal life; but he who does not obey the Son will not see life, but the wrath of God abides on him."

The Message

36 That is why whoever accepts and trusts the Son gets in on everything, life complete and forever! And that is also why the person who avoids and distrusts the Son is in the dark and doesn't see life. All he experiences of God is darkness, and an angry darkness at that."

Amplified Bible

36And he who believes in (has faith in, clings to, relies on) the Son has (now possesses) eternal life. But whoever disobeys (is unbelieving toward, refuses to trust in, disregards, is not subject to) the Son will never see (experience) life, but [instead] the wrath of God abides on him. [God's displeasure remains on him; His indignation hangs over him continually.]

New Living Translation

36 And anyone who believes in God's Son has eternal life. Anyone who doesn't obey the Son will never experience eternal life but remains under God's angry judgment."

Contemporary English Version

36Everyone who has faith in the Son has eternal life. But no one who rejects him will ever share in that life, and God will be angry with them forever.

Reflection

New King James Version

[36] He who believes in the Son has everlasting life; and he who does not believe the Son shall not see life, but the wrath of God abides on him."

God promises to pour His blessing upon your children.

Isaiah 44:3

New International Version

³ For I will pour water on the thirsty land, and streams on the dry ground; I will pour out my Spirit on your offspring, and my blessing on your descendants.

New American Standard Bible

³ 'For I will pour out water on the thirsty land And streams on the dry ground; I will pour out My Spirit on your offspring And My blessing on your descendants;

The Message

³ For I will pour water on the thirsty ground and send streams coursing through the parched earth. I will pour my Spirit into your descendants and my blessing on your children.

Amplified Bible

³For I will pour water upon him who is thirsty, and floods upon the dry ground. I will pour My Spirit upon your offspring, and My blessing upon your descendants.

New Living Translation

³ For I will pour out water to quench your thirst and to irrigate your parched fields. And I will pour out my Spirit on your descendants, and my blessing on your children.

Contemporary English Version

³ I will bless the thirsty land by sending streams of water; I will bless your descendants by giving them my Spirit.

New King James Version

³ For I will pour water on him who is thirsty, And floods on the dry ground; I will pour My Spirit on your descendants, And My blessing on your offspring;

Reflection

God promises that your enemies don't stand a chance against you and your children.

Psalm 127:3-5

New International Version

³ Children are a heritage from the LORD, offspring a reward from him. ⁴ Like arrows in the hands of a warrior are children born in one's youth. ⁵ Blessed is the man whose quiver is full of them. They will not be put to shame when they contend with their opponents in court.

New American Standard Bible

³Behold, children are a gift of the LORD, The fruit of the womb is a reward. ⁴Like arrows in the hand of a warrior, So are the children of one's youth. ⁵How (blessed is the man whose quiver is full of them; They will not be ashamed When they speak with their enemiesin the gate.

The Message

³⁻⁵ Don't you see that children are God's best gift? the fruit of the womb his generous legacy? Like a warrior's fistful of arrows are the children of a vigorous youth. Oh, how blessed are you parents, with your quivers full of children! Your enemies don't stand a chance against you; you'll sweep them right off your doorstep.

Amplified Bible

³Behold, children are a heritage from the Lord, the fruit of the womb a reward.⁴As arrows are in the hand of a warrior, so are the children of one's youth. ⁵Happy, blessed, and fortunate is the man whose quiver is filled with them! They will not be put to shame when they speak with their adversaries [in gatherings] at the [city's] gate.

Reflection

New Living Translation

[3] Children are a gift from the Lord; they are a reward from him. [4] Children born to a young man are like arrows in a warrior's hands. [5] How joyful is the man whose quiver is full of them! He will not be put to shame when he confronts his accusers at the city gates.

Contemporary English Version

[3] Children are a blessing and a gift from the LORD. [4]Having a lot of children to take care of you in your old age is like a warrior with a lot of arrows. [5]The more you have, the better off you will be, because they will protect you when your enemies attack with arguments.

New King James Version

[3] Behold, children are a heritage from the LORD, The fruit of the womb is a reward. [4] Like arrows in the hand of a warrior, So are the children of one's youth. [5] Happy is the man who has his quiver full of them; They shall not be ashamed, But shall speak with their enemies in the gate.

God promises to never let you down.

Psalm 22:24

New International Version

²⁴ For he has not despised or scorned the suffering of the afflicted one; he has not hidden his face from him but has listened to his cry for help.

New American Standard Bible

²⁴ For He has not despised nor abhorred the affliction of the afflicted; Nor has He hidden His face from him; But when he cried to Him for help, He heard.

The Message

²⁴ He has never let you down, never looked the other way when you were being kicked around. He has never wandered off to do his own thing; he has been right there, listening.

Amplified Bible

²⁴For He has not despised or abhorred the affliction of the afflicted; neither has He hidden His face from him, but when he cried to Him, He heard.

New Living Translation

²⁴ For he has not ignored or belittled the suffering of the needy. He has not turned his back on them, but has listened to their cries for help.

Contemporary English Version

²⁴The LORD doesn't hate or despise the helpless in all of their troubles. When I cried out, he listened and did not turn away.

New King James Version

²⁴ For He has not despised nor abhorred the affliction of the afflicted; Nor has He hidden His face from Him; But when He cried to Him, He heard.

Reflection

God promises that if you stumble you will not be down for long.

Psalm 37:24

New International Version

²⁴ though he may stumble, he will not fall, for the LORD upholds him with his hand.

New American Standard Bible

²⁴When he falls, he will not be hurled headlong, Because the LORD is the One who holds his hand.

The Message

²³⁻²⁴ Stalwart walks in step with God; his path blazed by God, he's happy. If he stumbles, he's not down for long; God has a grip on his hand.

Amplified Bible

²⁴Though he falls, he shall not be utterly cast down, for the Lord grasps his hand in support and upholds him.

New Living Translation

²⁴ Though they stumble, they will never fall, for the Lord holds them by the hand.

Contemporary English Version

²⁴The LORD will hold your hand, and if you stumble, you still won't fall.

New King James Version

²⁴ Though he fall, he shall not be utterly cast down; For the LORD upholds him with His hand.

Reflection

God promises to care for those who trust in Him.

Nahum 1:7

New International Version

⁷ The LORD is good, a refuge in times of trouble.
 He cares for those who trust in him,

New American Standard Bible

⁷The LORD is good, A stronghold in the day of trouble, And He knows those who take refuge in Him.

The Message

⁷ God is good, a hiding place in tough times He recognizes and welcomes anyone looking for help,

Amplified Bible

⁷The Lord is good, a Strength and Stronghold in the day of trouble; He knows (recognizes, has knowledge of, and understands) those who take refuge and trust in Him.

New Living Translation

⁷ The Lord is good, a strong refuge when trouble comes. He is close to those who trust in him.

Contemporary English Version

⁷The LORD is good. He protects those who trust him in times of trouble.

New King James Version

⁷ The LORD is good, A stronghold in the day of trouble; And He knows those who trust in Him.

Reflection

God promises that salvation comes from the Lord.

Psalm 37:39

New International Version

³⁹ The salvation of the righteous comes from the LORD;
　he is their stronghold in time of trouble.

New American Standard Bible

³⁹But the salvation of the righteous is from the LORD;
　He is their strength in time of trouble.

The Message

³⁹⁻⁴⁰ The spacious, free life is from God, it's also protected and safe. God-strengthened, we're delivered from evil—when we run to him, he saves us.

Amplified Bible

³⁹But the salvation of the [consistently] righteous is of the Lord; He is their Refuge and secure Stronghold in the time of trouble.

New Living Translation

³⁹ The Lord rescues the godly; he is their fortress in times of trouble.

Contemporary English Version

³⁹The LORD protects his people, and they can come to him in times of trouble.

New King James Version

³⁹ But the salvation of the righteous is from the LORD;
　He is their strength in the time of trouble.

Reflection

God promises that the righteous will never be shaken.

Psalm 55:22

New International Version

²² Cast your cares on the LORD and he will
    sustain you;
        he will never let the righteous be shaken.

New American Standard Bible

²²Cast your burden upon the LORD and He
    will sustain you;
        He will never allow the righteous to be
shaken.

The Message

²²⁻²³ Pile your troubles on God's shoulders—
        he'll carry your load, he'll help you out.

Amplified Bible

²²Cast your burden on the Lord [releasing the
weight of it] and He will sustain you; He will
never allow the [consistently] righteous to be
moved (made to slip, fall, or fail).

New Living Translation

²² Give your burdens to the Lord, and he will
    take care of you.
        He will not permit the godly to slip and
fall.

Contemporary English Version

²²Our LORD, we belong to you. We tell you
    what worries us,
        and you won't let us fall.

New King James Version

²² Cast your burden on the LORD,
    And He shall sustain you;
        He shall never permit the righteous to be moved.

Reflection

God promises that His word will bring perfect peace.

John 16:33

New International Version

[33] "I have told you these things, so that in me you may have peace. In this world you will have trouble. But take heart! I have overcome the world."

New American Standard Bible

[33] "These things I have spoken to you, so that in Me you may have peace In the world you have tribulation, but take courage; I have overcome the world."

The Message

[33] I've told you all this so that trusting me, you will be unshakable and assured, deeply at peace. In this godless world you will continue to experience difficulties. But take heart! I've conquered the world."

Amplified Bible

[33] I have told you these things, so that in Me you may have [perfect] peace and confidence. In the world you have tribulation and trials and distress and frustration; but be of good cheer [take courage; be confident, certain, undaunted]! For I have overcome the world. [I have deprived it of power to harm you and have conquered it for you.]

New Living Translation

[33] I have told you all this so that you may have peace in me. Here on earth you will have many trials and sorrows. But take heart, because I have overcome the world."

Contemporary English Version

[33] I have told you this, so that you might have peace in your hearts because of me. While you are in the world, you will have to suffer. But cheer up! I have defeated the world.

Reflection

New King James Version

[33] These things I have spoken to you, that in Me you may have peace. In the world you will have tribulation; but be of good cheer, I have overcome the world."

God promises to refresh our soul.

Matthew 11:28

New International Version

28 "Come to me, all you who are weary and burdened, and I will give you rest.

New American Standard Bible

28"Come to Me, all who are weary and heavy-laden, and I will give you rest.

The Message

28 "Are you tired? Worn out? Burned out on religion? Come to me. Get away with me and you'll recover your life. I'll show you how to take a real rest.

Amplified Bible

28Come to Me, all you who labor and are heavy-laden and overburdened, and I will cause you to rest. [I will ease and relieve and refresh your souls.]

New Living Translation

28 Then Jesus said, "Come to me, all of you who are weary and carry heavy burdens, and I will give you rest.

Contemporary English Version

28If you are tired from carrying heavy burdens, come to me and I will give you rest.

New King James Version

28 Come to Me, all you who labor and are heavy laden, and I will give you rest.

Reflection

God promises to be a sanctuary during bad times.

Psalm 9:9

New International Version

⁹ The LORD is a refuge for the oppressed,
a stronghold in times of trouble.

New American Standard Bible

⁹The LORD also will be a stronghold for the oppressed,
A stronghold in times of trouble;

The Message

⁹God's a safe-house for the battered,
a sanctuary during bad times.

Amplified Bible

⁹The Lord also will be a refuge and a high tower for the oppressed, a refuge and a stronghold in times of trouble (high cost, destitution, and desperation).

New Living Translation

⁹ The Lord is a shelter for the oppressed,
a refuge in times of trouble.

Contemporary English Version

⁹The poor can run to you because you are a fortress
in times of trouble.

New King James Version

⁹ The LORD also will be a refuge for the oppressed,
A refuge in times of trouble.

Reflection

God promises to redeem you because you belong to Him.

Isaiah 43:1

New International Version

¹ But now, this is what the LORD says—he who created you, Jacob, he who formed you, Israel: "Do not fear, for I have redeemed you; I have summoned you by name; you are mine.

New American Standard Bible

¹But now, thus says the LORD, your Creator, O Jacob, And He who formed you, O Israel, "Do not fear, for I have redeemed you; I have called you by name; you are Mine!

The Message

¹ But now, God's Message, the God who made you in the first place, Jacob, the One who got you started, Israel: "Don't be afraid, I've redeemed you. I've called your name. You're mine.

Amplified Bible

¹BUT NOW [in spite of past judgments for Israel's sins], thus says the Lord, He Who created you, O Jacob, and He Who formed you, O Israel: Fear not, for I have redeemed you [ransomed you by paying a price instead of leaving you captives]; I have called you by your name; you are Mine.

New Living Translation

¹ But now, O Jacob, listen to the Lord who created you.
  O Israel, the one who formed you says,
"Do not be afraid, for I have ransomed you. I have called you by name; you are mine.

Contemporary English Version

¹Descendants of Jacob, I, the LORD, created you and formed your nation. Israel, don't be afraid. I have rescued you. I have called you by name; now you belong to me.

Reflection

New King James Version

[1] But now, thus says the LORD, who created you, O Jacob, And He who formed you, O Israel: "Fear not, for I have redeemed you; I have called you by your name; You are Mine.

God promises with Him you will always be a majority.

2 Kings 6:16

New International Version

[16] "Don't be afraid," the prophet answered. "Those who are with us are more than those who are with them."

New American Standard Bible

[16]So he answered, "Do not fear, for those who are with us are more than those who are with them."

The Message

[16] He said, "Don't worry about it—there are more on our side than on their side."

Amplified Bible

[16][Elisha] answered, Fear not; for those with us are more than those with them.

New Living Translation

[16] "Don't be afraid!" Elisha told him. "For there are more on our side than on theirs!"

Contemporary English Version

[16]"Don't be afraid," Elisha answered. "There are more troops on our side than on theirs."

New King James Version

[16] So he answered, "Do not fear, for those who are with us are more than those who are with them."

Reflection

God promises that you will live in safety when you trust Him.

Psalm 37:3

New International Version

³ Trust in the LORD and do good;
dwell in the land and enjoy safe pasture.

New American Standard Bible

³Trust in the LORD and do good;
Dwell in the land and cultivate faithfulness.

The Message

³ Get insurance with God and do a good deed,
settle down and stick to your last.

Amplified Bible

³Trust (lean on, rely on, and be confident) in the Lord and do good; so shall you dwell in the land and feed surely on His faithfulness, and truly you shall be fed.

New Living Translation

³ Trust in the Lord and do good.
Then you will live safely in the land and prosper.

Contemporary English Version

³Trust the LORD and live right!
The land will be yours, and you will be safe.

New King James Version

³ Trust in the LORD, and do good;
Dwell in the land, and feed on His faithfulness.

Reflection

God promises to give strength to the weary.

Isaiah 40:29

New International Version

²⁹ He gives strength to the weary
  and increases the power of the weak.

New American Standard Bible

²⁹He gives strength to the weary,
  And to him who lacks might He increases power.

The Message

²⁹ He energizes those who get tired,
  gives fresh strength to dropouts.

Amplified Bible

²⁹He gives power to the faint and weary, and to him who has no might He increases strength [causing it to multiply and making it to abound].

New Living Translation

²⁹ He gives power to the weak
  and strength to the powerless.

Contemporary English Version

²⁹The LORD gives strength
  to those who are weary.

New King James Version

²⁹ He gives power to the weak,
  And to those who have no might He increases strength.

Reflection

God promises to strengthen the heart of those who put their trust in Him.

Psalm 31:24

New International Version

[24] Be strong and take heart,
 all you who hope in the LORD.

New American Standard Bible

[24]Be strong and let your heart take courage,
 All you who hope in the LORD.

The Message

[24] Be brave. Be strong. Don't give up.
 Expect God to get here soon.

Amplified Bible

[24]Be strong and let your heart take courage, all you who wait for and hope for and expect the Lord!

New Living Translation

[24] So be strong and courageous,
 all you who put your hope in the Lord!

Contemporary English Version

[24]All who trust the LORD,
 be cheerful and strong.

New King James Version

[24] Be of good courage,
 And He shall strengthen your heart,
 All you who hope in the LORD.

Reflection

God promises that you can do all things through Christ who gives you strength.

Philippians 4:12-13

New International Version

[12] I know what it is to be in need, and I know what it is to have plenty. I have learned the secret of being content in any and every situation, whether well fed or hungry, whether living in plenty or in want. [13] I can do all this through him who gives me strength.

New American Standard Bible

[12] I know how to get along with humble means, and I also know how to live in prosperity; in any and every circumstance I have learned the secret of being filled and going hungry, both of having abundance and suffering need. [13] I can do all things through Him who strengthens me.

The Message

[12-13] I've learned by now to be quite content whatever my circumstances. I'm just as happy with little as with much, with much as with little. I've found the recipe for being happy whether full or hungry, hands full or hands empty. Whatever I have, wherever I am, I can make it through anything in the One who makes me who I am.

Amplified Bible

[12] I know how to be abased and live humbly in straitened circumstances, and I know also how to enjoy plenty and live in abundance. I have learned in any and all circumstances the secret of facing every situation, whether well-fed or going hungry, having a sufficiency and enough to spare or going without and being in want. [13] I have strength for all things in Christ Who empowers me [I am ready for anything and equal to anything through Him Who infuses inner strength into me; I am self-sufficient in Christ's sufficiency].

Reflection

New Living Translation

[12] I know how to live on almost nothing or with everything. I have learned the secret of living in every situation, whether it is with a full stomach or empty, with plenty or little. [13] For I can do everything through Christ, who gives me strength.

Contemporary English Version

[12]I know what it is to be poor or to have plenty, and I have lived under all kinds of conditions. I know what it means to be full or to be hungry, to have too much or too little. [13]Christ gives me the strength to face anything.

New King James Version

[12] I know how to be abased, and I know how to abound. Everywhere and in all things I have learned both to be full and to be hungry, both to abound and to suffer need. [13] I can do all things through Christ who strengthens me.

God promises to take the sting out of death.

---

1 Corinthians 15:55

New International Version

⁵⁵ "Where, O death, is your victory?
  Where, O death, is your sting?"

New American Standard Bible

⁵⁵"O DEATH, WHERE IS YOUR VICTORY?
O DEATH, WHERE IS YOUR STING?"

The Message

⁵⁵ Death swallowed by triumphant Life!
  Who got the last word, oh, Death?
  Oh, Death, who's afraid of you now?

Amplified Bible

⁵⁵O death, where is your victory? O death,
where is your sting?

New Living Translation

⁵⁵ O death, where is your victory?
  O death, where is your sting?"

Contemporary English Version

⁵⁵Where is its victory?
  Where is its sting?"

New King James Version

⁵⁵ "O Death, where is your sting?
  O Hades, where is your victory?"

Reflection

God promises that the obedient will not see death.

John 8:51

New International Version

⁵¹ Very truly I tell you, whoever obeys my word will never see death."

New American Standard Bible

⁵¹"Truly, truly, I say to you, if anyone keeps My word he will never see death."

The Message

⁵¹ If you practice what I'm telling you, you'll never have to look death in the face."

Amplified Bible

⁵¹I assure you, most solemnly I tell you, if anyone observes My teaching [lives in accordance with My message, keeps My word], he will by no means ever see and experience death.

New Living Translation

⁵¹ I tell you the truth, anyone who obeys my teaching will never die!"

Contemporary English Version

⁵¹I tell you for certain that if you obey my words, you will never die."

New King James Version

⁵¹ Most assuredly, I say to you, if anyone keeps My word he shall never see death."

Reflection

God promises to redeem your life from the grave.

Psalm 49:15

New International Version

15 But God will redeem me from the realm of
the dead;
he will surely take me to himself.

New American Standard Bible

15But God will redeem my soul from the
power of Sheol,
For He will receive me. Selah.

The Message

15 God snatches me from the clutch of death,
he reaches down and grabs me.

Amplified Bible

15But God will redeem me from the power
of Sheol (the place of the dead); for He will
receive me. Selah [pause, and calmly think of
that]!

New Living Translation

15 But as for me, God will redeem my life.
He will snatch me from the power of the
grave.

Contemporary English Version

15But God will rescue me from the power of
death.

New King James Version

15 But God will redeem my soul from the
power of the grave,
For He shall receive me. Selah

Reflection

God promises to wipe every tear from your eyes.

Isaiah 25:8

New International Version

⁸ he will swallow up death forever. The Sovereign LORD will wipe away the tears from all faces;he will remove his people's disgrace from all the earth. The LORD has spoken.

New American Standard Bible

⁸He will swallow up death for all time, And the Lord GOD will wipe tears away from all faces, And He will remove the reproach of His people from all the earth; For the LORD has spoken.

The Message

⁸ Yes, he'll banish death forever. And God will wipe the tears from every face. He'll remove every sign of disgrace. From his people, wherever they are. Yes! God says so!

Amplified Bible

⁸He will swallow up death [in victory; He will abolish death forever]. And the Lord God will wipe away tears from all faces; and the reproach of His people He will take away from off all the earth; for the Lord has spoken it.

New Living Translation

⁸ He will swallow up death forever! The Sovereign Lord will wipe away all tears. He will remove forever all insults and mockery against his land and people. The Lord has spoken!

Contemporary English Version

⁸The LORD All-Powerful will destroy the power of death and wipe away all tears. No longer will his people be insulted everywhere. The LORD has spoken!

Reflection

New King James Version

[8] He will swallow up death forever, And the Lord GOD will wipe away tears from all faces; The rebuke of His people He will take away from all the earth; For the LORD has spoken.

God promises prosperity to the man of peace.

Psalm 37:37

New International Version

37 Consider the blameless, observe the upright;
   a future awaits those who seek peace.

New American Standard Bible

37 Mark the blameless man, and behold the
   upright;
      For the man of peace will have a posterity.

The Message

37-38 Keep your eye on the healthy soul,
   scrutinize the straight life;
      There's a future in strenuous wholeness.

Amplified Bible

37 Mark the blameless man and behold the
upright, for there is a happy end for the man
of peace.

New Living Translation

37 Look at those who are honest and good,
   for a wonderful future awaits those who
love peace.

Contemporary English Version

37 Think of the bright future waiting for all the
   families
      of honest and innocent and peace-loving
people.

New King James Version

37 Mark the blameless man, and observe the
   upright;
      For the future of that man is peace.

Reflection

God promises eternal life to those who believe in Jesus.

John 3:15

New International Version

[15] that everyone who believes may have eternal life in him."

New American Standard Bible

[15]so that whoever believes will in Him have eternal life.

The Message

[15] and everyone who looks up to him, trusting and expectant, will gain a real life, eternal life.

Amplified Bible

[15]In order that everyone who believes in Him [who cleaves to Him, trusts Him, and relies on Him] may not perish, but have eternal life and [actually] live forever!

New Living Translation

[15] so that everyone who believes in him will have eternal life.

Contemporary English Version

[15]Then everyone who has faith in the Son of Man will have eternal life.

New King James Version

[15] that whoever believes in Him should not perish but have eternal life

Reflection

God promises that the wicked will be no more.

Job 8:22

New International Version

²² Your enemies will be clothed in shame,
    and the tents of the wicked will be no
more."

New American Standard Bible

²²"Those who hate you will be clothed with
    shame,
    And the tent of the wicked will be no
longer."

The Message

²²With your enemies thoroughly discredited,
    their house of cards collapsed."

Amplified Bible

²²Those who hate you will be clothed with
shame, and the tents of the wicked shall be no
more.

New Living Translation

²² Those who hate you will be clothed with
    shame,
    and the home of the wicked will be
destroyed."

Contemporary English Version

²²But your evil enemies will be put to shame
    and disappear forever.

New King James Version

²² Those who hate you will be clothed with
    shame,
    And the dwelling place of the wicked will
come to nothing."

Reflection

God promises the enemies that attack you will be defeated before your face.

Deuteronomy 28:7

New International Version

7 The LORD will grant that the enemies who rise up against you will be defeated before you. They will come at you from one direction but flee from you in seven.

New American Standard Bible

7"The LORD shall cause your enemies who rise up against you to be defeated before you; they will come out against you one way and will flee before you seven ways.

The Message

7 God will defeat your enemies who attack you. They'll come at you on one road and run away on seven roads.

Amplified Bible

7The Lord shall cause your enemies who rise up against you to be defeated before your face; they shall come out against you one way and flee before you seven ways.

New Living Translation

7 "The Lord will conquer your enemies when they attack you. They will attack you from one direction, but they will scatter from you in seven!

Contemporary English Version

7The LORD will help you defeat your enemies and make them scatter in all directions.

New King James Version

7 "The LORD will cause your enemies who rise against you to be defeated before your face; they shall come out against you one way and flee before you seven ways.

Reflection

God promises that everything will work out for the best.

Isaiah 54:17

New International Version

[17] no weapon forged against you will prevail, and you will refute every tongue that accuses you. This is the heritage of the servants of the LORD, and this is their vindication from me," declares the LORD.

New American Standard Bible

[17]"No weapon that is formed against you will prosper; And every tongue that accuses you in judgment you will condemn This is the heritage of the servants of the LORD, And their vindication is from Me," declares the LORD.

The Message

[17]but no weapon that can hurt you has ever been forged. Any accuser who takes you to court will be dismissed as a liar. This is what God's servants can expect. I'll see to it that everything works out for the best." God's Decree.

Amplified Bible

[17]But no weapon that is formed against you shall prosper, and every tongue that shall rise against you in judgment you shall show to be in the wrong. This [peace, righteousness, security, triumph over opposition] is the heritage of the servants of the Lord [those in whom the ideal Servant of the Lord is reproduced]; this is the righteousness or the vindication which they obtain from Me [this is that which I impart to them as their justification], says the Lord.

New Living Translation

[17] But in that coming day no weapon turned against you will succeed. You will silence every voice raised up to accuse you. These benefits are enjoyed by the servants of the Lord; their vindication will come from me. I, the Lord, have spoken!

Reflection

Contemporary English Version

[17]Weapons made to attack you won't be successful; words spoken against you won't hurt at all. My servants, Jerusalem is yours! I, the LORD, promise to bless you with victory.

New King James Version

[17] No weapon formed against you shall prosper, And every tongue which rises against you in judgment You shall condemn. This is the heritage of the servants of the LORD, And their righteousness is from Me," Says the LORD.

God promises to keep you in a secure place during troubling times.

Psalm 27:5-6

New International Version

⁵ For in the day of trouble he will keep me safe in his dwelling; he will hide me in the shelter of his sacred tent and set me high upon a rock. ⁶ Then my head will be exalted above the enemies who surround me; at his sacred tent I will sacrifice with shouts of joy; I will sing and make music to the LORD.

New American Standard Bible

⁵For in the day of trouble He will conceal me in His tabernacle;In the secret place of His tent He will hide me;He will lift me up on a rock. ⁶And now my head will be lifted up above my enemies around me, And I will offer in His tent sacrifices with shouts of joy; I will sing, yes, I will sing praises to the LORD.

The Message

⁵ That's the only quiet, secure place in a noisy world, The perfect getaway, far from the buzz of traffic. ⁶ God holds me head and shoulders above all who try to pull me down. I'm headed for his place to offer anthems that will raise the roof! Already I'm singing God-songs; I'm making music to God.

Amplified Bible

⁵For in the day of trouble He will hide me in His shelter; in the secret place of His tent will He hide me; He will set me high upon a rock. ⁶And now shall my head be lifted up above my enemies round about me; in His tent I will offer sacrifices and shouting of joy; I will sing, yes, I will sing praises to the Lord.

New Living Translation

⁵ For he will conceal me there when troubles come; he will hide me in his sanctuary. He will place me out of reach on a high rock. ⁶ Then I will hold my head highabove

Reflection

my enemies who surround me. At his sanctuary I will offer sacrifices with shouts of joy, singing and praising the Lord with music.

Contemporary English Version

5In times of trouble, you will protect me. You will hide me in your tent and keep me safe on top of a mighty rock. 6You will let me defeat all of my enemies. Then I will celebrate, as I enter your tent with animal sacrifices and songs of praise.

New King James Version

5 For in the time of trouble He shall hide me in His pavilion; In the secret place of His tabernacle He shall hide me; He shall set me high upon a rock. 6 And now my head shall be lifted up above my enemies all around me; Therefore I will offer sacrifices of joy in His tabernacle; I will sing, yes, I will sing praises to the LORD.

God promises to bring justice for His chosen people.

Luke 18:7

New International Version

⁷ And will not God bring about justice for his chosen ones, who cry out to him day and night? Will he keep putting them off?

New American Standard Bible

⁷now, will not God bring about justice for His elect who cry to Him day and night, and will He delay long over them?

The Message

⁷ So what makes you think God won't step in and work justice for his chosen people, who continue to cry out for help? Won't he stick up for them?

Amplified Bible

⁷And will not [our just] God defend and protect and avenge His elect (His chosen ones), who cry to Him day and night? Will He defer them and delay help on their behalf?

New Living Translation

⁷ Even he rendered a just decision in the end. So don't you think God will surely give justice to his chosen people who cry out to him day and night? Will he keep putting them off?

Contemporary English Version

⁷Won't God protect his chosen ones who pray to him day and night? Won't he be concerned for them?

New King James Version

⁷ And shall God not avenge His own elect who cry out day and night to Him, though He bears long with them?

Reflection

God promises to deliver from the oppression of the enemy.

---

2 Kings 17:39

New International Version

³⁹ Rather, worship the LORD your God; it is he who will deliver you from the hand of all your enemies."

New American Standard Bible

³⁹"But the LORD your God you shall fear; and He will deliver you from the hand of all your enemies."

The Message

³⁹ And whatever you do, don't worship other gods! And the covenant he made with you, don't forget your part in that. And don't worship other gods! Worship God, and God only—he's the one who will save you from enemy oppression."

Amplified Bible

³⁹But the Lord your God you shall [reverently] fear; then He will deliver you out of the hands of all your enemies.

New Living Translation

³⁹ You must worship only the Lord your God. He is the one who will rescue you from all your enemies."

Contemporary English Version

³⁹except me. I am the LORD your God, and I will rescue you from all your enemies.

New King James Version

³⁹ But the LORD your God you shall fear; and He will deliver you from the hand of all your enemies."

Reflection

God promises to keep you safe and sound.

Proverbs 3:25-26

New International Version

[25] Have no fear of sudden disaster or of the ruin that overtakes the wicked, [26] for the LORD will be at your side and will keep your foot from being snared.

New American Standard Bible

[25] Do not be afraid of sudden fear Nor of the onslaught of the wicked when it comes; [26] For the LORD will be your confidence And will keep your foot from being caught.

The Message

[25-26] No need to panic over alarms or surprises, or predictions that doomsday's just around the corner, Because God will be right there with you; he'll keep you safe and sound.

Amplified Bible

[25] Be not afraid of sudden terror and panic, nor of the stormy blast or the storm and ruin of the wicked when it comes [for you will be guiltless], [26] For the Lord shall be your confidence, firm and strong, and shall keep your foot from being caught [in a trap or some hidden danger].

New Living Translation

[25] You need not be afraid of sudden disaster
  or the destruction that comes upon the
  wicked,
[26] for the Lord is your security.
  He will keep your foot from being caught
in a trap.

Contemporary English Version

[25] So don't be afraid of sudden disasters or storms that strike those who are evil. [26] You can be sure that the LORD will protect you from harm.

Reflection

New King James Version

[25] Do not be afraid of sudden terror,
   Nor of trouble from the wicked when it comes;
[26] For the LORD will be your confidence,
   And will keep your foot from being caught.

God promises to be your help always.

Hebrews 13:6

New International Version

⁶ So we say with confidence, "The Lord is my helper; I will not be afraid. What can mere mortals do to me?"

New American Standard Bible

⁶so that we confidently say, "THE LORD IS MY HELPER, I WILL NOT BE AFRAID. WHAT WILL MAN DO TO ME?"

The Message

⁶we can boldly quote, God is there, ready to help; I'm fearless no matter what. Who or what can get to me?

Amplified Bible

⁶So we take comfort and are encouraged and confidently and boldly say, The Lord is my Helper; I will not be seized with alarm [I will not fear or dread or be terrified]. What can man do to me?

New Living Translation

⁶ So we can say with confidence,

"The Lord is my helper,
so I will have no fear.
What can mere people do to me?"

Contemporary English Version

⁶That should make you feel like saying, "The Lord helps me! Why should I be afraid of what people can do to me?"

New King James Version

⁶ So we may boldly say: "The LORD is my helper;
I will not fear. What can man do to me?"

Reflection

God promises that those who believe in Him will live.

John 11:25-26

New International Version

²⁵ Jesus said to her, "I am the resurrection and the life. The one who believes in me will live, even though they die; ²⁶ and whoever lives by believing in me will never die. Do you believe this?"

New American Standard Bible

²⁵Jesus said to her, "I am the resurrection and the life; he who believes in Me will live even if he dies, ²⁶and everyone who lives and believes in Me will never die. Do you believe this?"

The Message

²⁵⁻²⁶"You don't have to wait for the End. I am, right now, Resurrection and Life. The one who believes in me, even though he or she dies, will live. And everyone who lives believing in me does not ultimately die at all. Do you believe this?"

Amplified Bible

²⁵Jesus said to her, I am [Myself] the Resurrection and the Life. Whoever believes in (adheres to, trusts in, and relies on) Me, although he may die, yet he shall live; ²⁶And whoever continues to live and believes in (has faith in, cleaves to, and relies on) Me shall never [actually] die at all. Do you believe this?

New Living Translation

²⁵ Jesus told her, "I am the resurrection and the life. Anyone who believes in me will live, even after dying. ²⁶ Everyone who lives in me and believes in me will never ever die. Do you believe this, Martha?"

Reflection

Contemporary English Version

[25]Jesus then said, "I am the one who raises the dead to life! Everyone who has faith in me will live, even if they die. [26]And everyone who lives because of faith in me will never really die. Do you believe this?"

New King James Version

[25] Jesus said to her, "I am the resurrection and the life. He who believes in Me, though he may die, he shall live. [26] And whoever lives and believes in Me shall never die. Do you believe this?"

God promises eternal life to those who believe in the name of Jesus.

1 John 5:13

New International Version

¹³ I write these things to you who believe in the name of the Son of God so that you may know that you have eternal life.

New American Standard Bible

¹³These things I have written to you who believe in the name of the Son of God, so that you may know that you have eternal life.

The Message

¹³My purpose in writing is simply this: that you who believe in God's Son will know beyond the shadow of a doubt that you have eternal life, the reality and not the illusion.

Amplified Bible

¹³I write this to you who believe in (adhere to, trust in, and rely on) the name of the Son of God [in the peculiar services and blessings conferred by Him on men], so that you may know [with settled and absolute knowledge] that you [already] have life, yes, eternal life.

New Living Translation

¹³ I have written this to you who believe in the name of the Son of God, so that you may know you have eternal life.

Contemporary English Version

¹³All of you have faith in the Son of God, and I have written to let you know that you have eternal life.

New King James Version

¹³ These things I have written to you who believe in the name of the Son of God, that you may know that you have eternal life, and that you may continue to believe in the name of the Son of God.

Reflection

God promises to restore life to your mortal body.

Romans 8:11

New International Version

¹¹ And if the Spirit of him who raised Jesus from the dead is living in you, he who raised Christ from the dead will also give life to your mortal bodies because of his Spirit who lives in you.

New American Standard Bible

¹¹But if the Spirit of Him who raised Jesus from the dead dwells in you, He who raised Christ Jesus from the dead will also give life to your mortal bodies through His Spirit who dwells in you.

The Message

¹¹ When God lives and breathes in you (and he does, as surely as he did in Jesus), you are delivered from that dead life. With his Spirit living in you, your body will be as alive as Christ's!

Amplified Bible

¹¹And if the Spirit of Him Who raised up Jesus from the dead dwells in you, [then] He Who raised up Christ Jesus from the dead will also restore to life your mortal (short-lived, perishable) bodies through His Spirit Who dwells in you.

New Living Translation

¹¹ The Spirit of God, who raised Jesus from the dead, lives in you. And just as God raised Christ Jesus from the dead, he will give life to your mortal bodies by this same Spirit living within you.

Contemporary English Version

¹¹Yet God raised Jesus to life! God's Spirit now lives in you, and he will raise you to life by his Spirit.

Reflection

New King James Version

[11] But if the Spirit of Him who raised Jesus from the dead dwells in you, He who raised Christ from the dead will also give life to your mortal bodies through His Spirit who dwells in you.

God promises that one day there will be no more death.

Revelation 21:4

New International Version

⁴ 'He will wipe every tear from their eyes. There will be no more death' or mourning or crying or pain, for the old order of things has passed away."

New American Standard Bible

⁴and He will wipe away every tear from their eyes; and there will no longer be any death; there will no longer be any mourning, or crying, or pain; the first things have passed away."

The Message

⁴ He'll wipe every tear from their eyes. Death is gone for good—tears gone, crying gone, pain gone—all the first order of things gone." The Enthroned continued, "Look! I'm making everything new. Write it all down—each word dependable and accurate."

Amplified Bible

⁴God will wipe away every tear from their eyes; and death shall be no more, neither shall there be anguish (sorrow and mourning) nor grief nor pain any more, for the old conditions and the former order of things have passed away.

New Living Translation

⁴ He will wipe every tear from their eyes, and there will be no more death or sorrow or crying or pain. All these things are gone forever."

Contemporary English Version

⁴He will wipe all tears from their eyes, and there will be no more death, suffering, crying, or pain. These things of the past are gone forever.

Reflection

New King James Version

[4] And God will wipe away every tear from their eyes; there shall be no more death, nor sorrow, nor crying. There shall be no more pain, for the former things have passed away."

God promises to give you the free gift of eternal life.

Romans 6:23

New International Version

23 For the wages of sin is death, but the gift of God is eternal life in Christ Jesus our Lord.

New American Standard Bible

23For the wages of sin is death, but the free gift of God is eternal life in Christ Jesus our Lord.

The Message

23 Work hard for sin your whole life and your pension is death. But God's gift is real life, eternal life, delivered by Jesus, our Master.

Amplified Bible

23For the wages which sin pays is death, but the [bountiful] free gift of God is eternal life through (in union with) Jesus Christ our Lord.

New Living Translation

23 For the wages of sin is death, but the free gift of God is eternal life through Christ Jesus our Lord.

Contemporary English Version

23Sin pays off with death. But God's gift is eternal life given by Jesus Christ our Lord.

New King James Version

23 For the wages of sin is death, but the gift of God is eternal life in Christ Jesus our Lord.

Reflection

God promises to prepare a place for you with Him.

John 14:2-3

New International Version

² My Father's house has many rooms; if that were not so, would I have told you that I am going there to prepare a place for you? ³ And if I go and prepare a place for you, I will come back and take you to be with me that you also may be where I am.

New American Standard Bible

²"In My Father's house are many dwelling places; if it were not so, I would have told you; for I go to prepare a place for you. ³"If I go and prepare a place for you, I will come again and receive you to Myself, that where I am, there you may be also.

The Message

²⁻³ There is plenty of room for you in my Father's home. If that weren't so, would I have told you that I'm on my way to get a room ready for you? And if I'm on my way to get your room ready, I'll come back and get you so you can live where I live."

Amplified Bible

²In My Father's house there are many dwelling places (homes). If it were not so, I would have told you; for I am going away to prepare a place for you. ³And when (if) I go and make ready a place for you, I will come back again and will take you to Myself, that where I am you may be also.

New Living Translation

² There is more than enough room in my Father's home. If this were not so, would I have told you that I am going to prepare a place for you? ³ When everything is ready, I will come and get you, so that you will always be with me where I am.

Reflection

Contemporary English Version

²There are many rooms in my Father's house. I wouldn't tell you this, unless it was true. I am going there to prepare a place for each of you. ³After I have done this, I will come back and take you with me. Then we will be together.

New King James Version

² In My Father's house are many mansions; if it were not so, I would have told you. I go to prepare a place for you. ³ And if I go and prepare a place for you, I will come again and receive you to Myself; that where I am, there you may be also.

RUDOLPH MOSELEY JR.

God promises that no one can snatch you out of His hands.

John 10:27-28

New International Version

²⁷ My sheep listen to my voice; I know them, and they follow me. ²⁸ I give them eternal life, and they shall never perish; no one will snatch them out of my hand.

New American Standard Bible

²⁷"My sheep hear My voice, and I know them, and they follow Me; ²⁸and I give eternal life to them, and they will never perish; and no one will snatch them out of My hand.

The Message

²⁷⁻²⁸ My sheep recognize my voice. I know them, and they follow me. I give them real and eternal life. They are protected from the Destroyer for good. No one can steal them from out of my hand. The Father who put them under my care is so much greater than the Destroyer and Thief. No one could ever get them away from him.

Amplified Bible

²⁷The sheep that are My own hear and are listening to My voice; and I know them, and they follow Me. ²⁸And I give them eternal life, and they shall never lose it or perish throughout the ages. [To all eternity they shall never by any means be destroyed.] And no one is able to snatch them out of My hand.

New Living Translation

²⁷ My sheep listen to my voice; I know them, and they follow me. ²⁸ I give them eternal life, and they will never perish. No one can snatch them away from me,

Reflection

Contemporary English Version

[27] My sheep know my voice, and I know them. They follow me, [28] and I give them eternal life, so that they will never be lost. No one can snatch them out of my hand.

New King James Version

[27] My sheep hear My voice, and I know them, and they follow Me. [28] And I give them eternal life, and they shall never perish; neither shall anyone snatch them out of My hand.

God promises life to those who participate in communion with Him.

John 6:54

New International Version

⁵⁴ Whoever eats my flesh and drinks my blood has eternal life, and I will raise them up at the last day.

New American Standard Bible

⁵⁴"He who eats My flesh and drinks My blood has eternal life, and I will raise him up on the last day.

The Message

⁵⁴The one who brings a hearty appetite to this eating and drinking has eternal life and will be fit and ready for the Final Day.

Amplified Bible

⁵⁴He who feeds on My flesh and drinks My blood has (possesses now) eternal life, and I will raise him up [from the dead] on the last day.

New Living Translation

⁵⁴ But anyone who eats my flesh and drinks my blood has eternal life, and I will raise that person at the last day.

Contemporary English Version

⁵⁴But if you do eat my flesh and drink my blood, you will have eternal life, and I will raise you to life on the last day.

New King James Version

⁵⁴ Whoever eats My flesh and drinks My blood has eternal life, and I will raise him up at the last day.

Reflection

God promises to deliver on things you have faith and confidence to believe Him for.

Hebrews 11

New International Version

¹ Now faith is confidence in what we hope for and assurance about what we do not see.

New American Standard Bible

¹Now faith is the assurance of things hoped for, the conviction of things not seen.

The Message

¹The fundamental fact of existence is that this trust in God, this faith, is the firm foundation under everything that makes life worth living. It's our handle on what we can't see.

Amplified Bible

¹NOW FAITH is the assurance (the confirmation, the title deed) of the things [we] hope for, being the proof of things [we] do not see and the conviction of their reality [faith perceiving as real fact what is not revealed to the senses].

New Living Translation

¹ Faith is the confidence that what we hope for will actually happen; it gives us assurance about things we cannot see.

Contemporary English Version

¹Faith makes us sure of what we hope for and gives us proof of what we cannot see.

New King James Version

¹ Now faith is the substance of things hoped for, the evidence of things not seen.

Reflection

God promises to give wisdom to those who ask for it.

James 1:5-6

New International Version

⁵ If any of you lacks wisdom, you should ask God, who gives generously to all without finding fault, and it will be given to you. ⁶ But when you ask, you must believe and not doubt, because the one who doubts is like a wave of the sea, blown and tossed by the wind.

New American Standard Bible

⁵But if any of you lacks wisdom, let him ask of God, who gives to all generously and without reproach, and it will be given to him. ⁶But he must ask in faith without any doubting, for the one who doubts is like the surf of the sea, driven and tossed by the wind.

The Message

⁵⁻⁶If you don't know what you're doing, pray to the Father. He loves to help. You'll get his help, and won't be condescended to when you ask for it. Ask boldly, believingly, without a second thought. People who "worry their prayers" are like wind-whipped waves.

Amplified Bible

⁵If any of you is deficient in wisdom, let him ask of the giving God [Who gives] to everyone liberally and ungrudgingly, without reproaching or faultfinding, and it will be given him. ⁶Only it must be in faith that he asks with no wavering (no hesitating, no doubting). For the one who wavers (hesitates, doubts) is like the billowing surge out at sea that is blown hither and thither and tossed by the wind.

New Living Translation

⁵ If you need wisdom, ask our generous God, and he will give it to you. He will not rebuke you for asking. ⁶ But when you ask him, be sure that your faith is in God

Reflection

alone. Do not waver, for a person with divided loyalty is as unsettled as a wave of the sea that is blown and tossed by the wind.

Contemporary English Version

⁵If any of you need wisdom, you should ask God, and it will be given to you. God is generous and won't correct you for asking. ⁶But when you ask for something, you must have faith and not doubt. Anyone who doubts is like an ocean wave tossed around in a storm.

New King James Version

⁵ If any of you lacks wisdom, let him ask of God, who gives to all liberally and without reproach, and it will be given to him. ⁶ But let him ask in faith, with no doubting, for he who doubts is like a wave of the sea driven and tossed by the wind.

God promises to grant anything you ask for in His name in line with His will.

Mark 11:22-23

New International Version

²² "Have faith in God," Jesus answered. ²³ "Truly I tell you, if anyone says to this mountain, 'Go, throw yourself into the sea,' and does not doubt in their heart but believes that what they say will happen, it will be done for them.

New American Standard Bible

²²And Jesus answered saying to them, "Have faith in God. ²³"Truly I say to you, whoever says to this mountain, 'Be taken up and cast into the sea,' and does not doubt in his heart, but believes that what he says is going to happen, it will be granted him.

The Message

²²⁻²³ Jesus was matter-of-fact: "Embrace this God-life. Really embrace it, and nothing will be too much for you. This mountain, for instance: Just say, 'Go jump in the lake'—no shuffling or shilly-shallying—and it's as good as done. That's why I urge you to pray for absolutely everything, ranging from small to large.

Amplified Bible

²²And Jesus, replying, said to them, Have faith in God [constantly]. ²³Truly I tell you, whoever says to this mountain, Be lifted up and thrown into the sea! and does not doubt at all in his heart but believes that what he says will take place, it will be done for him.

New Living Translation

²² Then Jesus said to the disciples, "Have faith in God. ²³ I tell you the truth, you can say to this mountain, 'May you be lifted up and thrown into the sea,' and it will happen. But you must really believe it will happen and have no doubt in your heart.

Reflection

Contemporary English Version

[22]Jesus told his disciples: Have faith in God! [23]If you have faith in God and don't doubt, you can tell this mountain to get up and jump into the sea, and it will.

New King James Version

[22] So Jesus answered and said to them, "Have faith in God. [23] For assuredly, I say to you, whoever says to this mountain, 'Be removed and be cast into the sea,' and does not doubt in his heart, but believes that those things he says will be done, he will have whatever he says.

God promises to be faithful even when we are not faithful.

---

2 Timothy 2:13

New International Version

[13] if we are faithless, he remains faithful, for he cannot disown himself.

New American Standard Bible

[13]If we are faithless, He remains faithful, for He cannot deny Himself.

The Message

[13]If we give up on him, he does not give up—for there's no way he can be false to himself.

Amplified Bible

[13]If we are faithless [do not believe and are untrue to Him], He remains true (faithful to His Word and His righteous character), for He cannot deny Himself.

New Living Translation

[13] If we are unfaithful, he remains faithful, for he cannot deny who he is.

Contemporary English Version

[13]If we are not faithful, he will still be faithful. Christ cannot deny who he is."

New King James Version

[13] If we are faithless,
   He remains faithful;
      He cannot deny Himself.

Reflection

God promises to be patient with everyone.

2 Peter 3:9

New International Version

⁹ The Lord is not slow in keeping his promise, as some understand slowness. Instead he is patient with you, not wanting anyone to perish, but everyone to come to repentance.

New American Standard Bible

⁹The Lord is not slow about His promise, as some count slowness, but is patient toward you, not wishing for any to perish but for all to come to repentance.

The Message

⁹ God isn't late with his promise as some measure lateness. He is restraining himself on account of you, holding back the End because he doesn't want anyone lost. He's giving everyone space and time to change.

Amplified Bible

⁹The Lord does not delay and is not tardy or slow about what He promises, according to some people's conception of slowness, but He is long-suffering (extraordinarily patient) toward you, not desiring that any should perish, but that all should turn to repentance.

New Living Translation

⁹ The Lord isn't really being slow about his promise, as some people think. No, he is being patient for your sake. He does not want anyone to be destroyed, but wants everyone to repent.

Contemporary English Version

⁹The Lord isn't slow about keeping his promises, as some people think he is. In fact, God is patient, because he wants everyone to turn from sin and no one to be lost.

Reflection

New King James Version

[9] The Lord is not slack concerning His promise, as some count slackness, but is longsuffering toward us, not willing that any should perish but that all should come to repentance.

God promises that not one of His words will fail.

1 Kings 8:56

New International Version

[56] "Praise be to the LORD, who has given rest to his people Israel just as he promised. Not one word has failed of all the good promises he gave through his servant Moses.

New American Standard Bible

[56]"Blessed be the LORD, who has given rest to His people Israel, according to all that He promised; not one word has failed of all His good promise, which He promised through Moses His servant.

The Message

[56]"Blessed be God, who has given peace to his people Israel just as he said he'd do. Not one of all those good and wonderful words that he spoke through Moses has misfired.

Amplified Bible

[56]Blessed be the Lord, Who has given rest to His people Israel, according to all that He promised. Not one word has failed of all His good promise which He promised through Moses His servant.

New Living Translation

[56] "Praise the Lord who has given rest to his people Israel, just as he promised. Not one word has failed of all the wonderful promises he gave through his servant Moses.

Contemporary English Version

[56]Praise the LORD! He has kept his promise and given us peace. Every good thing he promised to his servant Moses has happened.

Reflection

New King James Version

[56] "Blessed be the LORD, who has given rest to His people Israel, according to all that He promised. There has not failed one word of all His good promise, which He promised through His servant Moses.

God promises to continue to do wonderful things.

Isaiah 25:1

New International Version

¹ LORD, you are my God; I will exalt you and praise your name, for in perfect faithfulness you have done wonderful things, things planned long ago.

New American Standard Bible

¹O LORD, You are my God; I will exalt You, I will give thanks to Your name; For You have worked wonders, Plans formed long ago, with perfect faithfulness.

The Message

¹ God, you are my God. I celebrate you. I praise you. You've done your share of miracle-wonders, well-thought-out plans, solid and sure.

Amplified Bible

¹O LORD, You are my God; I will exalt You, I will praise Your name, for You have done wonderful things, even purposes planned of old [and fulfilled] in faithfulness and truth.

New Living Translation

¹ O Lord, I will honor and praise your name, for you are my God. You do such wonderful things! You planned them long ago, and now you have accomplished them.

Contemporary English Version

¹You, LORD, are my God! I will praise you for doing the wonderful things you had planned and promised since ancient times.

New King James Version

¹ O LORD, You are my God. I will exalt You, I will praise Your name, For You have done wonderful things; Your counsels of old are faithfulness and truth.

Reflection

God promises never to forsake those who seek Him.

Psalm 9:10

New International Version

[10] Those who know your name trust in you,
  for you, LORD, have never forsaken those
who seek you.

New American Standard Bible

[10]And those who know Your name will put
  their trust in You,
  For You, O LORD, have not forsaken
those who seek You.

The Message

[9-10] God's a safe-house for the battered, a
  sanctuary during bad times.
  The moment you arrive, you relax; you're
never sorry you knocked.

Amplified Bible

[10]And they who know Your name [who have
experience and acquaintance with Your mercy]
will lean on and confidently put their trust in
You, for You, Lord, have not forsaken those
who seek (inquire of and for) You [on the
authority of God's Word and the right of their
necessity].

New Living Translation

[10] Those who know your name trust in you,
  for you, O Lord, do not abandon those
who search for you

Contemporary English Version

[10]Everyone who honors your name can trust
you, because you are faithful to all who depend
on you.

Reflection

New King James Version

[10] And those who know Your name will put their trust in You;
  For You, LORD, have not forsaken those who seek You.

God promises that His promises are all fulfilled in Christ.

2 Corinthians 1:20

New International Version

[20] For no matter how many promises God has made, they are "Yes" in Christ. And so through him the "Amen" is spoken by us to the glory of God.

New American Standard Bible

[20]For as many as are the promises of God, in Him they are yes; therefore also through Him is our Amen to the glory of God through us.

The Message

[20] Whatever God has promised gets stamped with the Yes of Jesus. In him, this is what we preach and pray, the great Amen, God's Yes and our Yes together, gloriously evident.

Amplified Bible

[20]For as many as are the promises of God, they all find their Yes [answer] in Him [Christ]. For this reason we also utter the Amen (so be it) to God through Him [in His Person and by His agency] to the glory of God.

New Living Translation

[20] For all of God's promises have been fulfilled in Christ with a resounding "Yes!" And through Christ, our "Amen" (which means "Yes") ascends to God for his glory.

Contemporary English Version

[20]Christ says "Yes" to all of God's promises. That's why we have Christ to say "Amen" for us to the glory of God.

New King James Version

[20] For all the promises of God in Him are Yes, and in Him Amen, to the glory of God through us.

Reflection

God promises that His love for you will never be shaken.

Isaiah 54:10

New International Version

¹⁰ Though the mountains be shaken and the hills be removed, yet my unfailing love for you will not be shaken nor my covenant of peace be removed," says the LORD, who has compassion on you.

New American Standard Bible

¹⁰"For the mountains may be removed and the hills may shake, But My lovingkindness will not be removed from you, And My covenant of peace will not be shaken," Says the LORD who has compassion on you.

The Message

¹⁰For even if the mountains walk away and the hills fall to pieces, My love won't walk away from you, my covenant commitment of peace won't fall apart." The God who has compassion on you says so.

Amplified Bible

¹⁰For though the mountains should depart and the hills be shaken or removed, yet My love and kindness shall not depart from you, nor shall My covenant of peace and completeness be removed, says the Lord, Who has compassion on you.

New Living Translation

¹⁰ For the mountains may move and the hills disappear, but even then my faithful love for you will remain. My covenant of blessing will never be broken," says the Lord, who has mercy on you.

Contemporary English Version

¹⁰Every mountain and hill may disappear. But I will always be kind and merciful to you; I won't break my agreement to give your nation peace.

Reflection

New King James Version

[10] For the mountains shall depart And the hills be removed, But My kindness shall not depart from you, Nor shall My covenant of peace be removed," Says the LORD, who has mercy on you.

RUDOLPH MOSELEY JR.

God promises to fulfill what He has planned.

Isaiah 46:11

New International Version

¹¹From the east I summon a bird of prey; from a far-off land, a man to fulfill my purpose. What I have said, that I will bring about; what I have planned, that I will do.

New American Standard Bible

¹¹Calling a bird of prey from the east, The man of My purpose from a far country Truly I have spoken; truly I will bring it to pass. I have planned it, surely I will do it.

The Message

¹¹Calling that eagle, Cyrus, out of the east, from a far country the man I chose to help me. I've said it, and I'll most certainly do it. I've planned it, so it's as good as done.

Amplified Bible

¹¹Calling a ravenous bird from the east—the man [Cyrus] who executes My counsel from a far country. Yes, I have spoken, and I will bring it to pass; I have purposed it, and I will do it.

New Living Translation

¹¹I will call a swift bird of prey from the east a leader from a distant land to come and do my bidding. I have said what I would do, and I will do it.

Contemporary English Version

¹¹and brought someone from a distant land to do what I wanted. He attacked from the east, like a hawk swooping down. Now I will keep my promise and do what I planned.

Reflection

New King James Version

¹¹ Calling a bird of prey from the east, The man who executes My counsel, from a far country. Indeed I have spoken it; I will also bring it to pass. I have purposed it; I will also do it.

God promises to keep you from being trapped.

Proverbs 3:25-26

New International Version

²⁵ Have no fear of sudden disaster or of the ruin that overtakes the wicked, ²⁶ for the LORD will be at your side and will keep your foot from being snared.

New American Standard Bible

²⁵Do not be afraid of sudden fear Nor of the onslaught of the wicked when it comes; ²⁶For the LORD will be your confidence And will keep your foot from being caught.

The Message

²⁵⁻²⁶ No need to panic over alarms or surprises, or predictions that doomsday's just around the corner, Because God will be right there with you; he'll keep you safe and sound.

Amplified Bible

²⁵Be not afraid of sudden terror and panic, nor of the stormy blast or the storm and ruin of the wicked when it comes [for you will be guiltless], ²⁶For the Lord shall be your confidence, firm and strong, and shall keep your foot from being caught [in a trap or some hidden danger].

New Living Translation

²⁵ You need not be afraid of sudden disaster or the destruction that comes upon the wicked, ²⁶ for the Lord is your security. He will keep your foot from being caught in a trap.

Contemporary English Version

²⁵So don't be afraid of sudden disasters or storms that strike those who are evil. ²⁶You can be sure that the LORD will protect you from harm.

Reflection

New King James Version

[25] Do not be afraid of sudden terror, Nor of trouble from the wicked when it comes; [26] For the LORD will be your confidence, And will keep your foot from being caught.

God promises that you will live without fear of harm.

Proverbs 1:33

New International Version

³³ but whoever listens to me will live in safety
and be at ease, without fear of harm."

New American Standard Bible

³³"But he who listens to me shall live securely
And will be at ease from the dread of
evil."

The Message

³³ First pay attention to me, and then relax.
Now you can take it easy—you're in good
hands."

Amplified Bible

³³But whoso hearkens to me [Wisdom] shall
dwell securely and in confident trust and shall
be quiet, without fear or dread of evil.

New Living Translation

³³ But all who listen to me will live in peace,
untroubled by fear of harm."

Contemporary English Version

³³But if you listen to me, you will be safe and
secure
without fear of disaster."

New King James Version

³³ But whoever listens to me will dwell safely,
And will be secure, without fear of evil."

Reflection

God promises to give you rest.

Isaiah 14:3

New International Version

³ On the day the LORD gives you relief from your suffering and turmoil and from the harsh labor forced on you,

New American Standard Bible

³And it will be in the day when the LORD gives you rest from your pain and turmoil and harsh service in which you have been enslaved,

The Message

³⁻⁴When God has given you time to recover from the abuse and trouble and harsh servitude that you had to endure, you can amuse yourselves by taking up this satire, a taunt against the king of Babylon:

Amplified Bible

³When the Lord has given you rest from your sorrow and pain and from your trouble and unrest and from the hard service with which you were made to serve,

New Living Translation

³ In that wonderful day when the Lord gives his people rest from sorrow and fear, from slavery and chains,

Contemporary English Version

³The LORD will set you free from your sorrow, suffering, and slavery.

New King James Version

³ It shall come to pass in the day the LORD gives you rest from your sorrow, and from your fear and the hard bondage in which you were made to serve,

Reflection

God promises that you will enjoy your sleep.

Proverbs 3:24

New International Version

²⁴ When you lie down, you will not be afraid;
   when you lie down, your sleep will be
sweet.

New American Standard Bible

²⁴When you lie down, you will not be afraid;
   When you lie down, your sleep will be
sweet.

The Message

²⁴You'll take afternoon naps without a worry,
   you'll enjoy a good night's sleep.

Amplified Bible

²⁴When you lie down, you shall not be afraid;
yes, you shall lie down, and your sleep shall be
sweet.

New Living Translation

²⁴ You can go to bed without fear;
   you will lie down and sleep soundly.

Contemporary English Version

²⁴you will rest without a worry
   and sleep soundly.

New King James Version

²⁴ When you lie down, you will not be afraid;
   Yes, you will lie down and your sleep will
be sweet.

Reflection

God promises to be your helper.

Hebrews 13:6

New International Version

⁶ So we say with confidence, "The Lord is my helper; I will not be afraid. What can mere mortals do to me?"

New American Standard Bible

⁶so that we confidently say, "THE LORD IS MY HELPER, I WILL NOT BE AFRAID. WHAT WILL MAN DO TO ME?"

The Message

⁶ God is there, ready to help; I'm fearless no matter what. Who or what can get to me?

Amplified Bible

⁶So we take comfort and are encouraged and confidently and boldly say, The Lord is my Helper; I will not be seized with alarm [I will not fear or dread or be terrified]. What can man do to me?

New Living Translation

⁶ So we can say with confidence, "The Lord is my helper,
so I will have no fear. What can mere people do to me?"

Contemporary English Version

⁶That should make you feel like saying, "The Lord helps me!
Why should I be afraid of what people can do to me?"

New King James Version

⁶ So we may boldly say: "The LORD is my helper;
I will not fear. What can man do to me?"

Reflection

God promises to be a refuge and strength.

Psalm 46:1

New International Version

¹ God is our refuge and strength,
an ever-present help in trouble.

New American Standard Bible

¹God is our refuge and strength,
A very present help in trouble.

The Message

¹⁻² God is a safe place to hide, ready to help
when we need him.
We stand fearless at the cliff-edge of
doom,

Amplified Bible

¹GOD IS our Refuge and Strength [mighty and impenetrable to temptation], a very present and well-proved help in trouble.

New Living Translation

¹ God is our refuge and strength,
always ready to help in times of trouble.

Contemporary English Version

¹God is our mighty fortress, always ready to help in times of trouble.

New King James Version

¹ God is our refuge and strength,
A very present help in trouble.

Reflection

God promises to keep you safe when you trust in Him.

Proverbs 29:25

New International Version

²⁵ Fear of man will prove to be a snare,
but whoever trusts in the LORD is kept safe.

New American Standard Bible

²⁵The ear of man brings a snare,
But he who trusts in the LORD will be exalted.

The Message

²⁵ The fear of human opinion disables;
trusting in God protects you from that.

Amplified Bible

²⁵The fear of man brings a snare, but whoever leans on, trusts in, and puts his confidence in the Lord is safe and set on high.

New Living Translation

²⁵ Fearing people is a dangerous trap,
but trusting the Lord means safety.

Contemporary English Version

²⁵Don't fall into the trap of being a
coward—trust the LORD,
and you will be safe.

New King James Version

²⁵ The fear of man brings a snare,
But whoever trusts in the LORD shall be safe.

Reflection

God promises to fend off all harm from you.

Psalm 91:4-6

New International Version

⁴ He will cover you with his feathers, and under his wings you will find refuge; his faithfulness will be your shield and rampart. ⁵ You will not fear the terror of night, nor the arrow that flies by day, ⁶ nor the pestilence that stalks in the darkness, nor the plague that destroys at midday.

New American Standard Bible

⁴He will cover you with His pinions, And under His wings you may seek refuge; His faithfulness is a shield and bulwark. ⁵You will not be afraid of the terror by night, Or of the arrow that flies by day; ⁶Of the pestilence that stalks in darkness, Or of the destruction that lays waste at noon.

The Message

⁴⁻⁶ His huge outstretched arms protect you—under them you're perfectly safe; his arms fend off all harm. Fear nothing—not wild wolves in the night, not flying arrows in the day,

Amplified Bible

⁴[Then] He will cover you with His pinions, and under His wings shall you trust and find refuge; His truth and His faithfulness are a shield and a buckler. ⁵You shall not be afraid of the terror of the night, nor of the arrow (the evil plots and slanders of the wicked) that flies by day, ⁶Nor of the pestilence that stalks in darkness, nor of the destruction and sudden death that surprise and lay waste at noonday.

New Living Translation

⁴ He will cover you with his feathers. He will shelter you with his wings. His faithful promises are your armor and protection.⁵ Do not be afraid of the terrors

Reflection

of the night, nor the arrow that flies in the day.[6] Do not dread the disease that stalks in darkness, nor the disaster that strikes at midday.

Contemporary English Version

[4]He will spread his wings over you and keep you secure. His faithfulness is like a shield or a city wall. [5]You won't need to worry about dangers at night or arrows during the day. [6]And you won't fear diseases that strike in the dark or sudden disaster at noon.

New King James Version

[4] He shall cover you with His feathers, And under His wings you shall take refuge; His truth shall be your shield and buckler. [5] You shall not be afraid of the terror by night, Nor of the arrow that flies by day,[6] Nor of the pestilence that walks in darkness, Nor of the destruction that lays waste at noonday.

God promises that you will not be at a dead end during difficult times.

Isaiah 43:2

New International Version

² When you pass through the waters, I will be with you; and when you pass through the rivers,

they will not sweep over you. When you walk through the fire, you will not be burned; the flames will not set you ablaze.

New American Standard Bible

²"When you pass through the waters, I will be with you; And through the rivers, they will not overflow you When you walk through the fire, you will not be scorched, Nor will the flame burn you.

The Message

² When you're in over your head, I'll be there with you. When you're in rough waters, you will not go down. When you're between a rock and a hard place, it won't be a dead end—

Amplified Bible

²When you pass through the waters, I will be with you, and through the rivers, they will not overwhelm you. When you walk through the fire, you will not be burned or scorched, nor will the flame kindle upon you.

New Living Translation

² When you go through deep waters, I will be with you. When you go through rivers of difficulty, you will not drown. When you walk through the fire of oppression, you will not be burned up; the flames will not consume you.

Reflection

Contemporary English Version

[2]When you cross deep river, I will be with you, and you won't drown. When you walk through fire, you won't be burned or scorched by the flames.

New King James Version

[2] When you pass through the waters, I will be with you; And through the rivers, they shall not overflow you. When you walk through the fire, you shall not be burned, Nor shall the flame scorch you.

God promises to give you His peace.

John 14:27

New International Version

27 Peace I leave with you; my peace I give you. I do not give to you as the world gives. Do not let your hearts be troubled and do not be afraid.

New American Standard Bible

27"Peace I leave with you; My peace I give to you; not as the world gives do I give to you Do not let your heart be troubled, nor let it be fearful.

The Message

27 Peace. I don't leave you the way you're used to being left—feeling abandoned, bereft. So don't be upset. Don't be distraught.

Amplified Bible

27Peace I leave with you; My [own] peace I now give and bequeath to you. Not as the world gives do I give to you. Do not let your hearts be troubled, neither let them be afraid. [Stop allowing yourselves to be agitated and disturbed; and do not permit yourselves to be fearful and intimidated and cowardly and unsettled.]

New Living Translation

27 "I am leaving you with a gift—peace of mind and heart. And the peace I give is a gift the world cannot give. So don't be troubled or afraid.

Contemporary English Version

27I give you peace, the kind of peace that only I can give. It isn't like the peace that this world can give. So don't be worried or afraid.

New King James Version

27 Peace I leave with you, My peace I give to you; not as the world gives do I give to you. Let not your heart be troubled, neither let it be afraid.

Reflection

God promises to fill your cup to overflowing with His blessing.

Psalm 23:4-5

New International Version

[4] Even though I walk through the darkest valley, I will fear no evil, for you are with me; your rod and your staff, they comfort me. [5] You prepare a table before me in the presence of my enemies. You anoint my head with oil; my cup overflows.

New American Standard Bible

[4]Even though I (walk through the valley of the shadow of death, I fear no evil, for You are with me;Your rod and Your staff, they comfort me. [5]You prepare a table before me in the presence of my enemies;You have anointed my head with oil; My cup overflows.

The Message

[4] Even when the way goes through Death Valley, I'm not afraid when you walk at my side. Your trusty shepherd's crook makes me feel secure. [5] You serve me a six-course dinner right in front of my enemies. You revive my drooping head; my cup brims with blessing.

Amplified Bible

[4]Yes, though I walk through the [deep, sunless] valley of the shadow of death, I will fear or dread no evil, for You are with me; Your rod [to protect] and Your staff [to guide], they comfort me. [5]You prepare a table before me in the presence of my enemies. You anoint my head with [a]oil; my [brimming] cup runs over.

New Living Translation

[4] Even when I walkthrough the darkest valley,[a] I will not be afraid, for you are close beside me. Your rod and your staff protect and comfort me.[5] You prepare a feast for me in the presence of my enemies. You honor me by anointing my head with oil. My cup overflows with blessings.

Reflection

Contemporary English Version

[4]I may walk through valleys as dark as death, but I won't be afraid. You are with me, and your shepherd's rod makes me feel safe. [5]You treat me to a feast, while my enemies watch. You honor me as your guest, and you fill my cup until it overflows.

New King James Version

[4] Yea, though I walk through the valley of the shadow of death, I will fear no evil; For You are with me; Your rod and Your staff, they comfort me. [5] You prepare a table before me in the presence of my enemies; You anoint my head with oil; My cup runs over.

RUDOLPH MOSELEY JR.

God promises to protect, deliver and set free.

Psalm 27:1-3

New International Version

¹ The LORD is my light and my salvation—whom shall I fear? The LORD is the stronghold of my life—of whom shall I be afraid? ² When the wicked advance against me to devour me, it is my enemies and my foes who will stumble and fall.³ Though an army besiege me, my heart will not fear; though war break out against me, even then I will be confident.

New American Standard Bible

¹The LORD is my light and my salvation;Whom shall I fear?The LORD is the defense of my life; Whom shall I dread? ²When evildoers came upon me to devour my flesh, My adversaries and my enemies, they stumbled and fell. ³Though a host encamp against me, My heart will not fear;Though war arise against me, In spite of this I shall be confident.

The Message

¹ Light, space, zest—that's God! So, with him on my side I'm fearless, afraid of no one and nothing.² When vandal hordes ride down ready to eat me alive, Those bullies and toughs fall flat on their faces. ³ When besieged, I'm calm as a baby. When all hell breaks loose, I'm collected and cool.

Amplified Bible

¹THE LORD is my Light and my Salvation—whom shall I fear or dread? The Lord is the Refuge and Stronghold of my life—of whom shall I be afraid? ²When the wicked, even my enemies and my foes, came upon me to eat up my flesh, they stumbled and fell. ³Though a host encamp against me, my heart shall not fear; though war arise against me, [even then] in this will I be confident.

Reflection

New Living Translation

[1] The Lord is my light and my salvation—so why should I be afraid? The Lord is my fortress, protecting me from danger, so why should I tremble? [2] When evil people come to devour me, when my enemies and foes attack me, they will stumble and fall. [3] Though a mighty army surrounds me, my heart will not be afraid. Even if I am attacked, I will remain confident.

Contemporary English Version

[1] You, LORD, are the light that keeps me safe. I am not afraid of anyone. You protect me, and I have no fears. [2] Brutal people may attack and try to kill me, but they will stumble. Fierce enemies may attack, but they will fall. [3] Armies may surround me, but I won't be afraid; war may break out, but I will trust you.

New King James Version

[1] The LORD is my light and my salvation; Whom shall I fear? The LORD is the strength of my life; Of whom shall I be afraid? [2] When the wicked came against me To eat up my flesh, My enemies and foes, They stumbled and fell. [3] Though an army may encamp against me, My heart shall not fear; Though war may rise against me, In this I will be confident.

God promises that you are more than victorious in every area of your life.

Romans 8:37-39

New International Version [37] No, in all these things we are more than conquerors through him who loved us. [38] For I am convinced that neither death nor life, neither angels nor demons, neither the present nor the future, nor any powers, [39] neither height nor depth, nor anything else in all creation, will be able to separate us from the love of God that is in Christ Jesus our Lord.

New American Standard Bible [37]But in all these things we overwhelmingly conquer through (Him who loved us. [38]For I am convinced that neither death, nor life, nor angels, nor principalities, nor things present, nor things to come, nor powers, [39]nor height, nor depth, nor any other created thing, will be able to separate us from the love of God

The Message [37-39]Do you think anyone is going to be able to drive a wedge between us and Christ's love for us? There is no way! Not trouble, not hard times, not hatred, not hunger, not homelessness, not bullying threats, backstabbing, not even the worst sins listed in Scripture: They kill us in cold blood because they hate you. We're sitting ducks; they pick us off one by one. None of this fazes us because Jesus loves us. I'm absolutely convinced that nothing—nothing living or dead, angelic or demonic, today or tomorrow, high or low, thinkable or unthinkable—absolutely nothing can get between us and God's love because of the way that Jesus our Master has embraced us.

Amplified Bible [37]Yet amid all these things we are more than conquerors and gain a surpassing victory through Him Who loved us. [38]For I am persuaded beyond doubt (am sure) that neither death nor life, nor angels nor principalities, nor things impending and threatening nor things to

Reflection

come, nor powers, [39]Nor height nor depth, nor anything else in all creation will be able to separate us from the love of God which is in Christ Jesus our Lord.

New Living Translation [37] No, despite all these things, overwhelming victory is ours through Christ, who loved us. [38] And I am convinced that nothing can ever separate us from God's love. Neither death nor life, neither angels nor demons,[neither our fears for today nor our worries about tomorrow—not even the powers of hell can separate us from God's love. [39] No power in the sky above or in the earth below—indeed, nothing in all creation will ever be able to separate us from the love of God that is revealed in Christ Jesus our Lord.

Contemporary English Version [37]In everything we have won more than a victory because of Christ who loves us. [38]I am sure that nothing can separate us from God's love—not life or death, not angels or spirits, not the present or the future, [39]and not powers above or powers below. Nothing in all creation can separate us from God's love for us in Christ Jesus our Lord!

New King James Version [37] Yet in all these things we are more than conquerors through Him who loved us. [38] For I am persuaded that neither death nor life, nor angels nor principalities nor powers, nor things present nor things to come, [39] nor height nor depth, nor any other created thing, shall be able to separate us from the love of God which is in Christ Jesus our Lord.

RUDOLPH MOSELEY JR.

God promises to give you the best of the best.

Psalm 147:14

New International Version

¹⁴ He grants peace to your borders
    and satisfies you with the finest of wheat.

New American Standard Bible

¹⁴He (makes peace in your borders;
    He satisfies you with the finest of the wheat.

The Message

¹⁴He keeps the peace at your borders,
    he puts the best bread on your tables.

Amplified Bible

¹⁴He makes peace in your borders; He fills you with the finest of the wheat.

New Living Translation

¹⁴ He sends peace across your nation
    and satisfies your hunger with the finest wheat.

Contemporary English Version

¹⁴God lets you live in peace, and he gives you the very best wheat.

New King James Version

¹⁴ He makes peace in your borders,
    And fills you with the finest wheat.

Reflection

God promises to remember His promises from long ago.

Psalm 111:5

New International Version

⁵ He provides food for those who fear him;
    he remembers his covenant forever.

New American Standard Bible

⁵He has given food to those who fear Him;
    He will remember His covenant forever.

The Message

⁵ He gave food to those who fear him,
    He remembered to keep his ancient
promise.

Amplified Bible

⁵He has given food and provision to those who
reverently and worshipfully fear Him; He will
remember His covenant forever and imprint it
[on His mind].

New Living Translation

⁵ He gives food to those who fear him;
    he always remembers his covenant.

Contemporary English Version

⁵He gives food to his worshipers and always
keeps his agreement with them.

New King James Version

⁵ He has given food to those who fear Him;
    He will ever be mindful of His covenant.

Reflection

God promises to give to you, what give to others and more.

Luke 6:37-38

New International Version.[37] "Do not judge, and you will not be judged. Do not condemn, and you will not be condemned. Forgive, and you will be forgiven. [38] Give, and it will be given to you. A good measure, pressed down, shaken together and running over, will be poured into your lap. For with the measure you use, it will be measured to you."

New American Standard Bible [37]"Do not judge, and you will not be judged; and do not condemn, and you will not be condemned; pardon, and you will be pardoned. [38]"Give, and it will be given to you. They will pour into your lap a good measure—pressed down, shaken together, and running over. For by your standard of measure it will be measured to you in return."

The Message [37-38]"Don't pick on people, jump on their failures, criticize their faults—unless, of course, you want the same treatment. Don't condemn those who are down; that hardness can boomerang. Be easy on people; you'll find life a lot easier. Give away your life; you'll find life given back, but not merely given back—given back with bonus and blessing. Giving, not getting, is the way. Generosity begets generosity."

Amplified Bible [37]Judge not [neither pronouncing judgment nor subjecting to censure], and you will not be judged; do not condemn and pronounce guilty, and you will not be condemned and pronounced guilty; acquit and forgive and release (give up resentment, let it drop), and you will be acquitted and forgiven and released. [38]Give, and [gifts] will be given to you; good measure, pressed down, shaken together, and running over, will they pour into [the pouch formed by] the bosom [of your robe and used as a bag]. For with the

Reflection

measure you deal out [with the measure you use when you confer benefits on others], it will be measured back to you.

New Living Translation [37] "Do not judge others, and you will not be judged. Do not condemn others, or it will all come back against you. Forgive others, and you will be forgiven. [38] Give, and you will receive. Your gift will return to you in full—pressed down, shaken together to make room for more, running over, and poured into your lap. The amount you give will determine the amount you get back."

Contemporary English Version [37]Jesus said: Don't judge others, and God won't judge you. Don't be hard on others, and God won't be hard on you. Forgive others, and God will forgive you. [38]If you give to others, you will be given a full amount in return. It will be packed down, shaken together, and spilling over into your lap. The way you treat others is the way you will be treated.

New King James Version [37] "Judge not, and you shall not be judged. Condemn not, and you shall not be condemned. Forgive, and you will be forgiven. [38] Give, and it will be given to you: good measure, pressed down, shaken together, and running over will be put into your bosom. For with the same measure that you use, it will be measured back to you."

God promises to prosper whatever you do.

Psalm 1:3

New International Version

3 That person is like a tree planted by streams of water, which yields its fruit in season and whose leaf does not wither—whatever they do prospers.

New American Standard Bible

3 He will be like a tree firmly planted by streams of water, Which yields its fruit in its season And its leaf does not wither; And in whatever he does, he prospers.

The Message

2-3 Instead you thrill to God's Word, you chew on Scripture day and night. You're a tree replanted in Eden, bearing fresh fruit every month, Never dropping a leaf, always in blossom.

Amplified Bible

3 And he shall be like a tree firmly planted [and tended] by the streams of water, ready to bring forth its fruit in its season; its leaf also shall not fade or wither; and everything he does shall prosper [and come to maturity].

New Living Translation

3 They are like trees planted along the riverbank, bearing fruit each season. Their leaves never wither, and they prosper in all they do.

Contemporary English Version

3 They are like trees growing beside a stream, trees that produce fruit in season and always have leaves. Those people succeed in everything they do.

New King James Version

3 He shall be like a tree Planted by the rivers of water, That brings forth its fruit in its season, Whose leaf also shall not wither; And whatever he does shall prosper.

Reflection

God promises to keep you on track when you listen to Him.

Proverbs 3:6

New International Version

⁶ in all your ways submit to him,
    and he will make your paths straight.

New American Standard Bible

⁶In all your ways acknowledge Him,
    And He will make your paths straight.

The Message

⁶ Listen for God's voice in everything you do,
    everywhere you go;
        he's the one who will keep you on track.

Amplified Bible

⁶In all your ways know, recognize, and acknowledge Him, and He will direct and make straight and plain your paths.

New Living Translation

⁶ Seek his will in all you do,
    and he will show you which path to take.

Contemporary English Version

⁶Always let him lead you, and he will clear the road for you to follow.

New King James Version

⁶ In all your ways acknowledge Him,
    And He shall direct your paths.

Reflection

God promises to lead you to truth.

John 16:13

New International Version

[13] But when he, the Spirit of truth, comes, he will guide you into all the truth. He will not speak on his own; he will speak only what he hears, and he will tell you what is yet to come.

New American Standard Bible

[13]"But when He, the Spirit of truth, comes, He will guide you into all the truth; for He will not speak on His own initiative, but whatever He hears, He will speak; and He will disclose to you what is to come.

The Message

[13]when the Friend comes, the Spirit of the Truth, he will take you by the hand and guide you into all the truth there is. He won't draw attention to himself, but will make sense out of what is about to happen and, indeed, out of all that I have done and said.

Amplified Bible

[13]But when He, the Spirit of Truth (the Truth-giving Spirit) comes, He will guide you into all the Truth (the whole, full Truth). For He will not speak His own message [on His own authority]; but He will tell whatever He hears [from the Father; He will give the message that has been given to Him], and He will announce and declare to you the things that are to come [that will happen in the future].

New Living Translation

[13] When the Spirit of truth comes, he will guide you into all truth. He will not speak on his own but will tell you what he has heard. He will tell you about the future.

Reflection

Contemporary English Version

[13]The Spirit shows what is true and will come and guide you into the full truth. The Spirit doesn't speak on his own. He will tell you only what he has heard from me, and he will let you know what is going to happen.

New King James Version

[13] However, when He, the Spirit of truth, has come, He will guide you into all truth; for He will not speak on His own authority, but whatever He hears He will speak; and He will tell you things to come.

God promises to put His Spirit in you.

Ezekiel 36:27

New International Version

²⁷ And I will put my Spirit in you and move you to follow my decrees and be careful to keep my laws.

New American Standard Bible

²⁷"I will put My Spirit within you and cause you to walk in My statutes, and you will be careful to observe My ordinances.

The Message

²⁷ I'll put my Spirit in you and make it possible for you to do what I tell you and live by my commands.

Amplified Bible

²⁷And I will put my Spirit within you and cause you to walk in My statutes, and you shall heed My ordinances and do them.

New Living Translation

²⁷ And I will put my Spirit in you so that you will follow my decrees and be careful to obey my regulations.

Contemporary English Version

²⁷because I will put my Spirit in you and make you eager to obey my laws and teachings.

New King James Version

²⁷ I will put My Spirit within you and cause you to walk in My statutes, and you will keep My judgments and do them.

Reflection

God promises to give us the blessing of Abraham.

Galatians 3:14

New International Version

¹⁴ He redeemed us in order that the blessing given to Abraham might come to the Gentiles through Christ Jesus, so that by faith we might receive the promise of the Spirit.

New American Standard Bible

¹⁴in order that in Christ Jesus the blessing of Abraham might come to the Gentiles, so that we would receive the promise of the Spirit through faith.

The Message

¹⁴ And now, because of that, the air is cleared and we can see that Abraham's blessing is present and available for non-Jews, too. We are all able to receive God's life, his Spirit, in and with us by believing—just the way Abraham received it.

Amplified Bible

¹⁴To the end that through [their receiving] Christ Jesus, the blessing [promised] to Abraham might come upon the Gentiles, so that we through faith might [all] receive [the realization of] the promise of the [Holy] Spirit.

New Living Translation

¹⁴ Through Christ Jesus, God has blessed the Gentiles with the same blessing he promised to Abraham, so that we who are believers might receive the promised Holy Spirit through faith.

Reflection

Contemporary English Version

¹⁴And because of what Jesus Christ has done, the blessing that was promised to Abraham was taken to the Gentiles. This happened so that by faith we would be given the promised Holy Spirit.

New King James Version

[14] that the blessing of Abraham might come upon the Gentiles in Christ Jesus, that we might receive the promise of the Spirit through faith.

God promises to teach you all things through His anointing.

1 John 2:27

New International Version

²⁷ As for you, the anointing you received from him remains in you, and you do not need anyone to teach you. But as his anointing teaches you about all things and as that anointing is real, not counterfeit—just as it has taught you, remain in him.

New American Standard Bible

²⁷As for you, the anointing which you received from Him abides in you, and you have no need for anyone to teach you; but as His anointing teaches you about all things, and is true and is not a lie, and just as it has taught you, you abide in Him.

The Message

²⁷ But they're no match for what is embedded deeply within you—Christ's anointing, no less! You don't need any of their so-called teaching. Christ's anointing teaches you the truth on everything you need to know about yourself and him, uncontaminated by a single lie. Live deeply in what you were taught.

Amplified Bible

²⁷But as for you, the anointing (the sacred appointment, the unction) which you received from Him abides permanently] in you; [so] then you have no need that anyone should instruct you. But just as His anointing teaches you concerning everything and is true and is no falsehood, so you must abide in (live in, never depart from) Him [being rooted in Him, knit to Him], just as [His anointing] has taught you [to do].

Reflection

New Living Translation

[27] But you have received the Holy Spirit, and he lives within you, so you don't need anyone to teach you what is true. For the Spirit teaches you everything you need to know, and what he teaches is true—it is not a lie. So just as he has taught you, remain in fellowship with Christ.

Contemporary English Version

[27] But Christ has blessed you with the Holy Spirit. Now the Spirit stays in you, and you don't need any teachers. The Spirit is truthful and teaches you everything. So stay one in your heart with Christ, just as the Spirit has taught you to do.

New King James Version

[27] But the anointing which you have received from Him abides in you, and you do not need that anyone teach you; but as the same anointing teaches you concerning all things, and is true, and is not a lie, and just as it has taught you, you will abide in Him.

God promise to help us pray.

Romans 8:26-27

New International Version

²⁶ In the same way, the Spirit helps us in our weakness. We do not know what we ought to pray for, but the Spirit himself intercedes for us through wordless groans. ²⁷ And he who searches our hearts knows the mind of the Spirit, because the Spirit intercedes for God's people in accordance with the will of God.

New American Standard Bible

²⁶In the same way the Spirit also helps our weakness; for we do not know how to pray as we should, but the Spirit Himself intercedes for us with groanings too deep for words; ²⁷and He who searches the hearts knows what the mind of the Spirit is, because He intercedes for the saints according to the will of God.

The Message

²⁶⁻²⁷Meanwhile, the moment we get tired in the waiting, God's Spirit is right alongside helping us along. If we don't know how or what to pray, it doesn't matter. He does our praying in and for us, making prayer out of our wordless sighs, our aching groans. He knows us far better than we know ourselves, knows our pregnant condition, and keeps us present before God.

Amplified Bible

²⁶So too the [Holy] Spirit comes to our aid and bears us up in our weakness; for we do not know what prayer to offer nor how to offer it worthily as we ought, but the Spirit Himself goes to meet our supplication and pleads in our behalf with unspeakable yearnings and groanings too deep for utterance. ²⁷And He Who searches the hearts of men knows what is in the mind of the [Holy] Spirit [what His intent is], because the Spirit intercedes and pleads [before God] in behalf of the saints according to and in harmony with God's will.

Reflection

New Living Translation

[26] And the Holy Spirit helps us in our weakness. For example, we don't know what God wants us to pray for. But the Holy Spirit prays for us with groanings that cannot be expressed in words. [27] And the Father who knows all hearts knows what the Spirit is saying, for the Spirit pleads for us believers in harmony with God's own will.

Contemporary English Version

[26] In certain ways we are weak, but the Spirit is here to help us. For example, when we don't know what to pray for, the Spirit prays for us in ways that cannot be put into words. [27] All of our thoughts are known to God. He can understand what is in the mind of the Spirit, as the Spirit prays for God's people.

New King James Version

[26] Likewise the Spirit also helps in our weaknesses. For we do not know what we should pray for as we ought, but the Spirit Himself makes intercession for us[a] with groanings which cannot be uttered. [27] Now He who searches the hearts knows what the mind of the Spirit is, because He makes intercession for the saints according to the will of God.

God promises to make us His children.

Romans 8:15

New International Version

¹⁵ The Spirit you received does not make you slaves, so that you live in fear again; rather, the Spirit you received brought about your adoption to sonship. And by him we cry, "Abba, Father."

New American Standard Bible

¹⁵For you have not received a spirit of slavery leading to fear again, but you have received a spirit of adoption as sons by which we cry out, "Abba! Father!"

The Message

¹⁵⁻¹⁷This resurrection life you received from God is not a timid, grave-tending life. It's adventurously expectant, greeting God with a childlike "What's next, Papa?"

Amplified Bible

¹⁵For [the Spirit which] you have now received [is] not a spirit of slavery to put you once more in bondage to fear, but you have received the Spirit of adoption [the Spirit producing sonship] in [the bliss of] which we cry, Abba (Father)! Father!

New Living Translation

¹⁵ So you have not received a spirit that makes you fearful slaves. Instead, you received God's Spirit when he adopted you as his own children. [Now we call him, "Abba, Father."

Contemporary English Version

¹⁵God's Spirit doesn't make us slaves who are afraid of him. Instead, we become his children and call him our Father.

New King James Version

¹⁵ For you did not receive the spirit of bondage again to fear, but you received the Spirit of adoption by whom we cry out, "Abba, Father."

Reflection

God promises joy in the Holy Spirit.

Romans 14:17

New International Version

17 For the kingdom of God is not a matter of eating and drinking, but of righteousness, peace and joy in the Holy Spirit,

New American Standard Bible

17for the kingdom of God is not eating and drinking, but righteousness and peace and joy in the Holy Spirit.

The Message

17God's kingdom isn't a matter of what you put in your stomach, for goodness' sake. It's what God does with your life as he sets it right, puts it together, and completes it with joy.

Amplified Bible

17[After all] the kingdom of God is not a matter of [getting the] food and drink [one likes], but instead it is righteousness (that state which makes a person acceptable to God) and [heart] peace and joy in the Holy Spirit.

New Living Translation

17 For the Kingdom of God is not a matter of what we eat or drink, but of living a life of goodness and peace and joy in the Holy Spirit.

Contemporary English Version

17God's kingdom isn't about eating and drinking. It is about pleasing God, about living in peace, and about true happiness. All this comes from the Holy Spirit.

New King James Version

17 for the kingdom of God is not eating and drinking, but righteousness and peace and joy in the Holy Spirit.

Reflection

God promises to cloth you in righteousness.

Isaiah 61:10

New International Version

¹⁰ I delight greatly in the LORD; my soul rejoices in my God. For he has clothed me with garments of salvation and arrayed me in a robe of his righteousness, as a bridegroom adorns his head like a priest, and as a bride adorns herself with her jewels.

New American Standard Bible

¹⁰I will rejoice greatly in the LORD, My soul will exult in my God;For He has clothed me with garments of salvation, He has wrapped me with a robe of righteousness, As a bridegroom decks himself with a garland, And as a bride adorns herself with her jewels.

The Message

¹⁰⁻¹¹I will sing for joy in God, explode in praise from deep in my soul!He dressed me up in a suit of salvation, he outfitted me in a robe of righteousness, As a bridegroom who puts on a tuxedo and a bride a jeweled tiara.

Amplified Bible

¹⁰I will greatly rejoice in the Lord, my soul will exult in my God; for He has clothed me with the garments of salvation, He has covered me with the robe of righteousness, as a bridegroom decks himself with a garland, and as a bride adorns herself with her jewels.

New Living Translation

¹⁰ I am overwhelmed with joy in the Lord my God!For he has dressed me with the clothing of salvation and draped me in a robe of righteousness. I am like a bridegroom in his wedding suit or a bride with her jewels.

Reflection

Contemporary English Version

[10]I celebrate and shout because of my LORD God. His saving power and justice are the very clothes I wear. They are more beautiful than the jewelry worn by a bride or a groom.

New King James Version

[10] I will greatly rejoice in the LORD, My soul shall be joyful in my God; For He has clothed me with the garments of salvation, He has covered me with the robe of righteousness, As a bridegroom decks himself with ornaments, And as a bride adorns herself with her jewels.

God promises to be your strength.

Nehemiah 8:10

New International Version

[10] Nehemiah said, "Go and enjoy choice food and sweet drinks, and send some to those who have nothing prepared. This day is holy to our Lord. Do not grieve, for the joy of the LORD is your strength."

New American Standard Bible

[10]Then he said to them, "Go, eat of the fat, drink of the sweet, and (A)send portions to him who has nothing prepared; for this day is holy to our Lord. Do not be grieved, for the joy of the LORD is your strength."

The Message

[10] He continued, "Go home and prepare a feast, holiday food and drink; and share it with those who don't have anything: This day is holy to God. Don't feel bad. The joy of God is your strength!"

Amplified Bible

[10]Then [Ezra] told them, Go your way, eat the fat, drink the sweet drink, and send portions to him for whom nothing is prepared; for this day is holy to our Lord. And be not grieved and depressed, for the joy of the Lord is your strength and stronghold.

New Living Translation

[10] And Nehemiah continued, "Go and celebrate with a feast of rich foods and sweet drinks, and share gifts of food with people who have nothing prepared. This is a sacred day before our Lord. Don't be dejected and sad, for the joy of the Lord is your strength!"

Reflection

Contemporary English Version

[10]Nehemiah told the people, "Enjoy your good food and wine and share some with those who didn't have anything to bring. Don't be sad! This is a special day for the LORD, and he will make you happy and strong."

New King James Version

[10] Then he said to them, "Go your way, eat the fat, drink the sweet, and send portions to those for whom nothing is prepared; for this day is holy to our Lord. Do not sorrow, for the joy of the LORD is your strength."

God promises to satisfy you with long life.

Psalm 91:16

New International Version

¹⁶ With long life I will satisfy him
and show him my salvation."

New American Standard Bible

¹⁶"With a (A)long life I will satisfy him
And (B)let him see My salvation."

The Message

¹⁶ I'll give you a long life,
give you a long drink of salvation!"

Amplified Bible

¹⁶With long life will I satisfy him and show
him My salvation.

New Living Translation

¹⁶ I will reward them with a long life
and give them my salvation."

Contemporary English Version

¹⁶You will live a long life
and see my saving power."

New King James Version

¹⁶ With long life I will satisfy him,
And show him My salvation."

Reflection

God promises to add years to your life.

Proverbs 10:27

New International Version

²⁷ The fear of the LORD adds length to life,
but the years of the wicked are cut short.

New American Standard Bible

²⁷The fear of the LORD prolongs life,
But the years of the wicked will be
shortened.

The Message

²⁷ The Fear-of-God expands your life;
a wicked life is a puny life.

Amplified Bible

²⁷The reverent and worshipful fear of the Lord
prolongs one's days, but the years of the wicked
shall be made short.

New Living Translation

²⁷ Fear of the Lord lengthens one's life,
but the years of the wicked are cut short.

Contemporary English Version

²⁷If you respect the LORD, you will live longer;
if you keep doing wrong, your life will be cut
short.

New King James Version

²⁷ The fear of the LORD prolongs days,
But the years of the wicked will be
shortened.

Reflection

God promises to multiply your years.

Proverbs 9:11

New International Version

¹¹ For through wisdom your days will be
many,
and years will be added to your life.

New American Standard Bible

¹¹For by me your days will be multiplied,
And years of life will be added to you.

The Message

¹¹ It's through me, Lady Wisdom, that your
life deepens,
and the years of your life ripen.

Amplified Bible

¹¹For by me [Wisdom from God] your days
shall be multiplied, and the years of your life
shall be increased.

New Living Translation

¹¹ Wisdom will multiply your days
and add years to your life.

Contemporary English Version

¹¹I am Wisdom. If you follow me,
you will live a long time.

New King James Version

¹¹ For by me your days will be multiplied,
And years of life will be added to you.

Reflection

God promises to bless your life in more ways than one.

Deuteronomy 7:13

New International Version

¹³ He will love you and bless you and increase your numbers. He will bless the fruit of your womb, the crops of your land—your grain, new wine and olive oil—the calves of your herds and the lambs of your flocks in the land he swore to your ancestors to give you.

New American Standard Bible

¹³"He will love you and bless you and multiply you; He will also bless the fruit of your womb and the fruit of your ground, your grain and your new wine and your oil, the increase of your herd and the young of your flock, in the land which He swore to your forefathers to give you.

The Message

¹³ He will bless the babies from your womb and the harvest of grain, new wine, and oil from your fields; he'll bless the calves from your herds and lambs from your flocks in the country he promised your ancestors that he'd give you.

Amplified Bible

¹³And He will love you, bless you, and multiply you; He will also bless the fruit of your body and the fruit of your land, your grain, your new wine, and your oil, the increase of your cattle and the young of your flock in the land which He swore to your fathers to give you.

New Living Translation

¹³ He will love you and bless you, and he will give you many children. He will give fertility to your land and your animals. When you arrive in the land he swore to give your ancestors, you will have large harvests of grain, new wine, and olive oil, and great herds of cattle, sheep, and goats.

Reflection

Contemporary English Version

[13]The LORD will love you and bless you by giving you many children and plenty of food, wine, and olive oil. Your herds of cattle will have many calves, and your flocks of sheep will have many lambs.

New King James Version

[13] And He will love you and bless you and multiply you; He will also bless the fruit of your womb and the fruit of your land, your grain and your new wine and your oil, the increase of your cattle and the offspring of your flock, in the land of which He swore to your fathers to give you.

God promises to come near to you when you come near to Him.

James 4:7-8

New International Version

⁷ Submit yourselves, then, to God. Resist the devil, and he will flee from you. ⁸ Come near to God and he will come near to you. Wash your hands, you sinners, and purify your hearts, you double-minded.

New American Standard Bible

⁷Submit therefore to God Resist the devil and he will flee from you. ⁸Draw near to God and He will draw near to you Cleanse your hands, you sinners; and purify your hearts, you double-minded.

The Message

⁷⁻⁸So let God work his will in you. Yell a loud no to the Devil and watch him scamper. Say a quiet yes to God and he'll be there in no time. Quit dabbling in sin. Purify your inner life. Quit playing the field.

Amplified Bible

⁷So be subject to God. Resist the devil [stand firm against him], and he will flee from you. ⁸Come close to God and He will come close to you. [Recognize that you are] sinners, get your soiled hands clean; [realize that you have been disloyal] wavering individuals with divided interests, and purify your hearts [of your spiritual adultery].

New Living Translation

⁷ So humble yourselves before God. Resist the devil, and he will flee from you. ⁸ Come close to God, and God will come close to you. Wash your hands, you sinners; purify your hearts, for your loyalty is divided between God and the world.

Reflection

Contemporary English Version

[7]Surrender to God! Resist the devil, and he will run from you. [8]Come near to God, and he will come near to you. Clean up your lives, you sinners. Purify your hearts, you people who can't make up your mind.

New King James Version

[7] Therefore submit to God. Resist the devil and he will flee from you. [8] Draw near to God and He will draw near to you. Cleanse your hands, you sinners; and purify your hearts, you double-minded.

God promises that the poor and afflicted will be satisfied.

Psalm 22:26

New International Version

26 The poor will eat and be satisfied; those who seek the LORD will praise him—may your hearts live forever!

New American Standard Bible

26The afflicted will eat and be satisfied; Those who seek Him will praise the LORD Let your heart live forever!

The Message

26Down-and-outers sit at God's table and eat their fill. Everyone on the hunt for God is here, praising him. "Live it up, from head to toe. Don't ever quit!"

Amplified Bible

26The poor and afflicted shall eat and be satisfied; they shall praise the Lord—they who [diligently] seek for, inquire of and for Him, and require Him [as their greatest need]. May your hearts be quickened now and forever!

New Living Translation

26 The poor will eat and be satisfied. All who seek the Lord will praise him. Their hearts will rejoice with everlasting joy.

Contemporary English Version

26The poor will eat and be full, and all who worship you will be thankful and live in hope.

New King James Version

26 The poor shall eat and be satisfied; Those who seek Him will praise the LORD. Let your heart live forever!

Reflection

God promises to crown the humble with victory.

Psalm 149:4

New International Version

⁴ For the LORD takes delight in his people;
he crowns the humble with victory.

New American Standard Bible

⁴For the LORD takes pleasure in His people;
He will beautify the afflicted ones with salvation.

The Message

⁴ And why? Because God delights in his
people,
festoons plain folk with salvation
garlands!

Amplified Bible

⁴For the Lord takes pleasure in His people; He
will beautify the humble with salvation and
adorn the wretched with victory.

New Living Translation

⁴ For the Lord delights in his people;
he crowns the humble with victory.

Contemporary English Version

⁴The LORD is pleased with his people, and he
gives victory to those who are humble.

New King James Version

⁴ For the LORD takes pleasure in His people;
He will beautify the humble with
salvation.

Reflection

God promises to honor those with a quiet and gentle spirit.

1 Peter 3:4

New International Version

⁴ Rather, it should be that of your inner self, the unfading beauty of a gentle and quiet spirit, which is of great worth in God's sight.

New American Standard Bible

⁴but let it be the hidden person of the heart, with the imperishable quality of a gentle and quiet spirit, which is precious in the sight of God.

The Message

⁴ What matters is not your outer appearance—the styling of your hair, the jewelry you wear, the cut of your clothes—but your inner disposition.

Amplified Bible

⁴But let it be the inward adorning and beauty of the hidden person of the heart, with the incorruptible and unfading charm of a gentle and peaceful spirit, which [is not anxious or wrought up, but] is very precious in the sight of God.

New Living Translation

⁴ You should clothe yourselves instead with the beauty that comes from within, the unfading beauty of a gentle and quiet spirit, which is so precious to God.

Contemporary English Version

⁴Be beautiful in your heart by being gentle and quiet. This kind of beauty will last, and God considers it very special.

New King James Version

⁴ rather let it be the hidden person of the heart, with the incorruptible beauty of a gentle and quiet spirit, which is very precious in the sight of God.

Reflection

God promises that meek people will move in and take over.

Psalm 37:11

New International Version

¹¹ But the meek will inherit the land
and enjoy peace and prosperity.

New American Standard Bible

¹¹But the humble will inherit the land
And will delight themselves in abundant
prosperity.

The Message

¹¹Down-to-earth people will move in and take
over,
relishing a huge bonanza.

Amplified Bible

¹¹But the meek [in the end] shall inherit the
earth and shall delight themselves in the
abundance of peace.(A)

New Living Translation

¹¹ The lowly will possess the land
and will live in peace and prosperity.

Contemporary English Version

¹¹but the poor will take the land
and enjoy a big harvest.

New King James Version

¹¹ But the meek shall inherit the earth,
And shall delight themselves in the
abundance of peace.

Reflection

God promises that a gentle answer turns away wrath.

Proverbs 15:1

New International Version

¹ A gentle answer turns away wrath,
  but a harsh word stirs up anger.

New American Standard Bible

¹A gentle answer turns away wrath,
  But a harsh word stirs up anger.

The Message

¹ A gentle response defuses anger, but a sharp tongue kindles a temper-fire.

Amplified Bible

¹A SOFT answer turns away wrath, but grievous words stir up anger.

New Living Translation

¹ A gentle answer deflects anger,
  but harsh words make tempers flare.

Contemporary English Version

¹A kind answer soothes angry feelings,
  but harsh words stir them up.

New King James Version

¹ A soft answer turns away wrath,
  But a harsh word stirs up anger.

Reflection

God promises to bless when you do what you are told to do.

Deuteronomy 6:3

New International Version

³ Hear, Israel, and be careful to obey so that it may go well with you and that you may increase greatly in a land flowing with milk and honey, just as the LORD, the God of your ancestors, promised you.

New American Standard Bible

³"O Israel, you should listen and be careful to do it, that it may be well with you and that you may multiply greatly, just as the LORD, the God of your fathers, has promised you, in a land flowing with milk and honey.

The Message

³ Listen obediently, Israel. Do what you're told so that you'll have a good life, a life of abundance and bounty, just as God promised, in a land abounding in milk and honey.

Amplified Bible

³Hear therefore, O Israel, and be watchful to do them, that it may be well with you and that you may increase exceedingly, as the Lord, the God of your fathers, has promised you, in a land flowing with milk and honey.

New Living Translation

³ Listen closely, Israel, and be careful to obey. Then all will go well with you, and you will have many children in the land flowing with milk and honey, just as the Lord, the God of your ancestors, promised you.

Reflection

Contemporary English Version

³Pay attention, Israel! Our ancestors worshiped the LORD, and he promised to give us this land that is rich with milk and honey. Be careful to obey him, and you will become a successful and powerful nation.

New King James Version

[3] Therefore hear, O Israel, and be careful to observe it, that it may be well with you, and that you may multiply greatly as the LORD God of your fathers has promised you—'a land flowing with milk and honey.'

God promises to bless the faithful and obedient.

Deuteronomy 7:12

New International Version

¹² If you pay attention to these laws and are careful to follow them, then the LORD your God will keep his covenant of love with you, as he swore to your ancestors.

New American Standard Bible

¹²"Then it shall come about, because you listen to these judgments and keep and do them, that the LORD your God will keep with you His covenant and His lovingkindness which He swore to your forefathers.

The Message

¹² And this is what will happen: When you, on your part, will obey these directives, keeping and following them, God, on his part, will keep the covenant of loyal love that he made with your ancestors:

Amplified Bible

¹²And if you hearken to these precepts and keep and do them, the Lord your God will keep with you the covenant and the steadfast love which He swore to your fathers.

New Living Translation

¹² "If you listen to these regulations and faithfully obey them, the Lord your God will keep his covenant of unfailing love with you, as he promised with an oath to your ancestors.

Contemporary English Version

¹²If you completely obey these laws, the LORD your God will be loyal and keep the agreement he made with you, just as he promised our ancestors.

Reflection

New King James Version

[12] "Then it shall come to pass, because you listen to these judgments, and keep and do them, that the LORD your God will keep with you the covenant and the mercy which He swore to your fathers.

God promises to prosper the faithful and obedient.

Deuteronomy 29:9

New International Version

⁹ Carefully follow the terms of this covenant, so that you may prosper in everything you do.

New American Standard Bible

⁹"So keep the words of this covenant to do them, that you may prosper in all that you do.

The Message

⁹ Diligently keep the words of this Covenant. Do what they say so that you will live well and wisely in every detail.

Amplified Bible

⁹Therefore keep the words of this covenant and do them, that you may deal wisely and prosper in all that you do.

New Living Translation

⁹ "Therefore, obey the terms of this covenant so that you will prosper in everything you do.

Contemporary English Version

⁹Israel, the LORD has made an agreement with you, and if you keep your part, you will be successful in everything you do.

New King James Version

⁹ Therefore keep the words of this covenant, and do them, that you may prosper in all that you do.

Reflection

God promises to bless the children of the faithful and obedient.

Deuteronomy 5:29

New International Version

²⁹ Oh, that their hearts would be inclined to fear me and keep all my commands always, so that it might go well with them and their children forever!

New American Standard Bible

²⁹"Oh that they had such a heart in them, that they would fear Me and keep all My commandments always, that it may be well with them and with their sons forever!

The Message

²⁹What I wouldn't give if they'd always feel this way, continuing to revere me and always keep all my commands; they'd have a good life forever, they and their children!

Amplified Bible

²⁹Oh, that they had such a [mind and] heart in them always [reverently] to fear Me and keep all My commandments, that it might go well with them and with their children forever!

New Living Translation

²⁹ Oh, that they would always have hearts like this, that they might fear me and obey all my commands! If they did, they and their descendants would prosper forever.

Contemporary English Version

²⁹I wish they would always worship me with fear and trembling and be this willing to obey me! Then they and their children would always enjoy a successful life.

New King James Version

²⁹ Oh, that they had such a heart in them that they would fear Me and always keep all My commandments, that it might be well with them and with their children forever!

Reflection

God promises promotion to those who obey His word.

Matthew 5:19

New International Version

¹⁹ Therefore anyone who sets aside one of the least of these commands and teaches others accordingly will be called least in the kingdom of heaven, but whoever practices and teaches these commands will be called great in the kingdom of heaven.

New American Standard Bible

¹⁹"Whoever then annuls one of the least of these commandments, and teaches others to do the same, shall be called least in the kingdom of heaven; but whoever keeps and teaches them, he shall be called great in the kingdom of heaven.

The Message

¹⁹⁻²⁰"Trivialize even the smallest item in God's Law and you will only have trivialized yourself. But take it seriously, show the way for others, and you will find honor in the kingdom. Unless you do far better than the Pharisees in the matters of right living, you won't know the first thing about entering the kingdom.

Amplified Bible

¹⁹Whoever then breaks or does away with or relaxes one of the least [important] of these commandments and teaches men so shall be called least [important] in the kingdom of heaven, but he who practices them and teaches others to do so shall be called great in the kingdom of heaven.

New Living Translation

¹⁹ So if you ignore the least commandment and teach others to do the same, you will be called the least in the Kingdom of Heaven. But anyone who obeys God's laws and teaches them will be called great in the Kingdom of Heaven.

Reflection

Contemporary English Version

[19] If you reject even the least important command in the Law and teach others to do the same, you will be the least important person in the kingdom of heaven. But if you obey and teach others its commands, you will have an important place in the kingdom.

New King James Version

[19] Whoever therefore breaks one of the least of these commandments, and teaches men so, shall be called least in the kingdom of heaven; but whoever does and teaches them, he shall be called great in the kingdom of heaven.

God promises to protect the house of those who put His word into practice.

Matthew 7:24-25

New International Version

[24] "Therefore everyone who hears these words of mine and puts them into practice is like a wise man who built his house on the rock. [25] The rain came down, the streams rose, and the winds blew and beat against that house; yet it did not fall, because it had its foundation on the rock.

New American Standard Bible

[24]"Therefore everyone who hears these words of Mine and acts on them, may be compared to a wise man who built his house on the rock. [25]"And the rain fell, and the floods came, and the winds blew and slammed against that house; and yet it did not fall, for it had been founded on the rock.

The Message

[24-25]"These words I speak to you are not incidental additions to your life, homeowner improvements to your standard of living. They are foundational words, words to build a life on. If you work these words into your life, you are like a smart carpenter who built his house on solid rock. Rain poured down, the river flooded, a tornado hit—but nothing moved that house. It was fixed to the rock.

Amplified Bible

[24]So everyone who hears these words of Mine and acts upon them [obeying them] will be like a [a]sensible (prudent, practical, wise) man who built his house upon the rock. [25]And the rain fell and the floods came and the winds blew and beat against that house; yet it did not fall, because it had been founded on the rock.

Reflection

_____

_____

_____

_____

_____

_____

_____

_____

_____

_____

_____

_____

_____

_____

_____

_____

_____

_____

_____

_____

_____

_____

_____

_____

_____

_____

_____

_____

_____

_____

New Living Translation

[24] "Anyone who listens to my teaching and follows it is wise, like a person who builds a house on solid rock. [25] Though the rain comes in torrents and the floodwaters rise and the winds beat against that house, it won't collapse because it is built on bedrock.

Contemporary English Version

[24]Anyone who hears and obeys these teachings of mine is like a wise person who built a house on solid rock. [25]Rain poured down, rivers flooded, and winds beat against that house. But it did not fall, because it was built on solid rock.

New King James Version

[24] "Therefore whoever hears these sayings of Mine, and does them, I will liken him to a wise man who built his house on the rock: [25] and the rain descended, the floods came, and the winds blew and beat on that house; and it did not fall, for it was founded on the rock.

God promises to cause all things to work out into something good.

Romans 8:28

New International Version

²⁸ And we know that in all things God works for the good of those who love him, who have been called according to his purpose.

New American Standard Bible

²⁸And we know that God causes all things to work together for good to those who love God, to those who are called according to His purpose.

The Message

²⁸ That's why we can be so sure that every detail in our lives of love for God is worked into something good.

Amplified Bible

²⁸We are assured and know that God being a partner in their labor] all things work together and are [fitting into a plan] for good to and for those who love God and are called according to [His] design and purpose.

New Living Translation

²⁸ And we know that God causes everything to work together for the good of those who love God and are called according to his purpose for them.

Contemporary English Version

²⁸We know that God is always at work for the good of everyone who loves him. They are the ones God has chosen for his purpose,

New King James Version

²⁸ And we know that all things work together for good to those who love God, to those who are the called according to His purpose.

Reflection

God promises that those who hear His word and believe will be saved.

John 5:24

New International Version

²⁴ "Very truly I tell you, whoever hears my word and believes him who sent me has eternal life and will not be judged but has crossed over from death to life.

New American Standard Bible

²⁴"Truly, truly, I say to you, he who hears My word, and believes Him who sent Me, has eternal life, and does not come into judgment, but has passed out of death into life.

The Message

²⁴"It's urgent that you listen carefully to this: Anyone here who believes what I am saying right now and aligns himself with the Father, who has in fact put me in charge, has at this very moment the real, lasting life and is no longer condemned to be an outsider. This person has taken a giant step from the world of the dead to the world of the living.

Amplified Bible

²⁴I assure you, most solemnly I tell you, the person whose ears are open to My words [who listens to My message] and believes and trusts in and clings to and relies on Him Who sent Me has (possesses now) eternal life. And he does not come into judgment [does not incur sentence of judgment, will not come under condemnation], but he has already passed over out of death into life.

New Living Translation

²⁴ "I tell you the truth, those who listen to my message and believe in God who sent me have eternal life. They will never be condemned for their sins, but they have already passed from death into life.

Reflection

Contemporary English Version

[24] I tell you for certain that everyone who hears my message and has faith in the one who sent me has eternal life and will never be condemned. They have already gone from death to life.

New King James Version

[24] "Most assuredly, I say to you, he who hears My word and believes in Him who sent Me has everlasting life, and shall not come into judgment, but has passed from death into life.

RUDOLPH MOSELEY JR.

God promises that if we ask anything in accordance with His will He hears us.

1 John 5:14-15

New International Version

[14] This is the confidence we have in approaching God: that if we ask anything according to his will, he hears us. [15] And if we know that he hears us—whatever we ask—we know that we have what we asked of him.

New American Standard Bible

[14] This is the confidence which we have before Him, that, if we ask anything according to His will, He hears us. [15] And if we know that He hears us in whatever we ask, we know that we have the requests which we have asked from Him.

The Message

[13-15] My purpose in writing is simply this: that you who believe in God's Son will know beyond the shadow of a doubt that you have eternal life, the reality and not the illusion. And how bold and free we then become in his presence, freely asking according to his will, sure that he's listening. And if we're confident that he's listening, we know that what we've asked for is as good as ours.

Amplified Bible

[14] And this is the confidence (the assurance, the privilege of boldness) which we have in Him: [we are sure] that if we ask anything (make any request) according to His will (in agreement with His own plan), He listens to and hears us. [15] And if (since) we [positively] know that He listens to us in whatever we ask, we also know [with settled and absolute knowledge] that we have [granted us as our present possessions] the requests made of Him.

Reflection

New Living Translation

[14] And we are confident that he hears us whenever we ask for anything that pleases him. [15] And since we know he hears us when we make our requests, we also know that he will give us what we ask for.

Contemporary English Version

[14] We are certain that God will hear our prayers when we ask for what pleases him. [15] And if we know that God listens when we pray, we are sure that our prayers have already been answered.

New King James Version

[14] Now this is the confidence that we have in Him, that if we ask anything according to His will, He hears us. [15] And if we know that He hears us, whatever we ask, we know that we have the petitions that we have asked of Him.

God promises to do anything we ask in His name.

John 14:13-14

New International Version

[13] And I will do whatever you ask in my name, so that the Father may be glorified in the Son. [14] You may ask me for anything in my name, and I will do it.

New American Standard Bible

[13]"Whatever you ask in My name, that will I do, so that the Father may be glorified in the Son. [14]"If you ask Me anything in My name, I will do it.

The Message

[13-14]You can count on it. From now on, whatever you request along the lines of who I am and what I am doing, I'll do it. That's how the Father will be seen for who he is in the Son. I mean it. Whatever you request in this way, I'll do.

Amplified Bible

[13]And I will do [I Myself will grant] whatever you ask in My Name [as presenting all that I AM], so that the Father may be glorified and extolled in (through) the Son.[14][Yes] I will grant [I Myself will do for you] whatever you shall ask in My Name [as presenting all that I AM].

New Living Translation

[13] You can ask for anything in my name, and I will do it, so that the Son can bring glory to the Father. [14] Yes, ask me for anything in my name, and I will do it!

Contemporary English Version

[13]Ask me, and I will do whatever you ask. This way the Son will bring honor to the Father. [14]I will do whatever you ask me to do.

New King James Version

[13] And whatever you ask in My name, that I will do, that the Father may be glorified in the Son. [14] If you ask[a] anything in My name, I will do it.

Reflection

God promises that if you remain in His word you can ask Him for anything.

John 15:7

New International Version

⁷ If you remain in me and my words remain in you, ask whatever you wish, and it will be done for you.

New American Standard Bible

⁷"If you abide in Me, and My words abide in you, ask whatever you wish, and it will be done for you.

The Message

⁷ But if you make yourselves at home with me and my words are at home in you, you can be sure that whatever you ask will be listened to and acted upon.

Amplified Bible

⁷If you live in Me [abide vitally united to Me] and My words remain in you and continue to live in your hearts, ask whatever you will, and it shall be done for you.

New Living Translation

⁷ But if you remain in me and my words remain in you, you may ask for anything you want, and it will be granted!

Contemporary English Version

⁷Stay joined to me and let my teachings become part of you. Then you can pray for whatever you want, and your prayer will be answered.

New King James Version

⁷ If you abide in Me, and My words abide in you, you will ask what you desire, and it shall be done for you.

Reflection

God promises to hear you when you pray in secret.

Matthew 6:6

New International Version

⁶ But when you pray, go into your room, close the door and pray to your Father, who is unseen. Then your Father, who sees what is done in secret, will reward you.

New American Standard Bible

⁶"But you, when you pray, go into your inner room, close your door and pray to your Father who is in secret, and your Father who sees what is done in secret will reward you.

The Message

⁶"Here's what I want you to do: Find a quiet, secluded place so you won't be tempted to role-play before God. Just be there as simply and honestly as you can manage. The focus will shift from you to God, and you will begin to sense his grace.

Amplified Bible

⁶But when you pray, go into your [most] private room, and, closing the door, pray to your Father, Who is in secret; and your Father, Who sees in secret, will reward you in the open.

New Living Translation

⁶ But when you pray, go away by yourself, shut the door behind you, and pray to your Father in private. Then your Father, who sees everything, will reward you.

Contemporary English Version

⁶When you pray, go into a room alone and close the door. Pray to your Father in private.
He knows what is done in private, and he will reward you.

New King James Version

⁶ But you, when you pray, go into your room, and when you have shut your door, pray to your Father who is in the secret place; and your Father who sees in secret will reward you openly.

Reflection

God promises to hear the prayer of the righteous.

Proverbs 15:29

New International Version

²⁹ The LORD is far from the wicked,
but he hears the prayer of the righteous.

New American Standard Bible

²⁹The LORD is far from the wicked,
But He hears the prayer of the righteous.

The Message

²⁹ God keeps his distance from the wicked;
he closely attends to the prayers of
God-loyal people.

Amplified Bible

²⁹The Lord is far from the wicked, but He hears
the prayer of the [consistently] righteous (the
upright, in right standing with Him).

New Living Translation

²⁹ The Lord is far from the wicked,
but he hears the prayers of the righteous.

Contemporary English Version

²⁹The LORD never even hears the prayers of
the wicked,
but he answers the prayers of all who obey
him.

New King James Version

²⁹ The LORD is far from the wicked,
But He hears the prayer of the righteous.

Reflection

God promises that He will hear the prayer of His people.

Zechariah 13:9

New International Version

⁹ This third I will put into the fire; I will refine them like silver and test them like gold. They will call on my name and I will answer them; I will say, 'They are my people,' and they will say, 'The LORD is our God.'"

New American Standard Bible

⁹"And I will bring the third part through the fire, Refine them as silver is refined, And test them as gold is tested They will call on My name, And I will answer them; I will say, 'They are My people,' And they will say, 'The LORD is my God.'

The Message

⁹I'll deliver the surviving third to the refinery fires. I'll refine them as silver is refined, test them for purity as gold is tested. Then they'll pray to me by name and I'll answer them personally. I'll say, 'That's my people.' They'll say, 'God—my God!'"

Amplified Bible

⁹And I will bring the third part through the fire, and will refine them as silver is refined and will test them as gold is tested. They will call on My name, and I will hear and answer them. I will say, It is My people; and they will say, The Lord is my God.

New Living Translation

⁹ I will bring that group through the fire and make them pure. I will refine them like silver and purify them like gold. They will call on my name, and I will answer them. I will say, 'These are my people,' and they will say, 'The Lord is our God.'"

Reflection

Contemporary English Version

⁹Then I will purify them and put them to the test, just as gold and silver are purified and tested. They will pray in my name, and I will answer them. I will say, "You are my people," and they will reply, "You, LORD, are our God!"

New King James Version

⁹ I will bring the one-third through the fire, Will refine them as silver is refined, And test them as gold is tested. They will call on My name, And I will answer them. I will say, 'This is My people'; And each one will say, 'The LORD is my God.'"

God promises to answer when you call.

Jeremiah 33:3

New International Version

³ 'Call to me and I will answer you and tell you great and unsearchable things you do not know.'

New American Standard Bible

³'Call to Me and I will answer you, and I will tell you great and mighty things, which you do not know.'

The Message

²⁻³"This is God's Message, the God who made earth, made it livable and lasting, known everywhere as God: 'Call to me and I will answer you. I'll tell you marvelous and wondrous things that you could never figure out on your own.'

Amplified Bible

³Call to Me and I will answer you and show you great and mighty things, fenced in and hidden, which you do not know (do not distinguish and recognize, have knowledge of and understand).

New Living Translation

³ Ask me and I will tell you remarkable secrets you do not know about things to come.

Contemporary English Version

³Ask me, and I will tell you things that you don't know and can't find out.

New King James Version

³ 'Call to Me, and I will answer you, and show you great and mighty things, which you do not know.'

Reflection

God promises that you will receive what you believe Him for.

Mark 11:24

New International Version

²⁴ Therefore I tell you, whatever you ask for in prayer, believe that you have received it, and it will be yours.

New American Standard Bible

²⁴"Therefore I say to you, all things for which you pray and ask, believe that you have received them, and they will be granted you.

The Message

²⁴That's why I urge you to pray for absolutely everything, ranging from small to large. Include everything as you embrace this God-life, and you'll get God's everything.

Amplified Bible

²⁴For this reason I am telling you, whatever you ask for in prayer, believe (trust and be confident) that it is granted to you, and you will [get it].

New Living Translation

²⁴ I tell you, you can pray for anything, and if you believe that you've received it, it will be yours.

Contemporary English Version

²⁴Everything you ask for in prayer will be yours, if you only have faith.

New King James Version

²⁴ Therefore I say to you, whatever things you ask when you pray, believe that you receive them, and you will have them.

Reflection

God promises that when you listen to Him you are in good hands.

Proverbs 1:33

New International Version

[33] but whoever listens to me will live in safety and be at ease, without fear of harm."

New American Standard Bible

[33] "But he who listens to me shall live securely
And will be at ease from the dread of evil."

The Message

[33] First pay attention to me, and then relax.
Now you can take it easy—you're in good hands."

Amplified Bible

[33] But whoso hearkens to me [Wisdom] shall dwell securely and in confident trust and shall be quiet, without fear or dread of evil.

New Living Translation

[33] But all who listen to me will live in peace, untroubled by fear of harm."

Contemporary English Version

[33] But if you listen to me, you will be safe and secure without fear of disaster."

New King James Version

[33] But whoever listens to me will dwell safely,
And will be secure, without fear of evil."

Reflection

God promises that no plague will come near you.

Psalm 91:9-10

New International Version

[9] If you say, "The LORD is my refuge," and you make the Most High your dwelling, [10] no harm will overtake you, no disaster will come near your tent.

New American Standard Bible

[9]For you have made the LORD, my refuge, Even the Most High, your dwelling place. [10]No evil will befall you, Nor will any plague come near your tent.

The Message

[9-10] Yes, because God's your refuge, the High God your very own home, Evil can't get close to you, harm can't get through the door.

Amplified Bible

[9]Because you have made the Lord your refuge, and the Most High your dwelling place, [10]There shall no evil befall you, nor any plague or calamity come near your tent.

New Living Translation

[9] If you make the Lord your refuge, if you make the Most High your shelter,[10] no evil will conquer you; no plague will come near your home.

Contemporary English Version

[9]The LORD Most High is your fortress. Run to him for safety, [10]and no terrible disasters will strike you or your home.

New King James Version

[9] Because you have made the LORD, who is my refuge, Even the Most High, your dwelling place,[10] No evil shall befall you, Nor shall any plague come near your dwelling;

Reflection

God promises to surround you with favor.

Psalm 5:12

New International Version

12 Surely, LORD, you bless the righteous;
    you surround them with your favor as
with a shield.

New American Standard Bible

12For it is You who blesses the righteous man,
    O LORD,
        You surround him with favor as with a
shield.

The Message

12You are famous, God, for welcoming
    God-seekers,
        for decking us out in delight.

Amplified Bible

12For You, Lord, will bless the
[uncompromisingly] righteous [him who is
upright and in right standing with You]; as with
a shield You will surround him with goodwill
(pleasure and favor).

New Living Translation

12 For you bless the godly, O Lord;
    you surround them with your shield of
love.

Contemporary English Version

12Our LORD, you bless those who live right,
    and you shield them with your kindness.

New King James Version

12 For You, O LORD, will bless the righteous;
    With favor You will surround him as with
a shield.

Reflection

God promises save those who put their hope in the living God.

1 Timothy 4:9-10

New International Version

⁹ This is a trustworthy saying that deserves full acceptance. ¹⁰ That is why we labor and strive, because we have put our hope in the living God, who is the Savior of all people, and especially of those who believe.

New American Standard Bible

⁹It is a trustworthy statement deserving full acceptance. ¹⁰For it is for this we labor and strive, because we have fixed our hope on the living God, who is the Savior of all men, especially of believers.

The Message

⁹⁻¹⁰. You can count on this. Take it to heart. This is why we've thrown ourselves into this venture so totally. We're banking on the living God, Savior of all men and women, especially believers.

Amplified Bible

⁹This saying is reliable and worthy of complete acceptance by everybody. ¹⁰With a view to this we toil and strive, [yes and] suffer reproach, because we have [fixed our] hope on the living God, Who is the Savior (Preserver, Maintainer, Deliverer) of all men, especially of those who believe (trust in, rely on, and adhere to Him).

New Living Translation

⁹ This is a trustworthy saying, and everyone should accept it. ¹⁰ This is why we work hard and continue to struggle,[a] for our hope is in the living God, who is the Savior of all people and particularly of all believers.

Reflection

Contemporary English Version

9-10 As the saying goes, "Exercise is good for your body, but religion helps you in every way. It promises life now and forever." These words are worthwhile and should not be forgotten. ¹⁰We have put our hope in the living God, who is the Savior of everyone, but especially of those who have faith. That's why we work and struggle so hard.

New King James Version

⁹ This is a faithful saying and worthy of all acceptance. ¹⁰ For to this end we both labor and suffer reproach, because we trust in the living God, who is the Savior of all men, especially of those who believe.

God promises to heal the sick when we pray for them.

James 5:14-16

New International Version[14] Is anyone among you sick? Let them call the elders of the church to pray over them and anoint them with oil in the name of the Lord. [15] And the prayer offered in faith will make the sick person well; the Lord will raise them up. If they have sinned, they will be forgiven. [16] Therefore confess your sins to each other and pray for each other so that you may be healed. The prayer of a righteous person is powerful and effective.

New American Standard Bible [14]Is anyone among you sick? Then he must call for the elders of the church and they are to pray over him, anointing him with oil in the name of the Lord; [15]and the prayer offered in faith will restore the one who is sick, and the Lord will raise him up, and if he has committed sins, they will be forgiven him. [16]Therefore, confess your sins to one another, and pray for one another so that you may be healed The effective prayer of a righteous man can accomplish much.

The Message [14-16] Are you sick? Call the church leaders together to pray and anoint you with oil in the name of the Master. Believing-prayer will heal you, and Jesus will put you on your feet. And if you've sinned, you'll be forgiven—healed inside and out. Make this your common practice: Confess your sins to each other and pray for each other so that you can live together whole and healed. The prayer of a person living right with God is something powerful to be reckoned with.

Amplified Bible [14]Is anyone among you sick? He should call in the church elders (the spiritual guides). And they should pray over him, anointing him with oil in the Lord's name. [15]And the prayer [that is] of faith will save him who is sick, and the Lord will restore him; and if he has committed sins, he will be forgiven. [16]Confess to one another therefore your faults (your slips, your false steps, your offenses,

Reflection

your sins) and pray [also] for one another, that you may be healed and restored [to a spiritual tone of mind and heart]. The earnest (heartfelt, continued) prayer of a righteous man makes tremendous power available [dynamic in its working].

New Living Translation [14] Are any of you sick? You should call for the elders of the church to come and pray over you, anointing you with oil in the name of the Lord. [15] Such a prayer offered in faith will heal the sick, and the Lord will make you well. And if you have committed any sins, you will be forgiven. [16] Confess your sins to each other and pray for each other so that you may be healed. The earnest prayer of a righteous person has great power and produces wonderful results.

Contemporary English Version [14] If you are sick, ask the church leaders to come and pray for you. Ask them to put olive oil on you in the name of the Lord. [15] If you have faith when you pray for sick people, they will get well. The Lord will heal them, and if they have sinned, he will forgive them. [16] If you have sinned, you should tell each other what you have done. Then you can pray for one another and be healed. The prayer of an innocent person is powerful, and it can help a lot.

New King James Version [14] Is anyone among you sick? Let him call for the elders of the church, and let them pray over him, anointing him with oil in the name of the Lord. [15] And the prayer of faith will save the sick, and the Lord will raise him up. And if he has committed sins, he will be forgiven. [16] Confess your trespasses to one another, and pray for one another, that you may be healed. The effective, fervent prayer of a righteous man avails much.

God promises to take sickness away from you.

Exodus 23:25

New International Version

²⁵ Worship the LORD your God, and his blessing will be on your food and water. I will take away sickness from among you,

New American Standard Bible

²⁵"But you shall serve the LORD your God, and He will bless your bread and your water; and I will remove sickness from your midst.

The Message

²⁵⁻²⁶ "But you—you serve your God and he'll bless your food and your water. I'll get rid of the sickness among you; there won't be any miscarriages nor barren women in your land. I'll make sure you live full and complete lives.

Amplified Bible

²⁵You shall serve the Lord your God; He shall bless your bread and water, and I will take sickness from your midst.

New Living Translation

²⁵ "You must serve only the Lord your God. If you do, Iwill bless you with food and water, and I will protect you from illness.

Contemporary English Version

²⁵Worship only me, the LORD your God! I will bless you with plenty of food and water and keep you strong.

New King James Version

²⁵ "So you shall serve the LORD your God, and He will bless your bread and your water. And I will take sickness away from the midst of you.

Reflection

God promises to give you a new heart and a new spirit.

Ezekiel 36:25-26

New International Version

²⁵ I will sprinkle clean water on you, and you will be clean; I will cleanse you from all your impurities and from all your idols. ²⁶ I will give you a new heart and put a new spirit in you; I will remove from you your heart of stone and give you a heart of flesh.

New American Standard Bible

²⁵"Then I will sprinkle clean water on you, and you will be clean; I will cleanse you from all your filthiness and from all your idols. ²⁶"Moreover, I will give you a new heart and put a new spirit within you; and I will remove the heart of stone from your flesh and give you a heart of flesh.

The Message

²⁵⁻²⁶ I'll pour pure water over you and scrub you clean. I'll give you a new heart, put a new spirit in you. I'll remove the stone heart from your body and replace it with a heart that's God-willed, not self-willed. I'll put my Spirit in you and make it possible for you to do what I tell you and live by my commands.

Amplified Bible

²⁵Then will I sprinkle clean water upon you, and you shall be clean from all your uncleanness; and from all your idols will I cleanse you. ²⁶A new heart will I give you and a new spirit will I put within you, and I will take away the stony heart out of your flesh and give you a heart of flesh.

New Living Translation

²⁵ "Then I will sprinkle clean water on you, and you will be clean. Your filth will be washed away, and you will no longer worship idols. ²⁶ And I will give you a

Reflection

new heart, and I will put a new spirit in you. I will take out your stony, stubborn heart and give you a tender, responsive heart.

Contemporary English Version

[25]I will sprinkle you with clean water, and you will be clean and acceptable to me. I will wash away everything that makes you unclean, and I will remove your disgusting idols. [26]I will take away your stubborn heart and give you a new heart and a desire to be faithful. You will have only pure thoughts,

New King James Version

[25] Then I will sprinkle clean water on you, and you shall be clean; I will cleanse you from all your filthiness and from all your idols. [26] I will give you a new heart and put a new spirit within you; I will take the heart of stone out of your flesh and give you a heart of flesh.

RUDOLPH MOSELEY JR.

God promises to save His people.

Matthew 1:21

New International Version

²¹ She will give birth to a son, and you are to give him the name Jesus, because he will save his people from their sins."

New American Standard Bible

²¹"She will bear a Son; and you shall call His name Jesus, for He will save His people from their sins."

The Message

²¹She will bring a son to birth, and when she does, you, Joseph, will name him Jesus—'God saves'—because he will save his people from their sins.

Amplified Bible

²¹She will bear a Son, and you shall call His name Jesus [the Greek form of the Hebrew Joshua, which means Savior], for He will save His people from their sins [that is, prevent them from failing and missing the true end and scope of life, which is God].

New Living Translation

²¹ And she will have a son, and you are to name him Jesus, for he will save his people from their sins."

Contemporary English Version

²¹Then after her baby is born, name him Jesus, because he will save his people from their sins."

New King James Version

²¹ And she will bring forth a Son, and you shall call His name JESUS, for He will save His people from their sins."

Reflection

God promises to reward you when you bless those that hurt you.

Matthew 5:11-12

New International Version

[11] "Blessed are you when people insult you, persecute you and falsely say all kinds of evil against you because of me. [12] Rejoice and be glad, because great is your reward in heaven, for in the same way they persecuted the prophets who were before you.

New American Standard Bible

[11]"Blessed are you when people insult you and persecute you, and falsely say all kinds of evil against you because of Me. [12]"Rejoice and be glad, for your reward in heaven is great; for in the same way they persecuted the prophets who were before you.

The Message

[11-12]"Not only that—count yourselves blessed every time people put you down or throw you out or speak lies about you to discredit me. What it means is that the truth is too close for comfort and they are uncomfortable. You can be glad when that happens—give a cheer, even!—for though they don't like it, I do! And all heaven applauds. And know that you are in good company. My prophets and witnesses have always gotten into this kind of trouble.

Amplified Bible

[11]Blessed (happy, [a]to be envied, and [b] spiritually prosperous—[c]with life-joy and satisfaction in God's favor and salvation, regardless of your outward conditions) are you when people revile you and persecute you and say all kinds of evil things against you falsely on My account. [12]Be glad and supremely joyful, for your reward in heaven is great (strong and intense), for in this same way people persecuted the prophets who were before you. [II Chron. 36:16.]

Reflection

New Living Translation

[11] "God blesses you when people mock you and persecute you and lie about you and say all sorts of evil things against you because you are my followers. [12] Be happy about it! Be very glad! For a great reward awaits you in heaven. And remember, the ancient prophets were persecuted in the same way.

Contemporary English Version

[11]God will bless you when people insult you, mistreat you, and tell all kinds of evil lies about you because of me. [12]Be happy and excited! You will have a great reward in heaven. People did these same things to the prophets who lived long ago.

New King James Version

[11] "Blessed are you when they revile and persecute you, and say all kinds of evil against you falsely for My sake. [12] Rejoice and be exceedingly glad, for great is your reward in heaven, for so they persecuted the prophets who were before you.

God promises that you will bear fruit in your season.

Psalm 1:3

New International Version

³ That person is like a tree planted by streams of water, which yields its fruit in season and whose leaf does not wither—whatever they do prospers.

New American Standard Bible

³He will be like a tree firmly planted by streams of water, Which yields its fruit in its season And its leaf does not wither; And in whatever he does, he prospers.

The Message

³ You're a tree replanted in Eden, bearing fresh fruit every month,
    Never dropping a leaf, always in blossom.

Amplified Bible

³And he shall be like a tree firmly planted [and tended] by the streams of water, ready to bring forth its fruit in its season; its leaf also shall not fade or wither; and everything he does shall prosper [and come to maturity].

New Living Translation

³ They are like trees planted along the riverbank, bearing fruit each season. Their leaves never wither, and they prosper in all they do.

Contemporary English Version

³They are like trees growing beside a stream, trees that produce fruit in season and always have leaves. Those people succeed in everything they do.

New King James Version

³ He shall be like a tree Planted by the rivers of water, That brings forth its fruit in its season, Whose leaf also shall not wither; And whatever he does shall prosper.

Reflection

God promises to bless you when you come in and when you go out.

Deuteronomy 28:2-6

New International Version ² All these blessings will come on you and accompany you if you obey the LORD your God: ³ You will be blessed in the city and blessed in the country. ⁴ The fruit of your womb will be blessed, and the crops of your land and the young of your livestock—the calves of your herds and the lambs of your flocks. ⁵ Your basket and your kneading trough will be blessed. ⁶ You will be blessed when you come in and blessed when you go out.

New American Standard Bible ²"All these blessings will come upon you and overtake you if you obey the LORD your God: ³"Blessed shall you be in the city, and blessed shall you be in the country. ⁴"Blessed shall be the offspring of your body and the produce of your ground and the offspring of your beasts, the increase of your herd and the young of your flock. ⁵"Blessed shall be your basket and your kneading bowl. ⁶"Blessed shall you be when you come in, and blessed shall you be when you go out.

The Message ²⁻⁶ All these blessings will come down on you and spread out beyond you because you have responded to the Voice of God, your God: God's blessing inside the city, God's blessing in the country; God's blessing on your children, the crops of your land, the young of your livestock, the calves of your herds, the lambs of your flocks. God's blessing on your basket and bread bowl; God's blessing in your coming in, God's blessing in your going out.

Amplified Bible ²And all these blessings shall come upon you and overtake you if you heed the voice of the Lord your God. ³Blessed shall you be in the city and blessed shall you be in the field. ⁴Blessed shall be the fruit of your body and the

Reflection

fruit of your ground and the fruit of your beasts, the increase of your cattle and the young of your flock. [5]Blessed shall be your basket and your kneading trough. [6]Blessed shall you be when you come in and blessed shall you be when you go out.

New Living Translation [2] You will experience all these blessings if you obey the Lord your God: [3] Your towns and your fields will be blessed.[4] Your children and your crops will be blessed. The offspring of your herds and flocks will be blessed.[5] Your fruit baskets and breadboards will be blessed.[6] Wherever you go and whatever you do, you will be blessed.

Contemporary English Version [1-2]Today I am giving you the laws and teachings of the LORD your God. Always obey them, and the LORD will make Israel the most famous and important nation on earth, and he will bless you in many ways. [3]The LORD will make your businesses and your farms successful. [4]You will have many children. You will harvest large crops, and your herds of cattle and flocks of sheep and goats will produce many young. [5]You will have plenty of bread to eat. [6]The LORD will make you successful in your daily work.

New King James Version [2] And all these blessings shall come upon you and overtake you, because you obey the voice of the LORD your God:[3] "Blessed shall you be in the city, and blessed shall you be in the country. [4] "Blessed shall be the fruit of your body, the produce of your ground and the increase of your herds, the increase of your cattle and the offspring of your flocks. [5] "Blessed shall be your basket and your kneading bowl. [6] "Blessed shall you be when you come in, and blessed shall you be when you go out.

God promises to supply your every need because He knows them.

Matthew 6:31-32

New International Version

[31] So do not worry, saying, 'What shall we eat?' or 'What shall we drink?' or 'What shall we wear?' [32] For the pagans run after all these things, and your heavenly Father knows that you need them.

New American Standard Bible

[31]"Do not worry then, saying, 'What will we eat?' or 'What will we drink?' or 'What will we wear for clothing?' [32]"For the Gentiles eagerly seek all these things; for your heavenly Father knows that you need all these things.

The Message

[30-33]"If God gives such attention to the appearance of wildflowers—most of which are never even seen—don't you think he'll attend to you, take pride in you, do his best for you? What I'm trying to do here is to get you to relax, to not be so preoccupied with getting, so you can respond to God's giving. People who don't know God and the way he works fuss over these things, but you know both God and how he works. Steep your life in God-reality, God-initiative, God-provisions. Don't worry about missing out. You'll find all your everyday human concerns will be met.

Amplified Bible

[31]Therefore do not worry and be anxious, saying, What are we going to have to eat? or, What are we going to have to drink? or, What are we going to have to wear? [32]For the Gentiles (heathen) wish for and crave and diligently seek all these things, and your heavenly Father knows well that you need them all.

Reflection

New Living Translation

[31] "So don't worry about these things, saying, 'What will we eat? What will we drink? What will we wear?' [32] These things dominate the thoughts of unbelievers, but your heavenly Father already knows all your needs.

Contemporary English Version

[31] Don't worry and ask yourselves, "Will we have anything to eat? Will we have anything to drink? Will we have any clothes to wear?" [32] Only people who don't know God are always worrying about such things. Your Father in heaven knows that you need all of these.

New King James Version

[31] "Therefore do not worry, saying, 'What shall we eat?' or 'What shall we drink?' or 'What shall we wear?' [32] For after all these things the Gentiles seek. For your heavenly Father knows that you need all these things.

God promises that He genuinely cares for you.

1 Peter 5:7

New International Version

⁷ Cast all your anxiety on him because he cares for you.

New American Standard Bible

⁷casting all your anxiety on Him, because He cares for you.

The Message

⁶⁻⁷So be content with who you are, and don't put on airs. God's strong hand is on you; he'll promote you at the right time. Live carefree before God; he is most careful with you.

Amplified Bible

⁷Casting the whole of your care [all your anxieties, all your worries, all your concerns, once and for all] on Him, for He cares for you affectionately and cares about you watchfully.

New Living Translation

⁷ Give all your worries and cares to God, for he cares about you.

Contemporary English Version

⁷God cares for you, so turn all your worries over to him.

New King James Version

⁷ casting all your care upon Him, for He cares for you.

Reflection

God promises to bless you when you worship Him alone.

Psalm 40:4

New International Version

⁴ Blessed is the one who trusts in the LORD, who does not look to the proud, to those who turn aside to false gods.

New American Standard Bible

⁴How blessed is the man who has made the LORD his trust, And has not turned to the proud, nor to those who lapse into falsehood.

The Message

⁴ Blessed are you who give yourselves over to God, turn your backs on the world's "sure thing," ignore what the world worships; The world's a huge stockpile of God-wonders and God-thoughts.

Amplified Bible

⁴Blessed (happy, fortunate, to be envied) is the man who makes the Lord his refuge and trust, and turns not to the proud or to followers of false gods.

New Living Translation

⁴ Oh, the joys of those who trust the Lord, who have no confidence in the proud or in those who worship idols.

Contemporary English Version

⁴You bless all of those who trust you, LORD, and refuse to worship idols or follow false gods.

New King James Version

⁴ Blessed is that man who makes the LORD
     his trust,
          And does not respect the proud, nor such as turn aside to lies.

Reflection

God promises to be your support when you trust Him.

Psalm 125:1

New International Version

¹ Those who trust in the LORD are like
    Mount Zion,
        which cannot be shaken but endures
forever.

New American Standard Bible

¹Those who trust in the LORD
    Are as Mount Zion, which cannot be
moved but abides forever.

The Message

¹Those who trust in God are like Zion
Mountain: Nothing can move it, a rock-solid
mountain you can always depend on.

Amplified Bible

¹THOSE WHO trust in, lean on, and
confidently hope in the Lord are like Mount
Zion, which cannot be moved but abides and
stands fast forever.

New Living Translation

¹ Those who trust in the Lord are as secure as
    Mount Zion;
        they will not be defeated but will endure
forever.

Contemporary English Version

¹Everyone who trusts the LORD is like
    Mount Zion
        that cannot be shaken and will stand
forever.

New King James Version

¹ Those who trust in the LORD Are like Mount Zion,
    Which cannot be moved, but abides forever.

Reflection

**God promises to give you peace when you pray,
petition and give thanks.**

Philippians 4:6-7

New International Version

⁶ Do not be anxious about anything, but in every situation, by prayer and petition, with thanksgiving, present your requests to God. ⁷ And the peace of God, which transcends all understanding, will guard your hearts and your minds in Christ Jesus.

New American Standard Bible

⁶ Be anxious for nothing, but in everything by prayer and supplication with thanksgiving let your requests be made known to God. ⁷And the peace of God, which surpasses all comprehension, will guard your hearts and your minds in Christ Jesus.

The Message

⁶⁻⁷Don't fret or worry. Instead of worrying, pray. Let petitions and praises shape your worries into prayers, letting God know your concerns. Before you know it, a sense of God's wholeness, everything coming together for good, will come and settle you down. It's wonderful what happens when Christ displaces worry at the center of your life.

Amplified Bible

⁶Do not fret or have any anxiety about anything, but in every circumstance and in everything, by prayer and petition (definite requests), with thanksgiving, continue to make your wants known to God. ⁷And God's peace [shall be yours, that tranquil state of a soul assured of its salvation through Christ, and so fearing nothing from God and being content with its earthly lot of whatever sort that is, that peace] which transcends all understanding shall garrison and mount guard over your hearts and minds in Christ Jesus.

Reflection

New Living Translation

[6] Don't worry about anything; instead, pray about everything. Tell God what you need, and thank him for all he has done. [7] Then you will experience God's peace, which exceeds anything we can understand. His peace will guard your hearts and minds as you live in Christ Jesus.

Contemporary English Version

[6]Don't worry about anything, but pray about everything. With thankful hearts offer up your prayers and requests to God. [7]Then, because you belong to Christ Jesus, God will bless you with peace that no one can completely understand. And this peace will control the way you think and feel.

New King James Version

[6] Be anxious for nothing, but in everything by prayer and supplication, with thanksgiving, let your requests be made known to God; [7] and the peace of God, which surpasses all understanding, will guard your hearts and minds through Christ Jesus.

God promises to deliver and to honor you.

Psalm 91:15

New International Version

¹⁵ He will call on me, and I will answer him; I will be with him in trouble, I will deliver him and honor him.

New American Standard Bible

¹⁵"He will call upon Me, and I will answer him; I will be with him in trouble; I will rescue him and honor him.

The Message

¹⁵ Call me and I'll answer, be at your side in bad times;
   I'll rescue you, then throw you a party.

Amplified Bible

¹⁵He shall call upon Me, and I will answer him; I will be with him in trouble, I will deliver him and honor him.

New Living Translation

¹⁵ When they call on me, I will answer; I will be with them in trouble.
   I will rescue and honor them.

Contemporary English Version

¹⁵When you are in trouble, call out to me.
   I will answer and be there to protect and honor you.

New King James Version

¹⁵ He shall call upon Me, and I will answer him;
   I will be with him in trouble;
   I will deliver him and honor him.

Reflection

God promises never to leave us until all of his promises have been fulfilled.

Genesis 28:15

New International Version

¹⁵ I am with you and will watch over you wherever you go, and I will bring you back to this land. I will not leave you until I have done what I have promised you."

New American Standard Bible

¹⁵"Behold, I am with you and will keep you wherever you go, and will bring you back to this land; for I will not leave you until I have done what I have promised you."

The Message

¹⁵Yes. I'll stay with you, I'll protect you wherever you go, and I'll bring you back to this very ground. I'll stick with you until I've done everything I promised you."

Amplified Bible

¹⁵And behold, I am with you and will keep (watch over you with care, take notice of) you wherever you may go, and I will bring you back to this land; for I will not leave you until I have done all of which I have told you.

New Living Translation

¹⁵ What's more, I am with you, and I will protect you wherever you go. One day I will bring you back to this land. I will not leave you until I have finished giving you everything I have promised you."

Contemporary English Version

¹⁵Wherever you go, I will watch over you, then later I will bring you back to this land. I won't leave you—I will do all I have promised.

Reflection

New King James Version

[15] Behold, I am with you and will keep you wherever you go, and will bring you back to this land; for I will not leave you until I have done what I have spoken to you."

God promises to fight for us after we stand firm on His promises.

Exodus 14:13-14

New International Version

[13] Moses answered the people, "Do not be afraid. Stand firm and you will see the deliverance the LORD will bring you today. The Egyptians you see today you will never see again. [14] The LORD will fight for you; you need only to be still."

New American Standard Bible

[13] But Moses said to the people, "Do not fear! Stand by and see the salvation of the LORD which He will accomplish for you today; for the Egyptians whom you have seen today, you will never see them again forever. [14] "The LORD will fight for you while you keep silent."

The Message

[13] Moses spoke to the people: "Don't be afraid. Stand firm and watch God do his work of salvation for you today. Take a good look at the Egyptians today for you're never going to see them again. [14] God will fight the battle for you. And you? You keep your mouths shut!"

Amplified Bible

[13] Moses told the people, Fear not; stand still (firm, confident, undismayed) and see the salvation of the Lord which He will work for you today. For the Egyptians you have seen today you shall never see again. [14] The Lord will fight for you, and you shall hold your peace and remain at rest.

New Living Translation

[13] But Moses told the people, "Don't be afraid. Just stand still and watch the Lord rescue you today. The Egyptians you see today will never be seen again. [14] The Lord himself will fight for you. Just stay calm."

Reflection

Contemporary English Version

[13]But Moses answered, "Don't be afraid! Be brave, and you will see the LORD save you today. These Egyptians will never bother you again. [14]The LORD will fight for you, and you won't have to do a thing."

New King James Version

[13] And Moses said to the people, "Do not be afraid. Stand still, and see the salvation of the LORD, which He will accomplish for you today. For the Egyptians whom you see today, you shall see again no more forever. [14] The LORD will fight for you, and you shall hold your peace."

RUDOLPH MOSELEY JR.

God promises to drive out your enemies.

Exodus 34:24

New International Version

²⁴ I will drive out nations before you and enlarge your territory, and no one will covet your land when you go up three times each year to appear before the LORD your God.

New American Standard Bible

²⁴"For I will drive out nations before you and enlarge your borders, and no man shall covet your land when you go up three times a year to appear before the LORD your God.

The Message

²³⁻²⁴ "All your men are to appear before the Master, the God of Israel, three times a year. You won't have to worry about your land when you appear before your God three times each year, for I will drive out the nations before you and give you plenty of land. Nobody's going to be hanging around plotting ways to get it from you.

Amplified Bible

²⁴For I will cast out the nations before you and enlarge your borders; neither shall any man desire [and molest] your land when you go up to appear before the Lord your God three times in the year.

New Living Translation

²⁴ I will drive out the other nations ahead of you and expand your territory, so no one will covet and conquer your land while you appear before the Lord your God three times each year.

Reflection

Contemporary English Version

²⁴I will force the nations out of your land and enlarge your borders. Then no one will try to take your property when you come to worship me these three times each year.

New King James Version

²⁴ For I will cast out the nations before you and enlarge your borders; neither will any man covet your land when you go up to appear before the LORD your God three times in the year.

RUDOLPH MOSELEY JR.

God promises to break every yoke of bondage.

Leviticus 26:13

New International Version

[13] I am the LORD your God, who brought you out of Egypt so that you would no longer be slaves to the Egyptians; I broke the bars of your yoke and enabled you to walk with heads held high.

New American Standard Bible

[13] I am the LORD your God, who brought you out of the land of Egypt so that you would not be their slaves, and I broke the bars of your yoke and made you walk erect.

The Message

[11-13] "I'll set up my residence in your neighborhood; I won't avoid or shun you; I'll stroll through your streets. I'll be your God; you'll be my people. I am God, your personal God who rescued you from Egypt so that you would no longer be slaves to the Egyptians. I ripped off the harness of your slavery so that you can move about freely.

Amplified Bible

[13] I am the Lord your God, Who brought you forth out of the land of Egypt, that you should no more be slaves; and I have broken the bars of your yoke and made you walk erect [as free men].

New Living Translation

[13] I am the Lord your God, who brought you out of the land of Egypt so you would no longer be their slaves. I broke the yoke of slavery from your neck so you can walk with your heads held high.

Reflection

Contemporary English Version

[13]I am the LORD your God, and I rescued you from Egypt, so that you would never again be slaves. I have set you free; now walk with your heads held high.

New King James Version

[13] I am the LORD your God, who brought you out of the land of Egypt, that you should not be their slaves; I have broken the bands of your yoke and made you walk upright.

God promises to keep you at the top.

Deuteronomy 28:13

New International Version

¹³ The LORD will make you the head, not the tail. If you pay attention to the commands of the LORD your God that I give you this day and carefully follow them, you will always be at the top, never at the bottom.

New American Standard Bible

¹³"The LORD will make you the head and not the tail, and you only will be above, and you will not be underneath, if you listen to the commandments of the LORD your God, which I charge you today, to observe them carefully,

The Message

¹³⁻¹⁴ God will make you the head, not the tail; you'll always be the top dog, never the bottom dog, as you obediently listen to and diligently keep the commands of God, your God, that I am commanding you today. Don't swerve an inch to the right or left from the words that I command you today by going off following and worshiping other gods.

Amplified Bible

¹³And the Lord shall make you the head, and not the tail; and you shall be above only, and you shall not be beneath, if you heed the commandments of the Lord your God which I command you this day and are watchful to do them.

New Living Translation

¹³ If you listen to these commands of the Lord your God that I am giving you today, and if you carefully obey them, the Lord will make you the head and not the tail, and you will always be on top and never at the bottom.

Reflection

Contemporary English Version

[13]Obey the laws and teachings that I'm giving you today, and the LORD your God will make Israel a leader among the nations, and not a follower. Israel will be wealthy and powerful, not poor and weak.

New King James Version

[13] And the LORD will make you the head and not the tail; you shall be above only, and not be beneath, if you heed the commandments of the LORD your God, which I command you today, and are careful to observe them.

God promises to be your dwelling place

Deuteronomy 33:27

New International Version

[27] The eternal God is your refuge, and underneath are the everlasting arms. He will drive out your enemies before you, saying, 'Destroy them!'

New American Standard Bible

[27]"The eternal God is a dwelling place, And underneath are the everlasting arms;And He drove out the enemy from before you, And said, 'Destroy!'

The Message

[27]The ancient God is home on a foundation of everlasting arms. He drove out the enemy before you and commanded, "Destroy!"

Amplified Bible

[27]The eternal God is your refuge and dwelling place, and underneath are the everlasting arms; He drove the enemy before you and thrust them out, saying, Destroy!

New Living Translation

[27] The eternal God is your refuge, and his everlasting arms are under you. He drives out the enemy before you;he cries out, 'Destroy them!'

Contemporary English Version

[27]The eternal God is our hiding place; he carries us in his arms. When God tells you to destroy your enemies, he will make them run.

New King James Version

[27] The eternal God is your refuge, And underneath are the everlasting arms; He will thrust out the enemy from before you, And will say, 'Destroy!'

Reflection

God promises to be with you wherever you go so don't be afraid.

Joshua 1:9

New International Version

⁹ Have I not commanded you? Be strong and courageous. Do not be afraid; do not be discouraged, for the LORD your God will be with you wherever you go."

New American Standard Bible

⁹ Have I not commanded you? (A)Be strong and courageous! (B)Do not tremble or be dismayed, for the LORD your God is with you wherever you go."

The Message

⁹ Haven't I commanded you? Strength! Courage! Don't be timid; don't get discouraged. God, your God, is with you every step you take."

Amplified Bible

⁹Have not I commanded you? Be strong, vigorous, and very courageous. Be not afraid, neither be dismayed, for the Lord your God is with you wherever you go.

New Living Translation

⁹ This is my command—be strong and courageous! Do not be afraid or discouraged. For the Lord your God is with you wherever you go."

Contemporary English Version

⁹I've commanded you to be strong and brave. Don't ever be afraid or discouraged! I am the LORD your God, and I will be there to help you wherever you go.

Reflection

New King James Version

⁹ Have I not commanded you? Be strong and of good courage; do not be afraid, nor be dismayed, for the LORD your God is with you wherever you go."

God promises to give you victory over all of your enemies.

Joshua 10:24-25

New International Version ²⁴ When they had brought these kings to Joshua, he summoned all the men of Israel and said to the army commanders who had come with him, "Come here and put your feet on the necks of these kings." So they came forward and placed their feet on their necks. ²⁵ Joshua said to them, "Do not be afraid; do not be discouraged. Be strong and courageous. This is what the LORD will do to all the enemies you are going to fight."

New American Standard Bible ²⁴ When they brought these kings out to Joshua, Joshua called for all the men of Israel, and said to the chiefs of the men of war who had gone with him, "Come near, put your feet on the necks of these kings." So they came near and put their feet on their necks. ²⁵ Joshua then said to them, "Do not fear or be dismayed! Be strong and courageous, for thus the LORD will do to all your enemies with whom you fight."

The Message ²⁴ When they had them all there in front of Joshua, he called up the army and told the field commanders who had been with him, "Come here. Put your feet on the necks of these kings." They stepped up and put their feet on their necks. ²⁵ Joshua told them, "Don't hold back. Don't be timid. Be strong! Be confident! This is what God will do to all your enemies when you fight them."

Amplified Bible ²⁴When they brought out those kings to Joshua, [he] called for all the Israelites and told the commanders of the men of war who went with him, Come, put your feet on the necks of these kings. And they came and put their feet on the [kings'] necks. ²⁵Joshua said to them, Fear not nor be dismayed; be strong and of good courage. For thus shall the Lord do to all your enemies against whom you fight.

Reflection

New Living Translation ²⁴ When they brought them out, Joshua told the commanders of his army, "Come and put your feet on the kings' necks." And they did as they were told. ²⁵ "Don't ever be afraid or discouraged," Joshua told his men. "Be strong and courageous, for the Lord is going to do this to all of your enemies."

Contemporary English Version ²⁴After Joshua had called the army together, he forced the five kings to lie down on the ground. Then he called his officers forward and told them, "You fought these kings along with me, so put your feet on their necks." The officers did, ²⁵and Joshua continued, "Don't ever be afraid or discouraged. Be brave and strong. This is what the LORD will do to all your enemies."

New King James Version ²⁴ So it was, when they brought out those kings to Joshua, that Joshua called for all the men of Israel, and said to the captains of the men of war who went with him, "Come near, put your feet on the necks of these kings." And they drew near and put their feet on their necks. ²⁵ Then Joshua said to them, "Do not be afraid, nor be dismayed; be strong and of good courage, for thus the LORD will do to all your enemies against whom you fight."

God promises that your enemies will fall flat on their faces.

Psalm 27:1-2

New International Version

¹ The LORD is my light and my salvation—whom shall I fear? The LORD is the stronghold of my life— of whom shall I be afraid?² When the wicked advance against me to devour me, it is my enemies and my foes who will stumble and fall.

New American Standard Bible

¹ The LORD is my light and my salvation; Whom shall I fear? The LORD is the defense of my life; Whom shall I dread? ² When evildoers came upon me to devour my flesh, My adversaries and my enemies, they stumbled and fell.

The Message

¹ Light, space, zest—that's God! So, with him on my side I'm fearless, afraid of no one and nothing. ² When vandal hordes ride down ready to eat me alive, Those bullies and toughs fall flat on their faces.

Amplified Bible

¹THE LORD is my Light and my Salvation—whom shall I fear or dread? The Lord is the Refuge and Stronghold of my life—of whom shall I be afraid? ²When the wicked, even my enemies and my foes, came upon me to eat up my flesh, they stumbled and fell.

New Living Translation

¹ The Lord is my light and my salvation—so why should I be afraid? The Lord is my fortress, protecting me from danger, so why should I tremble?² When evil people come to devour me, when my enemies and foes attack me, they will stumble and fall.

Reflection

Contemporary English Version

¹You, LORD, are the light that keeps me safe. I am not afraid of anyone. You protect me, and I have no fears. ²Brutal people may attack and try to kill me, but they will stumble. Fierce enemies may attack, but they will fall.

New King James Version

¹ The LORD is my light and my salvation; Whom shall I fear? The LORD is the strength of my life; Of whom shall I be afraid? ² When the wicked came against me To eat up my flesh, My enemies and foes, They stumbled and fell.

God promises victory because of His mighty power.

Psalm 44:3

New International Version

³ It was not by their sword that they won the land, nor did their arm bring them victory; it was your right hand, your arm, and the light of your face, for you loved them.

New American Standard Bible

³ For by their own sword they did not possess the land, And their own arm did not save them, But Your right hand and Your arm and the light of Your presence, For You favored them.

The Message

³ We didn't fight for this land; we didn't work for it—it was a gift! You gave it, smiling as you gave it, delighting as you gave it.

Amplified Bible

³For they got not the land [of Canaan] in possession by their own sword, neither did their own arm save them; but Your right hand and Your arm and the light of Your countenance [did it], because You were favorable toward and did delight in them.

New Living Translation

³ They did not conquer the land with their swords; it was not their own strong arm that gave them victory. It was your right hand and strong arm and the blinding light from your face that helped them, for you loved them.

Contemporary English Version

³Their strength and weapons were not what won the land and gave them victory! You loved them and fought with your powerful arm and your shining glory.

Reflection

New King James Version

[3] For they did not gain possession of the land by their own sword, Nor did their own arm save them; But it was Your right hand, Your arm, and the light of Your countenance, Because You favored them.

God promises to confuse your enemies.

Psalm 55:9

New International Version

⁹ Lord, confuse the wicked, confound their
    words,
    for I see violence and strife in the city.

New American Standard Bible

⁹ Confuse, O Lord, divide their tongues,
    For I have seen violence and strife in the
city.

The Message

⁹ Come down hard, Lord—slit their tongues.
    I'm appalled how they've split the city

Amplified Bible

⁹Destroy [their schemes], O Lord, confuse their
tongues, for I have seen violence and strife in
the city.

New Living Translation

⁹ Confuse them, Lord, and frustrate their
    plans,
    for I see violence and conflict in the city.

Contemporary English Version

⁹Confuse my enemies, Lord! Upset their
    plans.
    Cruelty and violence are all I see in the
city,

New King James Version

⁹ Destroy, O Lord, and divide their tongues,
    For I have seen violence and strife in the
city.

Reflection

God promises to make your enemies flee when you call for help.

Psalm 56:9

New International Version

⁹ Then my enemies will turn back
   when I call for help.
      By this I will know that God is for me.

New American Standard Bible

⁹ Then my enemies will turn back in the day
   when I call;
      This I know, that God is for me.

The Message

⁹ If my enemies run away, turn tail when I yell
   at them,
      Then I'll know that God is on my side.

Amplified Bible

⁹Then shall my enemies turn back in the day
that I cry out; this I know, for God is for me.

New Living Translation

⁹ My enemies will retreat when I call to you
   for help.
      This I know: God is on my side!

Contemporary English Version

⁹When I pray, LORD God, my enemies will
retreat, because I know for certain that you are
with me.

New King James Version

⁹ When I cry out to You,
   Then my enemies will turn back;
      This I know, because God is for me.

Reflection

God promises to make you trample your enemies.

Psalm 60:12

New International Version

[12] With God we will gain the victory,
and he will trample down our enemies.

New American Standard Bible

[12] Through God we shall do valiantly,
And it is He who will tread down our
adversaries.

The Message

[12] In God we'll do our very best;
he'll flatten the opposition for good.

Amplified Bible

[12] Through God we shall do valiantly, for He it
is Who shall tread down our adversaries.

New Living Translation

[12] With God's help we will do mighty things,
for he will trample down our foes.

Contemporary English Version (CEV)

[12] You will give us victory
and crush our enemies.

New King James Version

[12] Through God we will do valiantly,
For it is He who shall tread down our
enemies.

Reflection

God promises to preserve your life.

Psalm 66:9

New International Version

⁹ he has preserved our lives
    and kept our feet from slipping.

New American Standard Bible

⁹ Who keeps us in life
    And does not allow our feet to slip.

The Message

⁹ Didn't he set us on the road to life?
    Didn't he keep us out of the ditch?

Amplified Bible

⁹Who put and kept us among the living, and has not allowed our feet to slip.

New Living Translation

⁹ Our lives are in his hands,
    and he keeps our feet from stumbling.

Contemporary English Version

⁹God protects us from death
    and keeps us steady.

New King James Version

⁹ Who keeps our soul among the living,
    And does not allow our feet to be moved.

Reflection

God promises that you will live.

Psalm 118:17

New International Version

[17] I will not die but live,
and will proclaim what the LORD has done.

New American Standard Bible

[17] I will not die, but live,
And tell of the works of the LORD.

The Message (MSG

[17] I didn't die. I lived!
And now I'm telling the world what God did.

Amplified Bible

[17] I shall not die but live, and shall declare the works and recount the illustrious acts of the Lord.

New Living Translation

[17] I will not die; instead, I will live
to tell what the Lord has done.

Contemporary English Version

[17] And so my life is safe, and I will live to tell
what the LORD has done.

New King James Version

[17] I shall not die, but live,
And declare the works of the LORD.

Reflection

God promises to revive you in the midst of trouble.

Psalm 138:7

New International Version

⁷ Though I walk in the midst of trouble, you preserve my life. You stretch out your hand against the anger of my foes; with your right hand you save me.

New American Standard Bible

⁷ Though I walk in the midst of trouble, You will revive me; You will stretch forth Your hand against the wrath of my enemies, And Your right hand will save me.

The Message

⁷ When I walk into the thick of trouble, keep me alive in the angry turmoil. With one hand strike my foes, With your other hand save me.

Amplified Bible

⁷Though I walk in the midst of trouble, You will revive me; You will stretch forth Your hand against the wrath of my enemies, and Your right hand will save me.

New Living Translation

⁷ Though I am surrounded by troubles, you will protect me from the anger of my enemies. You reach out your hand, and the power of your right hand saves me.

Contemporary English Version

⁷I am surrounded by trouble, but you protect me against my angry enemies. With your own powerful arm you keep me safe.

New King James Version

⁷ Though I walk in the midst of trouble, You will revive me; You will stretch out Your hand Against the wrath of my enemies, And Your right hand will save me.

Reflection

God promises to uphold you with His mighty right hand.

Isaiah 41:10

New International Version

[10] So do not fear, for I am with you; do not be dismayed, for I am your God. I will strengthen you and help you; I will uphold you with my righteous right hand.

New American Standard Bible

[10] 'Do not fear, for I am with you; Do not anxiously look about you, for I am your God. I will strengthen you, surely I will help you, Surely I will uphold you with My righteous right hand.'

The Message

[10] Don't panic. I'm with you. There's no need to fear for I'm your God. I'll give you strength. I'll help you. I'll hold you steady, keep a firm grip on you.

Amplified Bible

[10] Fear not [there is nothing to fear], for I am with you; do not look around you in terror and be dismayed, for I am your God. I will strengthen and harden you to difficulties, yes, I will help you; yes, I will hold you up and retain you with My [victorious] right hand of rightness and justice.

New Living Translation

[10] Don't be afraid, for I am with you. Don't be discouraged, for I am your God. I will strengthen you and help you. I will hold you up with my victorious right hand.

Contemporary English Version

[10] Don't be afraid. I am with you. Don't tremble with fear. I am your God. I will make you strong, as I protect you with my arm and give you victories.

New King James Version

[10] Fear not, for I am with you; Be not dismayed, for I am your God. I will strengthen you, Yes, I will help you, I will uphold you with My righteous right hand.'

Reflection

God promises no attack from your enemy will be successful.

Isaiah 54:17

New International Version

[17] no weapon forged against you will prevail, and you will refute every tongue that accuses you. This is the heritage of the servants of the LORD, and this is their vindication from me," declares the LORD.

New American Standard Bible

[17] "No weapon that is formed against you will prosper; And every tongue that accuses you in judgment you will condemn. This is the heritage of the servants of the LORD, And their vindication is from Me," declares the LORD.

The Message

[17] but no weapon that can hurt you has ever been forged. Any accuser who takes you to court will be dismissed as a liar. This is what God's servants can expect. I'll see to it that everything works out for the best." God's Decree.

Amplified Bible

[17] But no weapon that is formed against you shall prosper, and every tongue that shall rise against you in judgment you shall show to be in the wrong. This [peace, righteousness, security, triumph over opposition] is the heritage of the servants of the Lord [those in whom the ideal Servant of the Lord is reproduced]; this is the righteousness or the vindication which they obtain from Me [this is that which I impart to them as their justification], says the Lord.

Reflection

New Living Translation

[17] But in that coming day no weapon turned against you will succeed. You will silence every voice raised up to accuse you. These benefits are enjoyed by the servants of the Lord; their vindication will come from me. I, the Lord, have spoken!

Contemporary English Version

¹⁷Weapons made to attack you won't be successful; words spoken against you won't hurt at all. My servants, Jerusalem is yours! I, the LORD, promise to bless you with victory.

New King James Version

¹⁷ No weapon formed against you shall prosper, And every tongue which rises against you in judgment You shall condemn. This is the heritage of the servants of the LORD, And their righteousness is from Me," Says the LORD.

God promises to disgrace your persecutor.

Jeremiah 20:11

New International Version

[11] But the LORD is with me like a mighty warrior; so my persecutors will stumble and not prevail. They will fail and be thoroughly disgraced; their dishonor will never be forgotten.

New American Standard Bible

[11] But the LORD is with me like a dread champion;Therefore my persecutors will stumble and not prevail. They will be utterly ashamed, because they have failed, With an everlasting disgrace that will not be forgotten.

The Message

[11]But God, a most fierce warrior, is at my side. Those who are after me will be sent sprawling—Slapstick buffoons falling all over themselves, a spectacle of humiliation no one will ever forget.

Amplified Bible

[11]But the Lord is with me as a mighty and terrible One; therefore my persecutors will stumble, and they will not overcome [me]. They will be utterly put to shame, for they will not deal wisely or prosper [in their schemes]; their eternal dishonor will never be forgotten.

New Living Translation

[11] But the Lord stands beside me like a great warrior. Before him my persecutors will stumble. They cannot defeat me. They will fail and be thoroughly humiliated. Their dishonor will never be forgotten.

Contemporary English Version

[11]But you, LORD, are a mighty soldier, standing at my side. Those troublemakers will fall down and fail—terribly embarrassed, forever ashamed.

Reflection

New King James Version

[11] But the LORD is with me as a mighty, awesome One. Therefore my persecutors will stumble, and will not prevail. They will be greatly ashamed, for they will not prosper. Their everlasting confusion will never be forgotten.

God promises to rescue you from the day of destruction.

Jeremiah 39:17-18

New International Version

¹⁷ But I will rescue you on that day, declares the LORD; you will not be given into the hands of those you fear. ¹⁸ I will save you; you will not fall by the sword but will escape with your life, because you trust in me, declares the LORD.'"

New American Standard Bible

¹⁷ But I will deliver you on that day," declares the LORD, "and you will not be given into the hand of the men whom you dread. ¹⁸ For I will certainly rescue you, and you will not fall by the sword; but you will have your own life as booty, because you have trusted in Me," declares the LORD.'

The Message

¹⁷⁻¹⁸ But I'll deliver you on that doomsday. You won't be handed over to those men whom you have good reason to fear. Yes, I'll most certainly save you. You won't be killed. You'll walk out of there safe and sound because you trusted me.'" God's Decree.

Amplified Bible

¹⁷But I will deliver you [Ebed-melech] on that day, says the Lord, and you will not be given into the hands of the men of whom you are afraid. ¹⁸For I will surely deliver you; and you will not fall by the sword, but your life will be [as your only booty and] as a reward of battle to you, because you have put your trust in Me, says the Lord.

New Living Translation

¹⁷ but I will rescue you from those you fear so much. ¹⁸ Because you trusted me, I will give you your life as a reward. I will rescue you and keep you safe. I, the Lord, have spoken!'"

Reflection

Contemporary English Version

¹⁷⁻¹⁸But because you trusted me, I will protect you from the officials of Judah, and when Judah is struck by disaster, I will rescue you and keep you alive. I, the LORD, have spoken.

New King James Version

¹⁷ But I will deliver you in that day," says the LORD, "and you shall not be given into the hand of the men of whom you are afraid. ¹⁸ For I will surely deliver you, and you shall not fall by the sword; but your life shall be as a prize to you, because you have put your trust in Me," says the LORD.'"

God promises to take away your punishment.

Zephaniah 3:14-15

New International Version

14 Sing, Daughter Zion; shout aloud, Israel! Be glad and rejoice with all your heart, Daughter Jerusalem! 15 The LORD has taken away your punishment, he has turned back your enemy. The LORD, the King of Israel, is with you; never again will you fear any harm.

New American Standard Bible

14 Shout for joy, O daughter of Zion! Shout in triumph, O Israel! Rejoice and exult with all your heart, O daughter of Jerusalem! 15 The LORD has taken away His judgments against you, He has cleared away your enemies. The King of Israel, the LORD, is in your midst; You will fear disaster no more.

The Message

14-15So sing, Daughter Zion! Raise the rafters, Israel!Daughter Jerusalem, be happy! celebrate!God has reversed his judgments against you and sent your enemies off chasing their tails. From now on, God is Israel's king, in charge at the center. There's nothing to fear from evil ever again!

Amplified Bible

14Sing, O Daughter of Zion; shout, O Israel! Rejoice, be in high spirits and glory with all your heart, O Daughter of Jerusalem [in that day]. 15[For then it will be that] the Lord has taken away the judgments against you; He has cast out your enemy. The King of Israel, even the Lord [Himself], is in the midst of you; [and after He has come to you] you shall not experience or fear evil any more.

Reflection

New Living Translation

¹⁴ Sing, O daughter of Zion; shout aloud, O Israel! Be glad and rejoice with all your heart, O daughter of Jerusalem!¹⁵ For the Lord will remove his hand of judgment and will disperse the armies of your enemy. And the Lord himself, the King of Israel, will live among you! At last your troubles will be over, and you will never again fear disaster.

Contemporary English Version

¹⁴Everyone in Jerusalem and Judah, celebrate and shout with all your heart! ¹⁵Zion, your punishment is over. The LORD has forced your enemies to turn and retreat. Your LORD is King of Israel and stands at your side; you don't have to worry about any more troubles.

New King James Version

¹⁴ Sing, O daughter of Zion! Shout, O Israel! Be glad and rejoice with all your heart, O daughter of Jerusalem! ¹⁵ The LORD has taken away your judgments, He has cast out your enemy. The King of Israel, the LORD, is in your midst; You shall see disaster no more.

God promises that you will reign in life.

Romans 5:17

New International Version

¹⁷ For if, by the trespass of the one man, death reigned through that one man, how much more will those who receive God's abundant provision of grace and of the gift of righteousness reign in life through the one man, Jesus Christ!

New American Standard Bible

¹⁷ For if by the transgression of the one, death reigned through the one, much more those who receive the abundance of grace and of the gift of righteousness will reign in life through the One, Jesus Christ.

The Message

¹⁷If death got the upper hand through one man's wrongdoing, can you imagine the breathtaking recovery life makes, sovereign life, in those who grasp with both hands this wildly extravagant life-gift, this grand setting-everything-right, that the one man Jesus Christ provides?

Amplified Bible

¹⁷For if because of one man's trespass (lapse, offense) death reigned through that one, much more surely will those who receive [God's] overflowing grace (unmerited favor) and the free gift of righteousness [putting them into right standing with Himself] reign as kings in life through the one Man Jesus Christ (the Messiah, the Anointed One).

New Living Translation

¹⁷ For the sin of this one man, Adam, caused death to rule over many. But even greater is God's wonderful grace and his gift of righteousness, for all who receive it will live in triumph over sin and death through this one man, Jesus Christ.

Reflection

Contemporary English Version

[17]Death ruled like a king because Adam had sinned. But that cannot compare with what Jesus Christ has done. God has been so kind to us, and he has accepted us because of Jesus. And so we will live and rule like kings.

New King James Version

[17] For if by the one man's offense death reigned through the one, much more those who receive abundance of grace and of the gift of righteousness will reign in life through the One, Jesus Christ.)

God promises victory through the Lord Jesus Christ.

1 Corinthians 15:57-58

New International Version

57 But thanks be to God! He gives us the victory through our Lord Jesus Christ. 58 Therefore, my dear brothers and sisters, stand firm. Let nothing move you. Always give yourselves fully to the work of the Lord, because you know that your labor in the Lord is not in vain.

New American Standard Bible

57 but thanks be to God, who gives us the victory through our Lord Jesus Christ. 58 Therefore, my beloved brethren, be steadfast, immovable, always abounding in the work of the Lord, knowing that your toil is not in vain in the Lord.

The Message

57 But now in a single victorious stroke of Life, all three—sin, guilt, death—are gone, the gift of our Master, Jesus Christ. Thank God! 58With all this going for us, my dear, dear friends, stand your ground. And don't hold back. Throw yourselves into the work of the Master, confident that nothing you do for him is a waste of time or effort.

Amplified Bible

57But thanks be to God, Who gives us the victory [making us conquerors] through our Lord Jesus Christ. 58Therefore, my beloved brethren, be firm (steadfast), immovable, always abounding in the work of the Lord [always being superior, excelling, doing more than enough in the service of the Lord], knowing and being continually aware that your labor in the Lord is not futile [it is never wasted or to no purpose].

Reflection

New Living Translation

[57] But thank God! He gives us victory over sin and death through our Lord Jesus Christ. [58] So, my dear brothers and sisters, be strong and immovable. Always work enthusiastically for the Lord, for you know that nothing you do for the Lord is ever useless.

Contemporary English Version

[57] But thank God for letting our Lord Jesus Christ give us the victory! [58] My dear friends, stand firm and don't be shaken. Always keep busy working for the Lord. You know that everything you do for him is worthwhile.

New King James Version

[57] But thanks be to God, who gives us the victory through our Lord Jesus Christ. [58] Therefore, my beloved brethren, be steadfast, immovable, always abounding in the work of the Lord, knowing that your labor is not in vain in the Lord.

God promises to lead us in victory every time.

2 Corinthians 2:14

New International Version

14 But thanks be to God, who always leads us as captives in Christ's triumphal procession and uses us to spread the aroma of the knowledge of him everywhere.

New American Standard Bible

14 But thanks be to God, who always leads us in triumph in Christ, and manifests through us the sweet aroma of the knowledge of Him in every place.

The Message

14 In the Messiah, in Christ, God leads us from place to place in one perpetual victory parade. Through us, he brings knowledge of Christ. Everywhere we go, people breathe in the exquisite fragrance.

Amplified Bible

14But thanks be to God, Who in Christ always leads us in triumph [as trophies of Christ's victory] and through us spreads and makes evident the fragrance of the knowledge of God everywhere,

New Living Translation

14 But thank God! He has made us his captives and continues to lead us along in Christ's triumphal procession. Now he uses us to spread the knowledge of Christ everywhere, like a sweet perfume.

Contemporary English Version

14I am grateful that God always makes it possible for Christ to lead us to victory. God also helps us spread the knowledge about Christ everywhere, and this knowledge is like the smell of perfume.

Reflection

New King James Version

[14] Now thanks be to God who always leads us in triumph in Christ, and through us diffuses the fragrance of His knowledge in every place.

God promises to strengthen you and place you on a firm foundation every time.

Thessalonians 3:3

New International Version

³ But the Lord is faithful, and he will strengthen you and protect you from the evil one.

New American Standard Bible

³ But the Lord is faithful, and He will strengthen and protect you from the evil one.

The Message

³ But the Master never lets us down. He'll stick by you and protect you from evil.

Amplified Bible

³Yet the Lord is faithful, and He will strengthen [you] and set you on a firm foundation and guard you from the evil [one].

New Living Translation

³ But the Lord is faithful; he will strengthen you and guard you from the evil one.

Contemporary English Version

³But the Lord can be trusted to make you strong and protect you from harm.

New King James Version

³ But the Lord is faithful, who will establish you and guard you from the evil one.

Reflection

God promises to stand by you as you proclaim His message.

Timothy 4:17-18

New International Version [17] But the Lord stood at my side and gave me strength, so that through me the message might be fully proclaimed and all the Gentiles might hear it. And I was delivered from the lion's mouth. [18] The Lord will rescue me from every evil attack and will bring me safely to his heavenly kingdom. To him be glory for ever and ever. Amen.

New American Standard Bible [17] But the Lord stood with me and strengthened me, so that through me the proclamation might be fully accomplished, and that all the Gentiles might hear; and I was rescued out of the lion's mouth. [18] The Lord will rescue me from every evil deed, and will bring me safely to His heavenly kingdom; to Him be the glory forever and ever. Amen.

The Message [17-18] But it doesn't matter—the Master stood by me and helped me spread the Message loud and clear to those who had never heard it. I was snatched from the jaws of the lion! God's looking after me, keeping me safe in the kingdom of heaven. All praise to him, praise forever! Oh, yes!

Amplified Bible [17] But the Lord stood by me and strengthened me, so that through me the [Gospel] message might be fully proclaimed and all the Gentiles might hear it. So I was delivered out of the jaws of the lion. [18][And indeed] the Lord will certainly deliver and draw me to Himself from every assault of evil. He will preserve and bring me safe unto His heavenly kingdom. To Him be the glory forever and ever. Amen (so be it).

New Living Translation [17] But the Lord stood with me and gave me strength so that I might preach the Good News in its entirety for all the Gentiles to hear. And

Reflection

he rescued me from certain death.[¹⁸ Yes, and the Lord will deliver me from every evil attack and will bring me safely into his heavenly Kingdom. All glory to God forever and ever! Amen.

Contemporary English Version ¹⁷But the Lord stood beside me. He gave me the strength to tell his full message, so that all Gentiles would hear it. And I was kept safe from hungry lions. ¹⁸The Lord will always keep me from being harmed by evil, and he will bring me safely into his heavenly kingdom. Praise him forever and ever! Amen.

New King James Version ¹⁷ But the Lord stood with me and strengthened me, so that the message might be preached fully through me, and that all the Gentiles might hear. Also I was delivered out of the mouth of the lion. ¹⁸ And the Lord will deliver me from every evil work and preserve me for His heavenly kingdom. To Him be glory forever and ever. Amen!

RUDOLPH MOSELEY JR.

God promises that He is our healer.

Exodus 15:26

New International Version

²⁶ He said, "If you listen carefully to the LORD your God and do what is right in his eyes, if you pay attention to his commands and keep all his decrees, I will not bring on you any of the diseases I brought on the Egyptians, for I am the LORD, who heals you."

New American Standard Bible

²⁶ And He said, "If you will give earnest heed to the voice of the LORD your God, and do what is right in His sight, and give ear to His commandments, and keep all His statutes, I will put none of the diseases on you which I have put on the Egyptians; for I, the LORD, am your healer."

The Message

²⁶ That's the place where God set up rules and procedures; that's where he started testing them. God said, "If you listen, listen obediently to how God tells you to live in his presence, obeying his commandments and keeping all his laws, then I won't strike you with all the diseases that I inflicted on the Egyptians; I am God your healer."

Amplified Bible

²⁶Saying, If you will diligently hearken to the voice of the Lord your God and will do what is right in His sight, and will listen to and obey His commandments and keep all His statutes, I will put none of the diseases upon you which I brought upon the Egyptians, for I am the Lord Who heals you.

New Living Translation

²⁶ He said, "If you will listen carefully to the voice of the Lord your God and do what is right in his sight, obeying his commands and keeping all his decrees, then

Reflection

I will not make you suffer any of the diseases I sent on the Egyptians; for I am the Lord who heals you."

Contemporary English Version

[26]Then he said, "I am the LORD your God, and I cure your diseases. If you obey me by doing right and by following my laws and teachings, I won't punish you with the diseases I sent on the Egyptians."

New King James Version

[26] and said, "If you diligently heed the voice of the LORD your God and do what is right in His sight, give ear to His commandments and keep all His statutes, I will put none of the diseases on you which I have brought on the Egyptians. For I am the LORD who heals you."

God promises to take away our sickness

Exodus 23:25

New International Version

[25] Worship the LORD your God, and his blessing will be on your food and water. I will take away sickness from among you,

New American Standard Bible

[25] But you shall serve the LORD your God, and He will bless your bread and your water; and I will remove sickness from your midst.

The Message

[25-26] "But you—you serve your God and he'll bless your food and your water. I'll get rid of the sickness among you; there won't be any miscarriages nor barren women in your land. I'll make sure you live full and complete lives.

Amplified Bible

[25] You shall serve the Lord your God; He shall bless your bread and water, and I will take sickness from your midst.

New Living Translation

[25] "You must serve only the Lord your God. If you do, I will bless you with food and water, and I will protect you from illness.

Contemporary English Version

[25] Worship only me, the LORD your God! I will bless you with plenty of food and water and keep you strong.

New King James Version

[25] "So you shall serve the LORD your God, and He will bless your bread and your water. And I will take sickness away from the midst of you.

Reflection

God promises to forgive our sin and to heal all our diseases.

Psalm 103:2-5

New International Version 2 Praise the LORD, my soul, and forget not all his benefits—3 who forgives all your sins and heals all your diseases, 4 who redeems your life from the pit and crowns you with love and compassion, 5 who satisfies your desires with good things so that your youth is renewed like the eagle's.

New American Standard Bible 2 Bless the LORD, O my soul, And forget none of His benefits; 3 Who pardons all your iniquities, Who heals all your diseases; 4 Who redeems your life from the pit, Who crowns you with lovingkindness and compassion; 5 Who satisfies your years with good things, So that your youth is renewed like the eagle.

The Message 1-2 O my soul, bless God. From head to toe, I'll bless his holy name! O my soul, bless God, don't forget a single blessing! 3-5 He forgives your sins—every one. He heals your diseases—every one. He redeems you from hell—saves your life! He crowns you with love and mercy—a paradise crown. He wraps you in goodness—beauty eternal. He renews your youth—you're always young in his presence.

Amplified Bible 2Bless (affectionately, gratefully praise) the Lord, O my soul, and forget not [one of] all His benefits—3Who forgives [every one of] all your iniquities, Who heals [each one of] all your diseases, 4Who redeems your life from the pit and corruption, Who beautifies, dignifies, and crowns you with loving-kindness and tender mercy; 5Who satisfies your mouth [your necessity and desire at your personal age and situation] with good so that your youth, renewed, is like the eagle's [strong, overcoming, soaring]!

New Living Translation 2 Let all that I am praise the Lord; may I never forget the good things he does for me.3 He forgives all my sins and heals all my diseases. 4 He redeems me from death and crowns me with love and tender mercies.[5] He fills my life with good things. My youth is renewed like the eagle's!

Contemporary English Version [2]With all my heart I praise the LORD! I will never forget how kind he has been. [3]The LORD forgives our sins, heals us when we are sick, [4]and protects us from death. His kindness and love are a crown on our heads. [5]Each day that we live, he provides for our needs and gives us the strength of a young eagle.

New King James Version [2] Bless the LORD, O my soul, And forget not all His benefits: [3] Who forgives all your iniquities, Who heals all your diseases, [4] Who redeems your life from destruction, Who crowns you with lovingkindness and tender mercies, [5] Who satisfies your mouth with good things, So that your youth is renewed like the eagle's.

God promises to deliver and to prosper you.

Psalm 105:37

New International Version

37 He brought out Israel, laden with silver and
  gold,
    and from among their tribes no one
faltered.

New American Standard Bible

37 Then He brought them out with silver and
  gold,
    And among His tribes there was not one
who stumbled.

The Message

37 He led Israel out, their arms filled with loot,
    and not one among his tribes even
stumbled.

Amplified Bible

37He brought [Israel] forth also with silver
and gold, and there was not one feeble person
among their tribes.

New Living Translation

37 The Lord brought his people out of Egypt,
loaded with silver and gold; and not one among
the tribes of Israel even stumbled.

Contemporary English Version

37When God led Israel from Egypt, they took
silver and gold, and no one was left behind.

New King James Version

37 He also brought them out with silver and
  gold,
    And there was none feeble among His
tribes.

Reflection

God promises to heal by His word.

Psalm 107:20

New International Version

20 He sent out his word and healed them;
he rescued them from the grave.

New American Standard Bible

20 He sent His word and healed them,
And delivered them from their
destructions.

The Message

20 He spoke the word that healed you,
that pulled you back from the brink of
death.

Amplified Bible

20He sends forth His word and heals them and
rescues them from the pit and destruction.(A)

New Living Translation

20 He sent out his word and healed them,
snatching them from the door of death.

Contemporary English Version

20By the power of his own word, he healed you
and saved you from destruction.

New King James Version

20 He sent His word and healed them,
And delivered them from their
destructions.

Reflection

God promises that you will live and tell others about what God has done.

Psalm 118:17

New International Version

¹⁷ I will not die but live,
and will proclaim what the LORD has done.

New American Standard Bible

¹⁷ I will not die, but live,
And tell of the works of the LORD.

The Message

¹⁷ I didn't die. I lived!
And now I'm telling the world what God did.

Amplified Bible

¹⁷I shall not die but live, and shall declare the works and recount the illustrious acts of the Lord.

New Living Translation

¹⁷ I will not die; instead, I will live
to tell what the Lord has done.

Contemporary English Version

¹⁷And so my life is safe, and I will live to tell what the LORD has done.

New King James Version

¹⁷ I shall not die, but live,
And declare the works of the LORD.

Reflection

God promises that His words are life to your whole body.

Proverbs 4:20-22

New International Version

[20] My son, pay attention to what I say; turn your ear to my words. [21] Do not let them out of your sight, keep them within your heart; [22] for they are life to those who find them and health to one's whole body.

New American Standard Bible

[20] My son, give attention to my words; Incline your ear to my sayings. [21] Do not let them depart from your sight; Keep them in the midst of your heart. [22] For they are life to those who find them And health to all their body.

The Message

[20-22] Dear friend, listen well to my words; tune your ears to my voice. Keep my message in plain view at all times. Concentrate! Learn it by heart! Those who discover these words live, really live; body and soul, they're bursting with health.

Amplified Bible

[20] My son, attend to my words; consent and submit to my sayings. [21] Let them not depart from your sight; keep them in the center of your heart. [22] For they are life to those who find them, healing and health to all their flesh.

New Living Translation

[20] My child, pay attention to what I say. Listen carefully to my words. [21] Don't lose sight of them. Let them penetrate deep into your heart, [22] for they bring life to those who find them, and healing to their whole body.

Reflection

Contemporary English Version

[20]My child, listen carefully to everything I say. [21]Don't forget a single word, but think about it all. [22]Knowing these teachings will mean true life and good health for you.

New King James Version

[20] My son, give attention to my words; Incline your ear to my sayings. [21] Do not let them depart from your eyes; Keep them in the midst of your heart; [22] For they are life to those who find them, And health to all their flesh.

God promises to renew your strength when you wait on Him.

Isaiah 40:30-31

New International Version

[30] Even youths grow tired and weary, and young men stumble and fall; [31] but those who hope in the LORD will renew their strength. They will soar on wings like eagles; they will run and not grow weary, they will walk and not be faint.

New American Standard Bible

[30] Though youths grow weary and tired, And vigorous young men stumble badly, [31] Yet those who wait for the LORD Will gain new strength; They will mount up with wings like eagles, They will run and not get tired, They will walk and not become weary.

The Message

[30-31] For even young people tire and drop out, young folk in their prime stumble and fall. But those who wait upon God get fresh strength. They spread their wings and soar like eagles, They run and don't get tired, they walk and don't lag behind.

Amplified Bible

[30] Even youths shall faint and be weary, and [selected] young men shall feebly stumble and fall exhausted; [31] But those who wait for the Lord [who expect, look for, and hope in Him] shall change and renew their strength and power; they shall lift their wings and mount up [close to God] as eagles [mount up to the sun]; they shall run and not be weary, they shall walk and not faint or become tired.

New Living Translation

[30] Even youths will become weak and tired, and young men will fall in exhaustion. [31] But those who trust in the Lord will find new strength. They will soar high on wings like eagles. They will run and not grow weary. They will walk and not faint.

Reflection

Contemporary English Version

[30]Even young people get tired, then stumble and fall. [31]But those who trust the LORD will find new strength. They will be strong like eagles soaring upward on wings; they will walk and run without getting tired.

New King James Version

[30] Even the youths shall faint and be weary, And the young men shall utterly fall, [31] But those who wait on the LORD Shall renew their strength; They shall mount up with wings like eagles, They shall run and not be weary, They shall walk and not faint.

God promises that we have been healed by the stripes of Jesus.

Isaiah 53:4-6

New International Version ⁴ Surely he took up our pain and bore our suffering, yet we considered him punished by God, stricken by him, and afflicted. ⁵ But he was pierced for our transgressions, he was crushed for our iniquities; the punishment that brought us peace was on him, and by his wounds we are healed. ⁶ We all, like sheep, have gone astray, each of us has turned to our own way; and the LORD has laid on him the iniquity of us all.

New American Standard Bible ⁴ Surely our griefs He Himself bore, And our sorrows He carried; Yet we ourselves esteemed Him stricken, Smitten of God, and afflicted. ⁵ But He was pierced through for our transgressions, He was crushed for our iniquities; The chastening for our well-being fell upon Him, And by His scourging we are healed. ⁶ All of us like sheep have gone astray, Each of us has turned to his own way; But the LORD has caused the iniquity of us all To fall on Him.

The Message ⁴⁻⁶But the fact is, it was our pains he carried—our disfigurements, all the things wrong with us. We thought he brought it on himself, that God was punishing him for his own failures. But it was our sins that did that to him, that ripped and tore and crushed him—our sins! He took the punishment, and that made us whole. Through his bruises we get healed. We're all like sheep who've wandered off and gotten lost. We've all done our own thing, gone our own way. And God has piled all our sins, everything we've done wrong, on him, on him.

Amplified Bible ⁴Surely He has borne our griefs (sicknesses, weaknesses, and distresses) and carried our sorrows and pains [of punishment], yet we [ignorantly] considered Him stricken, smitten, and afflicted by God [as if with leprosy].⁵But He was wounded for our transgressions, He was bruised for our guilt and

Reflection

iniquities; the chastisement [needful to obtain] peace and well-being for us was upon Him, and with the stripes [that wounded] Him we are healed and made whole. ⁶All we like sheep have gone astray, we have turned every one to his own way; and the Lord has made to light upon Him the guilt and iniquity of us all.

New Living Translation ⁴ Yet it was our weaknesses he carried; it was our sorrows that weighed him down. And we thought his troubles were a punishment from God, a punishment for his own sins! ⁵ But he was pierced for our rebellion, crushed for our sins. He was beaten so we could be whole. He was whipped so we could be healed.⁶ All of us, like sheep, have strayed away. We have left God's paths to follow our own. Yet the Lord laid on him the sins of us all.

Contemporary English Version ⁴He suffered and endured great pain for us, but we thought his suffering was punishment from God. ⁵He was wounded and crushed because of our sins; by taking our punishment, he made us completely well. ⁶All of us were like sheep that had wandered off. We had each gone our own way, but the LORD gave him the punishment we deserved.

New King James Version ⁴ Surely He has borne our griefs And carried our sorrows; Yet we esteemed Him stricken, Smitten by God, and afflicted. ⁵ But He was wounded for our transgressions, He was bruised for our iniquities; The chastisement for our peace was upon Him, And by His stripes we are healed. ⁶ All we like sheep have gone astray; We have turned, every one, to his own way; And the LORD has laid on Him the iniquity of us all.

God promises to restore your health.

Jeremiah 30:17

New International Version

¹⁷ But I will restore you to health and heal your wounds,' declares the LORD, 'because you are called an outcast, Zion for whom no one cares.'

New American Standard Bible

¹⁷ 'For I will restore you to health And I will heal you of your wounds,' declares the LORD, 'Because they have called you an outcast, saying: "It is Zion; no one cares for her."'

The Message

¹⁷ As for you, I'll come with healing, curing the incurable, Because they all gave up on you and dismissed you as hopeless—that good-for-nothing Zion.'

Amplified Bible

¹⁷For I will restore health to you, and I will heal your wounds, says the Lord, because they have called you an outcast, saying, This is Zion, whom no one seeks after and for whom no one cares!

New Living Translation

¹⁷ I will give you back your health and heal your wounds," says the Lord. "For you are called an outcast— 'Jerusalem for whom no one cares.'"

Contemporary English Version

¹⁷No one wants you as a friend or cares what happens to you.
But I will heal your injuries, and you will get well.

New King James Version

¹⁷ For I will restore health to you And heal you of your wounds,' says the LORD, 'Because they called you an outcast saying:" This is Zion; No one seeks her."'

Reflection

God promises healing, security and abundant prosperity.

Jeremiah 33:6

New International Version

6 "'Nevertheless, I will bring health and healing to it; I will heal my people and will let them enjoy abundant peace and security.

New American Standard Bible

6 Behold, I will bring to it health and healing, and I will heal them; and I will reveal to them an abundance of peace and truth.

The Message

6"But now take another look. I'm going to give this city a thorough renovation, working a true healing inside and out. I'm going to show them life whole, life brimming with blessings.

Amplified Bible

6Behold, [in the future restored Jerusalem] I will lay upon it health and healing, and I will cure them and will reveal to them the abundance of peace (prosperity, security, stability) and truth.

New Living Translation

6 "Nevertheless, the time will come when I will heal Jerusalem's wounds and give it prosperity and true peace.

Contemporary English Version

6Then someday, I will heal this place and my people as well, and let them enjoy unending peace.

New King James Version

6 Behold, I will bring it health and healing; I will heal them and reveal to them the abundance of peace and truth.

Reflection

God promises to heal you when you worship.

Malachi 4:2

New International Version

² But for you who revere my name, the sun of righteousness will rise with healing in its rays. And you will go out and frolic like well-fed calves.

New American Standard Bible

² "But for you who fear My name, the sun of righteousness will rise with healing in its wings; and you will go forth and skip about like calves from the stall.

The Message

² But for you, sunrise! The sun of righteousness will dawn on those who honor my name, healing radiating from its wings. You will be bursting with energy, like colts frisky and frolicking. And you'll tromp on the wicked.

Amplified Bible

²But unto you who revere and worshipfully fear My name shall the Sun of Righteousness arise with healing in His wings and His beams, and you shall go forth and gambol like calves [released] from the stall and leap for joy.

New Living Translation

² "But for you who fear my name, the Sun of Righteousness will rise with healing in his wings.[a] And you will go free, leaping with joy like calves let out to pasture.

Contemporary English Version

²But for you that honor my name, victory will shine like the sun with healing in its rays, and you will jump around like calves at play.

New King James Version

² But to you who fear My name The Sun of Righteousness shall arise With healing in His wings; And you shall go out And grow fat like stall-fed calves.

Reflection

God promises to heal you because it is His will.

Matthew 8:2-3

New International Version

² A man with leprosycame and knelt before him and said, "Lord, if you are willing, you can make me clean." ³ Jesus reached out his hand and touched the man. "I am willing," he said. "Be clean!" Immediately he was cleansed of his leprosy.

New American Standard Bible

² And a leper came to Him and bowed down before Him, and said, "Lord, if You are willing, You can make me clean." ³ Jesus stretched out His hand and touched him, saying, "I am willing; be cleansed." And immediately his leprosy was cleansed.

The Message

² Then a leper appeared and went to his knees before Jesus, praying, "Master, if you want to, you can heal my body." ³ Jesus reached out and touched him, saying, "I want to. Be clean." Then and there, all signs of the leprosy were gone.

Amplified Bible

²And behold, a leper came up to Him and, prostrating himself, worshiped Him, saying, Lord, if You are willing, You are able to cleanse me by curing me. ³And He reached out His hand and touched him, saying, I am willing; be cleansed by being cured. nd instantly his leprosy was cured and cleansed.

New Living Translation

² Suddenly, a man with leprosy approached him and knelt before him. "Lord," the man said, "if you are willing, you can heal me and make me clean." ³ Jesus reached out and touched him. "I am willing," he said. "Be healed!" And instantly the leprosy disappeared.

Reflection

Contemporary English Version

²Suddenly a man with leprosy came and knelt in front of Jesus. He said, "Lord, you have the power to make me well, if only you wanted to." ³Jesus put his hand on the man and said, "I want to! Now you are well." At once the man's leprosy disappeared.

New King James Version

² And behold, a leper came and worshiped Him, saying, "Lord, if You are willing, You can make me clean." ³ Then Jesus put out His hand and touched him, saying, "I am willing; be cleansed." Immediately his leprosy was cleansed.

God promises to take our infirmities, and diseases away.

Matthew 8:17

New International Version

[17] This was to fulfill what was spoken through the prophet Isaiah: "He took up our infirmities and bore our diseases."

New American Standard Bible

[17] This was to fulfill what was spoken through Isaiah the prophet: "HE HIMSELF TOOK OUR INFIRMITIES AND CARRIED AWAY OUR DISEASES."

The Message

[16-17]That evening a lot of demon-afflicted people were brought to him. He relieved the inwardly tormented. He cured the bodily ill. He fulfilled Isaiah's well-known sermon: He took our illnesses, He carried our diseases.

Amplified Bible

[17]And thus He fulfilled what was spoken by the prophet Isaiah, He Himself took in order to carry away] our weaknesses and infirmities and bore away our diseases.

New Living Translation

[17] This fulfilled the word of the Lord through the prophet Isaiah, who said, "He took our sicknesses and removed our diseases."

Contemporary English Version

[17]So God's promise came true, just as the prophet Isaiah had said, "He healed our diseases and made us well."

New King James Version

[17] that it might be fulfilled which was spoken by Isaiah the prophet, saying: "He Himself took our infirmities And bore our sicknesses."

Reflection

God promises to heal because He has done it before.

Matthew 9:35

New International Version

³⁵ Jesus went through all the towns and villages, teaching in their synagogues, proclaiming the good news of the kingdom and healing every disease and sickness.

New American Standard Bible

³⁵ Jesus was going through all the cities and villages, teaching in their synagogues and proclaiming the gospel of the kingdom, and healing every kind of disease and every kind of sickness.

The Message

³⁵Then Jesus made a circuit of all the towns and villages. He taught in their meeting places, reported kingdom news, and healed their diseased bodies, healed their bruised and hurt lives. hands!"

Amplified Bible

³⁵And Jesus went about all the cities and villages, teaching in their synagogues and proclaiming the good news (the Gospel) of the kingdom and curing all kinds of disease and every weakness and infirmity.

New Living Translation

³⁵ Jesus traveled through all the towns and villages of that area, teaching in the synagogues and announcing the Good News about the Kingdom. And he healed every kind of disease and illness.

Contemporary English Version

³⁵Jesus went to every town and village. He taught in their meeting places and preached the good news about God's kingdom. Jesus also healed every kind of disease and sickness.

Reflection

New King James Version

[35] Then Jesus went about all the cities and villages, teaching in their synagogues, preaching the gospel of the kingdom, and healing every sickness and every disease among the people.

God promises to heal those who touch Him in faith.

Matthew 14:36

New International Version

[36] and begged him to let the sick just touch the edge of his cloak, and all who touched it were healed.

New American Standard Bible

[36] and they implored Him that they might just touch the fringe of His cloak; and as many as touched it were cured.

The Message

[34-36]On return, they beached the boat at Gennesaret. When the people got wind that he was back, they sent out word through the neighborhood and rounded up all the sick, who asked for permission to touch the edge of his coat. And whoever touched him was healed.

Amplified Bible

[36]And begged Him to let them merely touch the fringe of His garment; and as many as touched it were perfectly restored.

New Living Translation

[36] They begged him to let the sick touch at least the fringe of his robe, and all who touched him were healed.

Contemporary English Version

[36]They begged him just to let them touch his clothes, and everyone who did was healed.

New King James Version

[36] and begged Him that they might only touch the hem of His garment. And as many as touched it were made perfectly well.

Reflection

God promises to heal people using you.

Mark 16:17-18

New International Version

17 And these signs will accompany those who believe: In my name they will drive out demons; they will speak in new tongues; 18 they will pick up snakes with their hands; and when they drink deadly poison, it will not hurt them at all; they will place their hands on sick people, and they will get well."

New American Standard Bible

17 These signs will accompany those who have believed: in My name they will cast out demons, they will speak with new tongues; 18 they will pick up serpents, and if they drink any deadly poison, it will not hurt them; they will lay hands on the sick, and they will recover."

The Message

17-18"These are some of the signs that will accompany believers: They will throw out demons in my name, they will speak in new tongues, they will take snakes in their hands, they will drink poison and not be hurt, they will lay hands on the sick and make them well."

Amplified Bible

17And these attesting signs will accompany those who believe: in My name they will drive out demons; they will speak in new languages; 18They will pick up serpents; and [even] if they drink anything deadly, it will not hurt them; they will lay their hands on the sick, and they will get well.

New Living Translation

17 These miraculous signs will accompany those who believe: They will cast out demons in my name, and they will speak in new languages.[a] 18 They will be able

Reflection

_____
_____
_____
_____
_____
_____
_____
_____
_____
_____
_____
_____
_____
_____
_____
_____
_____
_____
_____
_____
_____
_____
_____
_____
_____
_____
_____
_____
_____
_____
_____
_____
_____

to handle snakes with safety, and if they drink anything poisonous, it won't hurt them. They will be able to place their hands on the sick, and they will be healed."

Contemporary English Version

[17]Everyone who believes me will be able to do wonderful things. By using my name they will force out demons, and they will speak new languages. [18]They will handle snakes and will drink poison and not be hurt. They will also heal sick people by placing their hands on them.

New King James Version

[17] And these signs will follow those who believe: In My name they will cast out demons; they will speak with new tongues; [18] they[a] will take up serpents; and if they drink anything deadly, it will by no means hurt them; they will lay hands on the sick, and they will recover."

God promises to heal all who are bound by the devil.

Acts 10:38

New International Version

[38] how God anointed Jesus of Nazareth with the Holy Spirit and power, and how he went around doing good and healing all who were under the power of the devil, because God was with him.

New American Standard Bible

[38] You know of Jesus of Nazareth, how God anointed Him with the Holy Spirit and with power, and how He went about doing good and healing all who were oppressed by the devil, for God was with Him.

The Message

[38] Then Jesus arrived from Nazareth, anointed by God with the Holy Spirit, ready for action. He went through the country helping people and healing everyone who was beaten down by the Devil. He was able to do all this because God was with him.

Amplified Bible

[38]How God anointed and consecrated Jesus of Nazareth with the [Holy] Spirit and with strength and ability and power; how He went about doing good and, in particular, curing all who were harassed and oppressed by [the power of] the devil, for God was with Him.

New Living Translation

[38] And you know that God anointed Jesus of Nazareth with the Holy Spirit and with power. Then Jesus went around doing good and healing all who were oppressed by the devil, for God was with him.

Reflection

Contemporary English Version

[38]God gave the Holy Spirit and power to Jesus from Nazareth. He was with Jesus, as he went around doing good and healing everyone who was under the power of the devil.

New King James Version

[38] how God anointed Jesus of Nazareth with the Holy Spirit and with power, who went about doing good and healing all who were oppressed by the devil, for God was with Him.

God promises to revive your mortal body in the same way Jesus was revived.

Romans 8:11

New International Version

[11] And if the Spirit of him who raised Jesus from the dead is living in you, he who raised Christ from the dead will also give life to your mortal bodies because of his Spirit who lives in you.

New American Standard Bible

[11] But if the Spirit of Him who raised Jesus from the dead dwells in you, He who raised Christ Jesus from the dead will also give life to your mortal bodies through His Spirit who dwells in you.

The Message

[11]It stands to reason, doesn't it, that if the alive-and-present God who raised Jesus from the dead moves into your life, he'll do the same thing in you that he did in Jesus, bringing you alive to himself? When God lives and breathes in you (and he does, as surely as he did in Jesus), you are delivered from that dead life. With his Spirit living in you, your body will be as alive as Christ's!

Amplified Bible

[11]And if the Spirit of Him Who raised up Jesus from the dead dwells in you, [then] He Who raised up Christ Jesus from the dead will also restore to life your mortal (short-lived, perishable) bodies through His Spirit Who dwells in you.

New Living Translation

[11] The Spirit of God, who raised Jesus from the dead, lives in you. And just as God raised Christ Jesus from the dead, he will give life to your mortal bodies by this same Spirit living within you.

Reflection

Contemporary English Version

[11]Yet God raised Jesus to life! God's Spirit now lives in you, and he will raise you to life by his Spirit.

New King James Version

[11] But if the Spirit of Him who raised Jesus from the dead dwells in you, He who raised Christ from the dead will also give life to your mortal bodies through His Spirit who dwells in you.

God promises that you will be healed when you confess your sin to each other.

James 5:15-16

New International Version [15] And the prayer offered in faith will make the sick person well; the Lord will raise them up. If they have sinned, they will be forgiven. [16] Therefore confess your sins to each other and pray for each other so that you may be healed. The prayer of a righteous person is powerful and effective.

New American Standard Bible [15] and the prayer offered in faith will restore the one who is sick, and the Lord will raise him up, and if he has committed sins, they will be forgiven him. [16] Therefore, confess your sins to one another, and pray for one another so that you may be healed. The effective prayer of a righteous man can accomplish much.

The Message [15-16]Are you hurting? Pray. Do you feel great? Sing. Are you sick? Call the church leaders together to pray and anoint you with oil in the name of the Master. Believing-prayer will heal you, and Jesus will put you on your feet. And if you've sinned, you'll be forgiven—healed inside and out. [16-18]Make this your common practice: Confess your sins to each other and pray for each other so that you can live together whole and healed. The prayer of a person living right with God is something powerful to be reckoned with.

Amplified Bible [15]And the prayer [that is] of faith will save him who is sick, and the Lord will restore him; and if he has committed sins, he will be forgiven. [16]Confess to one another therefore your faults (your slips, your false steps, your offenses, your sins) and pray [also] for one another, that you may be healed and restored [to a spiritual tone of mind and heart]. The earnest (heartfelt, continued) prayer of a righteous man makes tremendous power available [dynamic in its working].

Reflection

New Living Translation [15] Such a prayer offered in faith will heal the sick, and the Lord will make you well. And if you have committed any sins, you will be forgiven. [16] Confess your sins to each other and pray for each other so that you may be healed. The earnest prayer of a righteous person has great power and produces wonderful results.

Contemporary English Version [15]If you have faith when you pray for sick people, they will get well. The Lord will heal them, and if they have sinned, he will forgive them. [16]If you have sinned, you should tell each other what you have done. Then you can pray for one another and be healed. The prayer of an innocent person is powerful, and it can help a lot.

New King James Version [15] And the prayer of faith will save the sick, and the Lord will raise him up. And if he has committed sins, he will be forgiven. [16] Confess your trespasses to one another, and pray for one another, that you may be healed. The effective, fervent prayer of a righteous man avails much.

God promises to heal you because of what Jesus went through.

---

1 Peter 2:24

New International Version

[24] "He himself bore our sins" in his body on the cross, so that we might die to sins and live for righteousness; "by his wounds you have been healed."

New American Standard Bible

[24] and He Himself bore our sins in His body on the cross, so that we might die to sin and live to righteousness; for by His wounds you were healed.

The Message

[24] He used his servant body to carry our sins to the Cross so we could be rid of sin, free to live the right way. His wounds became your healing.

Amplified Bible

[24]He personally bore our sins in His [own] body on the tree [as on an altar and offered Himself on it], that we might die (cease to exist) to sin and live to righteousness. By His wounds you have been healed.

New Living Translation

[24] He personally carried our sins in his body on the cross so that we can be dead to sin and live for what is right. By his wounds you are healed.

Contemporary English Version

[24]Christ carried the burden of our sins. He was nailed to the cross, so that we would stop sinning and start living right. By his cuts and bruises you are healed.

Reflection

New King James Version

[24] who Himself bore our sins in His own body on the tree, that we, having died to sins, might live for righteousness—by whose stripes you were healed.

God promises to heal you even as He prospers you.

3 John 1:2

New International Version

² Dear friend, I pray that you may enjoy good health and that all may go well with you, even as your soul is getting along well.

New American Standard Bible

² Beloved, I pray that in all respects you may prosper and be in good health, just as your soul prospers.

The Message

² We're the best of friends, and I pray for good fortune in everything you do, and for your good health—that your everyday affairs prosper, as well as your soul!

Amplified Bible

²Beloved, I pray that you may prosper in every way and [that your body] may keep well, even as [I know] your soul keeps well and prospers.

New Living Translation

² Dear friend, I hope all is well with you and that you are as healthy in body as you are strong in spirit.

Contemporary English Version

²dear friend, and I pray that all goes well for you. I hope that you are as strong in body, as I know you are in spirit.

New King James Version

² Beloved, I pray that you may prosper in all things and be in health, just as your soul prospers.

Reflection

God promises to surround you with His favor.

Psalm 5:12

New International Version

¹² Surely, LORD, you bless the righteous;
you surround them with your favor as with a shield.

New American Standard Bible

¹² For it is You who blesses the righteous man, O LORD,
You surround him with favor as with a shield.

The Message

¹¹⁻¹² But you'll welcome us with open arms when we run for cover to you. Let the party last all night! Stand guard over our celebration. You are famous, God, for welcoming God-seekers, for decking us out in delight.

Amplifed Bible (AMP)

²For You, Lord, will bless the [uncompromisingly] righteous [him who is upright and in right standing with You]; as with a shield You will surround him with goodwill (pleasure and favor).

New Living Translation

¹² For you bless the godly, O Lord; you surround them with your shield of love.

Contemporary English Version

¹²Our LORD, you bless those who live right, and you shield them with your kindness.

New King James Version

¹² For You, O LORD, will bless the righteous;
With favor You will surround him as with a shield.

Reflection

God promises that you will rest secure.

Psalm 16:8-9

New International Version

⁸ I keep my eyes always on the LORD. With him at my right hand, I will not be shaken. ⁹ Therefore my heart is glad and my tongue rejoices; my body also will rest secure,

New American Standard Bible

⁸ I have set the LORD continually before me; Because He is at my right hand, I will not be shaken. ⁹ Therefore my heart is glad and my glory rejoices; My flesh also will dwell securely.

The Message

⁸ Day and night I'll stick with God; I've got a good thing going and I'm not letting go. ⁹I'm happy from the inside out, and from the outside in, I'm firmly formed.

Amplified Bible

⁸I have set the Lord continually before me; because He is at my right hand, I shall not be moved. ⁹Therefore my heart is glad and my glory [my inner self] rejoices; my body too shall rest and confidently dwell in safety,

New Living Translation

⁸ I know the Lord is always with me. I will not be shaken, for he is right beside me. ⁹ No wonder my heart is glad, and I rejoice. My body rests in safety.

Contemporary English Version

⁸I will always look to you, as you stand beside me and protect me from fear. ⁹With all my heart, I will celebrate, and I can safely rest.

Reflection

New King James Version

⁸ I have set the LORD always before me; Because He is at my right hand I shall not be moved. ⁹ Therefore my heart is glad, and my glory rejoices; My flesh also will rest in hope.

RUDOLPH MOSELEY JR.

God promises to make your life secure because of His favor.

Psalm 30:7

New International Version

⁷ LORD, when you favored me, you made my royal mountain stand firm; but when you hid your face, I was dismayed.

New American Standard Bible

⁷ O LORD, by Your favor You have made my mountain to stand strong; You hid Your face, I was dismayed.

The Message

⁷ I'm God's favorite. He made me king of the mountain." Then you looked the other way and I fell to pieces.

Amplified Bible

⁷By Your favor, O Lord, You have established me as a strong mountain; You hid Your face, and I was troubled.

New Living Translation

⁷ Your favor, O Lord, made me as secure as a mountain. Then you turned away from me, and I was shattered.

Contemporary English Version

⁷You, LORD, were my friend, and you made me strong as a mighty mountain. But when you hid your face, I was crushed.

New King James Version

⁷ LORD, by Your favor You have made my
   mountain stand strong;
   You hid Your face, and I was troubled.

Reflection

God promises the gift of victory.

Psalm 44:3

New International Version

³ It was not by their sword that they won the land, nor did their arm bring them victory; it was your right hand, your arm, and the light of your face, for you loved them.

New American Standard Bible

³ For by their own sword they did not possess the land, And their own arm did not save them, But Your right hand and Your arm and the light of Your presence, For You favored them.

The Message

³ We didn't fight for this land; we didn't work for it—it was a gift! You gave it, smiling as you gave it, delighting as you gave it.

Amplified Bible

³For they got not the land [of Canaan] in possession by their own sword, neither did their own arm save them; but Your right hand and Your arm and the light of Your countenance [did it], because You were favorable toward and did delight in them.

New Living Translation

³ They did not conquer the land with their swords; it was not their own strong arm that gave them victory. It was your right hand and strong arm and the blinding light from your face that helped them, for you loved them.

Contemporary English Version

³Their strength and weapons were not what won the land and gave them victory! You loved them and fought with your powerful arm and your shining glory.

Reflection

New King James Version

[3] For they did not gain possession of the land by their own sword, Nor did their own arm save them; But it was Your right hand, Your arm, and the light of Your countenance, Because You favored them.

God promises that your enemies will run when you call out to Him.

Psalm 56:9

New International Version

⁹ Then my enemies will turn back when I call
   for help.
      By this I will know that God is for me.

New American Standard Bible

⁹ Then my enemies will turn back in the day
   when I call;
      This I know, that God is for me.

The Message

⁹ If my enemies run away, turn tail when I yell
   at them,
      Then I'll know that God is on my side.

Amplified Bible

⁹Then shall my enemies turn back in the day
that I cry out; this I know, for God is for
me.(A)

New Living Translation

⁹ My enemies will retreat when I call to you
   for help.
      This I know: God is on my side!

Contemporary English Version

⁹When I pray, LORD God, my enemies will
retreat, because I know for certain that you are
with me.

New King James Version

⁹ When I cry out to You, Then my enemies
   will turn back;
      This I know, because God is for me.

Reflection

God promises to show His strength as He did in the past.

Psalm 68:28

New International Version

²⁸ Summon your power, God;
    show us your strength, our God, as you
have done before.

New American Standard Bible

²⁸ Your God has commanded your strength;
    Show Yourself strong, O God, who have
acted on our behalf.

The Message

²⁸ Parade your power, O God,
    the power, O God, that made us what we
are.

Amplified Bible

²⁸Your God has commanded your strength
[your might in His service and impenetrable
hardness to temptation]; O God, display Your
might and strengthen what You have wrought
for us!

New Living Translation

²⁸ Summon your might, O God.
    Display your power, O God, as you have
in the past.

Contemporary English Version

²⁸Our God, show your strength!
    Show us once again.

New King James Version

²⁸ Your God has commanded your strength;
    Strengthen, O God, what You have done
for us.

Reflection

God promises to be faithful in your life causing you to tell everyone.

Psalm 71:16

New International Version

¹⁶ I will come and proclaim your mighty acts,
Sovereign LORD;
I will proclaim your righteous deeds, yours alone.

New American Standard Bible

¹⁶ I will come with the mighty deeds of the
Lord GOD;
I will make mention of Your righteousness,
Yours alone.

The Message

¹⁶ I come in the power of the Lord God,
I post signs marking his right-of-way.

Amplified Bible

¹⁶ I will come in the strength and with the mighty acts of the Lord God; I will mention and praise Your righteousness, even Yours alone.

New Living Translation

¹⁶ I will praise your mighty deeds, O
Sovereign Lord.
I will tell everyone that you alone are just.

Contemporary English Version

¹⁶I will praise you, LORD God, for your
mighty deeds
and your power to save.

New King James Version

¹⁶ I will go in the strength of the Lord GOD;
I will make mention of Your righteousness,
of Yours only.

Reflection

God promises to grant you favor because of His glory.

Psalm 89:17

New International Version

¹⁷ For you are their glory and strength,
  and by your favor you exalt our horn.

New American Standard Bible

¹⁷ For You are the glory of their strength,
  And by Your favor our horn is exalted.

The Message

¹⁷ Your vibrant beauty has gotten inside us—you've been so good to us! We're walking on air! All we are and have we owe to God,

Amplified Bible

¹⁷For You are the glory of their strength [their proud adornment], and by Your favor our horn is exalted and we walk with uplifted faces!

New Living Translation

¹⁷ You are their glorious strength.
  It pleases you to make us strong.

Contemporary English Version

¹⁷Your own glorious power makes us strong,
  and because of your kindness, our strength increases.

New King James Version

¹⁷ For You are the glory of their strength,
  And in Your favor our horn is exalted.

Reflection

God promises to show you favor at the appointed time.

Psalm 102:13

New International Version

¹³ You will arise and have compassion on
   Zion,
      for it is time to show favor to her;
      the appointed time has come.

New American Standard Bible

¹³ You will arise and have compassion on Zion;
For it is time to be gracious to her, For the
appointed time has come.

The Message

¹³ You'll get up from your throne and help
   Zion—
      it's time for compassionate help.

Amplified Bible

¹³You will arise and have mercy and
loving-kindness for Zion, for it is time to have
pity and compassion for her; yes, the set time
has come [the moment designated].

New Living Translation

¹³ You will arise and have mercy on
   Jerusalem—
      and now is the time to pity her,
      now is the time you promised to help.

Contemporary English Version

¹³You will show pity to Zion
      because the time has come.

New King James Version

¹³ You will arise and have mercy on Zion;
      For the time to favor her,
      Yes, the set time, has come.

Reflection

God promises to crown you with love and compassion.

Psalm 103:4-5

New International Version

⁴ who redeems your life from the pit and crowns you with love and compassion, ⁵ who satisfies your desires with good things so that your youth is renewed like the eagle's.

New American Standard Bible

⁴ Who redeems your life from the pit, Who crowns you with lovingkindness and compassion; ⁵ Who satisfies your years with good things, So that your youth is renewed like the eagle.

The Message

³⁻⁵ He forgives your sins—every one. He heals your diseases—every one. He redeems you from hell—saves your life! He crowns you with love and mercy—a paradise crown. He wraps you in goodness—beauty eternal. He renews your youth—you're always young in his presence.

Amplified Bible

⁴Who redeems your life from the pit and corruption, Who beautifies, dignifies, and crowns you with loving-kindness and tender mercy; ⁵Who satisfies your mouth [your necessity and desire at your personal age and situation] with good so that your youth, renewed, is like the eagle's [strong, overcoming, soaring]!

New Living Translation

⁴ He redeems me from death and crowns me with love and tender mercies. ⁵ He fills my life with good things. My youth is renewed like the eagle's!

Reflection

Contemporary English Version

⁴and protects us from death. His kindness and love are a crown on our heads. ⁵Each day that we live, he provides for our needs and gives us the strength of a young eagle.

New King James Version

⁴ Who redeems your life from destruction, Who crowns you with lovingkindness and tender mercies, ⁵ Who satisfies your mouth with good things, So that your youth is renewed like the eagle's

God promises that you will be bursting with health.

Proverbs 4:20-22

New International Version

²⁰ My son, pay attention to what I say; turn your ear to my words. ²¹ Do not let them out of your sight, keep them within your heart; ²² for they are life to those who find them and health to one's whole body.

New American Standard Bible

²⁰ My son, give attention to my words; Incline your ear to my sayings. ²¹ Do not let them depart from your sight; Keep them in the midst of your heart. ²² For they are life to those who find them And health to all their body.

The Message

Learn It by Heart

²⁰⁻²² Dear friend, listen well to my words; tune your ears to my voice. Keep my message in plain view at all times. Concentrate! Learn it by heart!Those who discover these words live, really live; body and soul, they're bursting with health.

Amplified Bible

²⁰My son, attend to my words; consent and submit to my sayings. ²¹Let them not depart from your sight; keep them in the center of your heart. ²²For they are life to those who find them, healing and health to all their flesh.

New Living Translation

²⁰ My child, pay attention to what I say. Listen carefully to my words. ²¹ Don't lose sight of them. Let them penetrate deep into your heart. ²² for they bring life to those who find them, and healing to their whole body.

Reflection

Contemporary English Version

[20]My child, listen carefully to everything I say. [21]Don't forget a single word, but think about it all. [22]Knowing these teachings will mean true life and good health for you.

New King James Version

[20] My son, give attention to my words; Incline your ear to my sayings. [21] Do not let them depart from your eyes; Keep them in the midst of your heart; [22] For they are life to those who find them, And health to all their flesh.

God promises that you will be at peace with your enemies.

Proverbs 16:7

New International Version

7 When the LORD takes pleasure in anyone's
way,
he causes their enemies to make peace
with them.

New American Standard Bible

7 When a man's ways are pleasing to the
LORD,
He (A)makes even his enemies to be at
peace with him.

The Message

7 When God approves of your life,
even your enemies will end up shaking
your hand.

Amplified Bible

7When a man's ways please the Lord, He makes
even his enemies to be at peace with him.

New Living Translation

7 When people's lives please the Lord,
even their enemies are at peace with
them.

Contemporary English Version

7When we please the LORD, even our
enemies
make friends with us.

New King James Version

7 When a man's ways please the LORD,
He makes even his enemies to be at peace
with him.

Reflection

God promises to turn to you so that you will be blessed.

Ezekiel 36:9

New International Version

⁹ I am concerned for you and will look on you with favor; you will be plowed and sown,

New American Standard Bible

⁹ For, behold, I am for you, and I will turn to you, and you will be cultivated and sown.

Th Message (MSG)

⁹ My people are coming home! Do you see? I'm back again. I'm on your side. You'll teem with life—human and animal.

Amplified Bible

⁹For behold, I am for you and I will turn to you; and you shall be tilled and sown,

New Living Translation

⁹ See, I care about you, and I will pay attention to you. Your ground will be plowed and your crops planted.

Contemporary English Version

⁹I will take care of you by plowing your soil and planting crops on your fertile slopes.

New King James Version

⁹ For indeed I am for you, and I will turn to you, and you shall be tilled and sown.

Reflection

God promises to bring home the exiles.

Isaiah 45:13

New International Version

13 I will raise up Cyrus in my righteousness: I will make all his ways straight. He will rebuild my city and set my exiles free, but not for a price or reward, says the LORD Almighty."

New American Standard Bible

13 "I have aroused him in righteousness And I will make all his ways smooth; He will build My city and will let My exiles go free, Without any payment or reward," says the LORD of hosts.

The Message

13 And now I've got Cyrus on the move. I've rolled out the red carpet before him. He will build my city. He will bring home my exiles. I didn't hire him to do this. I told him. I, God-of-the-Angel-Armies.

Amplfied Bible (AMP)

13 I will raise [Cyrus] up in righteousness [willing in every way that which is right and proper], and I will direct all his ways; he will build My city, and he will let My captives go, not for hire or for a bribe, says the Lord of hosts.

New Living Translation

13 I will raise up Cyrus to fulfill my righteous purpose, and I will guide his actions. He will restore my city and free my captive people—without seeking a reward! I, the Lord of Heaven's Armies, have spoken!"

Reflection

Contemporary English Version

13 I have done the right thing by placing Cyrus in power, and I will make the roads easy for him to follow. I am the LORD All-Powerful! Cyrus will rebuild my city and set my people free without being paid a thing. I, the LORD, have spoken.

New King James Version

[13] I have raised him up in righteousness, And I will direct all his ways; He shall build My city And let My exiles go free, Not for price nor reward," Says the LORD of hosts.

God promises to wake you up to give you important instruction.

Isaiah 50:4

New International Version

4 The Sovereign LORD has given me a well-instructed tongue, to know the word that sustains the weary. He wakens me morning by morning, wakens my ear to listen like one being instructed.

New American Standard Bible

4 The Lord GOD has given Me the tongue of disciples, That I may know how to sustain the weary one with a word. He awakens Me morning by morning, He awakens My ear to listen as a disciple.

The Message

4 The Master, God, has given me a well-taught tongue, So I know how to encourage tired people. He wakes me up in the morning, Wakes me up, opens my ears to listen as one ready to take orders.

Amplified Bible

4[The [a]Servant of God says] The Lord God has given Me the tongue of a disciple and of one who is taught, that I should know how to speak a word in season to him who is weary. He wakens Me morning by morning, He wakens My ear to hear as a disciple [as one who is taught].

New Living Translation

4 The Sovereign Lord has given me his words of wisdom, so that I know how to comfort the weary. Morning by morning he wakens me and opens my understanding to his will.

Contemporary English Version

4The LORD God gives me the right words to encourage the weary. Each morning he awakens me eager to learn his teaching;

Reflection

[4] "The Lord GOD has given Me The tongue of the learned, That I should know how to speak A word in season to him who is weary. He awakens Me morning by morning, He awakens My ear To hear as the learned.

God promises to put His word in your mouth because you are His people.

Isaiah 51:16

New International Version

¹⁶ I have put my words in your mouth and covered you with the shadow of my hand—I who set the heavens in place, who laid the foundations of the earth, and who say to Zion, 'You are my people.'"

New American Standard Bible

¹⁶ I have put My words in your mouth and have covered you with the shadow of My hand, to establish the heavens, to found the earth, and to say to Zion, 'You are My people.'"

The Message

¹⁶ I teach you how to talk, word by word, and personally watch over you, Even while I'm unfurling the skies, setting earth on solid foundations, and greeting Zion: 'Welcome, my people!'"

Amplified Bible

¹⁶And I have put My words in your mouth and have covered you with the shadow of My hand, that I may fix the [new] heavens as a tabernacle and lay the foundations of a [new] earth and say to Zion, You are My people.

New Living Translation

¹⁶ And I have put my words in your mouthand hidden you safely in my hand. I stretched out the sky like a canopy and laid the foundations of the earth. I am the one who says to Israel, 'You are my people!'"

Contemporary English Version

¹⁶I have told you what to say, and I will keep you safe in the palm of my hand. I spread out the heavens and laid foundations for the earth. Now I say, "Jerusalem, your people are mine."

Reflection

New King James Version

[16] And I have put My words in your mouth; I have covered you with the shadow of My hand, That I may plant the heavens, Lay the foundations of the earth, And say to Zion, 'You are My people.'"

God promises that your life will glow in the darkness.

Isaiah 58:10

New International Version

[10] and if you spend yourselves in behalf of the hungry and satisfy the needs of the oppressed, then your light will rise in the darkness, and your night will become like the noonday.

New American Standard Bible

[10] And if you give yourself to the hungry And satisfy the desire of the afflicted, Then your light will rise in darkness And your gloom will become like midday.

The Message

[10] If you are generous with the hungry and start giving yourselves to the down-and-out, Your lives will begin to glow in the darkness, your shadowed lives will be bathed in sunlight.

Amplified Bible

[10]And if you pour out that with which you sustain your own life for the hungry and satisfy the need of the afflicted, then shall your light rise in darkness, and your obscurity and gloom become like the noonday.

New Living Translation

[10] Feed the hungry, and help those in trouble. Then your light will shine out from the darkness, and the darkness around you will be as bright as noon.

Contemporary English Version

[10]Give your food to the hungry and care for the homeless. Then your light will shine in the dark; your darkest hour will be like the noonday sun.

New King James Version

[10] If you extend your soul to the hungry And satisfy the afflicted soul, Then your light shall dawn in the darkness, And your darkness shall be as the noonday.

Reflection

God promises to bless your life more abundantly

John 10:10

New International Version

[10] The thief comes only to steal and kill and destroy; I have come that they may have life, and have it to the full.

New American Standard Bible

[10] The thief comes only to steal and kill and destroy; I came that they may have life, and have it abundantly.

The Message

[10] A thief is only there to steal and kill and destroy. I came so they can have real and eternal life, more and better life than they ever dreamed of.

Amplified Bible

[10] The thief comes only in order to steal and kill and destroy. I came that they may have and enjoy life, and have it in abundance (to the full, till it overflows).

New Living Translation

[10] The thief's purpose is to steal and kill and destroy. My purpose is to give them a rich and satisfying life.

Contemporary English Version

[10] A thief comes only to rob, kill, and destroy. I came so that everyone would have life, and have it in its fullest.

New King James Version

[10] The thief does not come except to steal, and to kill, and to destroy. I have come that they may have life, and that they may have it more abundantly.

Reflection

God promises to give you all things.

Romans 8:32

New International Version

³² He who did not spare his own Son, but gave him up for us all—how will he not also, along with him, graciously give us all things?

New American Standard Bible

³² He who did not spare His own Son, but delivered Him over for us all, how will He not also with Him freely give us all things?

The Message

³² If God didn't hesitate to put everything on the line for us, embracing our condition and exposing himself to the worst by sending his own Son, is there anything else he wouldn't gladly and freely do for us?

Amplified Bible

³²He who did not withhold or spare [even] His own Son but gave Him up for us all, will He not also with Him freely and graciously give us all [other] things?

New Living Translation

³² Since he did not spare even his own Son but gave him up for us all, won't he also give us everything else?

Contemporary English Version

³²God did not keep back his own Son, but he gave him for us. If God did this, won't he freely give us everything else?

New King James Version

³² He who did not spare His own Son, but delivered Him up for us all, how shall He not with Him also freely give us all things?

Reflection

God promises to enrich you in every way.

1 Corinthians 1:5

New International Version

⁵ For in him you have been enriched in every way—with all kinds of speech and with all knowledge—

New American Standard Bible

⁵ that in everything you were enriched in Him, in all speech and all knowledge,

The Message

⁴⁻⁶Every time I think of you—and I think of you often!—I thank God for your lives of free and open access to God, given by Jesus. There's no end to what has happened in you—it's beyond speech, beyond knowledge. The evidence of Christ has been clearly verified in your lives.

Amplified Bible

⁵[So] that in Him in every respect you were enriched, in full power and readiness of speech [to speak of your faith] and complete knowledge and illumination [to give you full insight into its meaning].

New Living Translation

⁵ Through him, God has enriched your church in every way—with all of your eloquent words and all of your knowledge.

Contemporary English Version

⁵who helps you speak and understand so well.

New King James Version

⁵ that you were enriched in everything by Him in all utterance and all knowledge,

Reflection

God promises that He is your redemption from sin.

1 Corinthians 1:30

New International Version

³⁰ It is because of him that you are in Christ Jesus, who has become for us wisdom from God—that is, our righteousness, holiness and redemption.

New American Standard Bible

³⁰ But by His doing you are in Christ Jesus, who became to us wisdom from God, and righteousness and sanctification, and redemption,

The Message

³⁰ Everything that we have—right thinking and right living, a clean slate and a fresh start—comes from God by way of Jesus Christ.

Amplified Bible

³⁰But it is from Him that you have your life in Christ Jesus, Whom God made our Wisdom from God, [revealed to us a knowledge of the divine plan of salvation previously hidden, manifesting itself as] our Righteousness [thus making us upright and putting us in right standing with God], and our Consecration [making us pure and holy], and our Redemption [providing our ransom from eternal penalty for sin].

New Living Translation

³⁰ God has united you with Christ Jesus. For our benefit God made him to be wisdom itself. Christ made us right with God; he made us pure and holy, and he freed us from sin.

Reflection

Contemporary English Version

[30]You are God's children. He sent Christ Jesus to save us and to make us wise, acceptable, and holy.

New King James Version

[30] But of Him you are in Christ Jesus, who became for us wisdom from God—and righteousness and sanctification and redemption—

God promises to give us life by His Spirit.

2 Corinthians 3:5-6

New International Version

[5] Not that we are competent in ourselves to claim anything for ourselves, but our competence comes from God. [6] He has made us competent as ministers of a new covenant—not of the letter but of the Spirit; for the letter kills, but the Spirit gives life.

New American Standard Bible

[5] Not that we are adequate in ourselves to consider anything as coming from ourselves, but our adequacy is from God, [6] who also made us adequate as servants of a new covenant, not of the letter but of the Spirit; for the letter kills, but the Spirit gives life.

The Message

[4-6] We couldn't be more sure of ourselves in this—that you, written by Christ himself for God, are our letter of recommendation. We wouldn't think of writing this kind of letter about ourselves. Only God can write such a letter. His letter authorizes us to help carry out this new plan of action. The plan wasn't written out with ink on paper, with pages and pages of legal footnotes, killing your spirit. It's written with Spirit on spirit, his life on our lives!

Amplified Bible

[5] Not that we are fit (qualified and sufficient in ability) of ourselves to form personal judgments or to claim or count anything as coming from us, but our power and ability and sufficiency are from God. [6] [It is He] Who has qualified us [making us to be fit and worthy and sufficient] as ministers and dispensers of a new covenant [of salvation through Christ], not [ministers] of the letter (of legally written code) but of the Spirit; for the code [of the Law] kills, but the [Holy] Spirit makes alive.

Reflection

New Living Translation

[5] It is not that we think we are qualified to do anything on our own. Our qualification comes from God. [6] He has enabled us to be ministers of his new covenant. This is a covenant not of written laws, but of the Spirit. The old written covenant ends in death; but under the new covenant, the Spirit gives life.

Contemporary English Version

[5] We don't have the right to claim that we have done anything on our own. God gives us what it takes to do all that we do. [6] He makes us worthy to be the servants of his new agreement that comes from the Holy Spirit and not from a written Law. After all, the Law brings death, but the Spirit brings life.

New King James Version

[5] Not that we are sufficient of ourselves to think of anything as being from ourselves, but our sufficiency is from God, [6] who also made us sufficient as ministers of the new covenant, not of the letter but of the Spirit;[a] for the letter kills, but the Spirit gives life.

God promises to bless you abundantly in every good work.

2 Corinthians 9:8

New International Version

[8] And God is able to bless you abundantly, so that in all things at all times, having all that you need, you will abound in every good work.

New American Standard Bible

[8] And God is able to make all grace abound to you, so that always having all sufficiency in everything, you may have an abundance for every good deed;

The Message

[8] God can pour on the blessings in astonishing ways so that you're ready for anything and everything, more than just ready to do what needs to be done.

Amplified Bible

[8] And God is able to make all grace (every favor and earthly blessing) come to you in abundance, so that you may always and under all circumstances and whatever the need be self-sufficient [possessing enough to require no aid or support and furnished in abundance for every good work and charitable donation].

New Living Translation

Contemporary English Version

[8] God can bless you with everything you need, and you will always have more than enough to do all kinds of good things for others.

New King James Version

[8] And God is able to make all grace abound toward you, that you, always having all sufficiency in all things, may have an abundance for every good work. [8] And God will generously provide all you need. Then you will always have everything you need and plenty left over to share with others.

Reflection

God promises to strengthen you when you are weak.

2 Corinthians 12:9

New International Version

⁹ But he said to me, "My grace is sufficient for you, for my power is made perfect in weakness." Therefore I will boast all the more gladly about my weaknesses, so that Christ's power may rest on me.

New American Standard Bible

⁹ And He has said to me, "My grace is sufficient for you, for power is perfected in weakness." Most gladly, therefore, I will rather boast about my weaknesses, so that the power of Christ may dwell in me.

The Message

⁷⁻¹⁰Because of the extravagance of those revelations, and so I wouldn't get a big head, I was given the gift of a handicap to keep me in constant touch with my limitations. Satan's angel did his best to get me down; what he in fact did was push me to my knees. No danger then of walking around high and mighty! At first I didn't think of it as a gift, and begged God to remove it. Three times I did that, and then he told me, My grace is enough; it's all you need. My strength comes into its own in your weakness.

Amplified Bible

⁹But He said to me, My grace (My favor and loving-kindness and mercy) is enough for you [sufficient against any danger and enables you to bear the trouble manfully]; for My strength and power are made perfect (fulfilled and completed) and [a]show themselves most effective in [your] weakness. Therefore, I will all the more gladly glory in my weaknesses and infirmities, that the strength and power of Christ (the Messiah) may rest (yes, may [b]pitch a tent over and dwell) upon me!

Reflection

New Living Translation

⁹ Each time he said, "My grace is all you need. My power works best in weakness." So now I am glad to boast about my weaknesses, so that the power of Christ can work through me.

Contemporary English Version

⁹But he replied, "My kindness is all you need. My power is strongest when you are weak." So if Christ keeps giving me his power, I will gladly brag about how weak I am.

New King James Version

⁹ And He said to me, "My grace is sufficient for you, for My strength is made perfect in weakness." Therefore most gladly I will rather boast in my infirmities, that the power of Christ may rest upon me.

God promises that He that is in you, is greater than the one in the world.

1 John 4:4

New International Version

⁴ You, dear children, are from God and have overcome them, because the one who is in you is greater than the one who is in the world.

New American Standard Bible

⁴ You are from God, little children, and have overcome them; because greater is He who is in you than he who is in the world.

The Message

⁴ My dear children, you come from God and belong to God. You have already won a big victory over those false teachers, for the Spirit in you is far stronger than anything in the world.

Amplified Bible

⁴Little children, you are of God [you belong to Him] and have [already] defeated and overcome them [the agents of the antichrist], because He Who lives in you is greater (mightier) than he who is in the world.

New Living Translation

⁴ But you belong to God, my dear children. You have already won a victory over those people, because the Spirit who lives in you is greater than the spirit who lives in the world.

Contemporary English Version

⁴Children, you belong to God, and you have defeated these enemies. God's Spirit is in you and is more powerful than the one that is in the world.

New King James Version

⁴ You are of God, little children, and have overcome them, because He who is in you is greater than he who is in the world.

Reflection

God promises to enlarge your territory.

Exodus 34:24

New International Version

²⁴ I will drive out nations before you and enlarge your territory, and no one will covet your land when you go up three times each year to appear before the LORD your God.

New American Standard Bible

²⁴ For I will drive out nations before you and enlarge your borders, and no man shall covet your land when you go up three times a year to appear before the LORD your God.

The Message

²⁴ for I will drive out the nations before you and give you plenty of land. Nobody's going to be hanging around plotting ways to get it from you.

Amplified Bible

²⁴For I will cast out the nations before you and enlarge your borders; neither shall any man desire [and molest] your land when you go up to appear before the Lord your God three times in the year.

New Living Translation

²⁴ I will drive out the other nations ahead of you and expand your territory, so no one will covet and conquer your land while you appear before the Lord your God three times each year.

Contemporary English Version

²⁴I will force the nations out of your land and enlarge your borders. Then no one will try to take your property when you come to worship me these three times each year.

Reflection

New King James Version

²⁴ For I will cast out the nations before you and enlarge your borders; neither will any man covet your land when you go up to appear before the LORD your God three times in the year.

God promises to do amazing things in your life.

Joshua 3:5-7

New International Version ⁵ Joshua told the people, "Consecrate yourselves, for tomorrow the LORD will do amazing things among you." ⁶ Joshua said to the priests, "Take up the ark of the covenant and pass on ahead of the people." So they took it up and went ahead of them. ⁷ And the LORD said to Joshua, "Today I will begin to exalt you in the eyes of all Israel, so they may know that I am with you as I was with Moses.

New American Standard Bible ⁵ Then Joshua said to the people, "Consecrate yourselves, for tomorrow the LORD will do wonders among you." ⁶ And Joshua spoke to the priests, saying, "Take up the ark of the covenant and cross over ahead of the people." So they took up the ark of the covenant and went ahead of the people. ⁷ Now the LORD said to Joshua, "This day I will begin to exalt you in the sight of all Israel, that they may know that just as I have been with Moses, I will be with you.

The Message ⁵ Then Joshua addressed the people: "Sanctify yourselves. Tomorrow God will work miracle-wonders among you." ⁶ Joshua instructed the priests, "Take up the Chest of the Covenant and step out before the people." So they took it up and processed before the people. ⁷⁻⁸ God said to Joshua, "This very day I will begin to make you great in the eyes of all Israel. They'll see for themselves that I'm with you in the same way that I was with Moses.

Amplified Bible ⁵And Joshua said to the people, Sanctify yourselves [that is, separate yourselves for a special holy purpose], for tomorrow the Lord will do wonders among you. ⁶Joshua said to the priests, Take up the ark of the covenant and pass over before the people. And they took it up and went on before the people. ⁷The

Reflection

Lord said to Joshua, This day I will begin to magnify you in the sight of all Israel, so they may know that as I was with Moses, so I will be with you.

New Living Translation [5] Then Joshua told the people, "Purify yourselves, for tomorrow the Lord will do great wonders among you." [6] In the morning Joshua said to the priests, "Lift up the Ark of the Covenant and lead the people across the river." And so they started out and went ahead of the people. [7] The Lord told Joshua, "Today I will begin to make you a great leader in the eyes of all the Israelites. They will know that I am with you, just as I was with Moses.

Contemporary English Version [5] Joshua told the people, "Make yourselves acceptable to worship the LORD, because he is going to do some amazing things for us." [6] Then Joshua turned to the priests and said, "Take the chest and cross the Jordan River ahead of us." So the priests picked up the chest by its carrying poles and went on ahead. [7] The LORD told Joshua, "Beginning today I will show the people that you are their leader, and they will know that I am helping you as I helped Moses.

New King James Version [5] And Joshua said to the people, "Sanctify yourselves, for tomorrow the LORD will do wonders among you." [6] Then Joshua spoke to the priests, saying, "Take up the ark of the covenant and cross over before the people." So they took up the ark of the covenant and went before the people. [7] And the LORD said to Joshua, "This day I will begin to exalt you in the sight of all Israel, that they may know that, as I was with Moses, so I will be with you.

God promises to lead you to safety because He delights in you.

---

2 Samuel 22:20

New International Version

[20] He brought me out into a spacious place;
he rescued me because he delighted in me.

New American Standard Bible

[20] "He also brought me forth into a broad place;
He rescued me, because He delighted in me.

The Message

[20] He stood me up on a wide-open field;
I stood there saved—surprised to be loved!

Amplified Bible

[20]He brought me forth into a large place; He delivered me because He delighted in me.

New Living Translation

[20] He led me to a place of safety;
he rescued me because he delights in me.

Contemporary English Version

[20]When I was fenced in, you freed and rescued me
because you love me.

New King James Version

[20] He also brought me out into a broad place;
He delivered me because He delighted in me.

Reflection

God promises to keep you from harm and to be free from pain.

1 Chronicles 4:10

New International Version

¹⁰ Jabez cried out to the God of Israel, "Oh, that you would bless me and enlarge my territory! Let your hand be with me, and keep me from harm so that I will be free from pain." And God granted his request.

New American Standard Bible

¹⁰ Now Jabez called on the God of Israel, saying, "Oh that You would bless me indeed and enlarge my border, and that Your hand might be with me, and that You would keep me from harm that it may not pain me!" And God granted him what he requested.

The Message

¹⁰ Jabez prayed to the God of Israel: "Bless me, O bless me! Give me land, large tracts of land. And provide your personal protection—don't let evil hurt me." God gave him what he asked.

Amplified Bible

¹⁰Jabez cried to the God of Israel, saying, Oh, that You would bless me and enlarge my border, and that Your hand might be with me, and You would keep me from evil so it might not hurt me! And God granted his request.

New Living Translation

¹⁰ He was the one who prayed to the God of Israel, "Oh, that you would bless me and expand my territory! Please be with me in all that I do, and keep me from all trouble and pain!" And God granted him his request.

Contemporary English Version

¹⁰One day he prayed to Israel's God, "Please bless me and give me a lot of land. Be with me so I will be safe from harm." And God did just what Jabez had asked.

Reflection

New King James Version

[10] And Jabez called on the God of Israel saying, "Oh, that You would bless me indeed, and enlarge my territory, that Your hand would be with me, and that You would keep me from evil, that I may not cause pain!" So God granted him what he requested.

RUDOLPH MOSELEY JR.

God promises to make your name great.

1 Chronicles 17:7-8

New International Version [7] "Now then, tell my servant David, 'This is what the LORD Almighty says: I took you from the pasture, from tending the flock, and appointed you ruler over my people Israel. [8] I have been with you wherever you have gone, and I have cut off all your enemies from before you. Now I will make your name like the names of the greatest men on earth.

New American Standard Bible [7] Now, therefore, thus shall you say to My servant David, 'Thus says the LORD of hosts, "I took you from the pasture, from following the sheep, to be leader over My people Israel. [8] I have been with you wherever you have gone, and have cut off all your enemies from before you; and I will make you a name like the name of the great ones who are in the earth.

The Message [7] "So here is what you are to tell my servant David: The God-of-theAngel-Armies has this word for you: I took you from the pasture, tagging after sheep, and made you prince over my people Israel. I was with you everywhere you went and mowed your enemies down before you; and now I'm about to make you famous, ranked with the great names on earth.

Amplified Bible [7] Now therefore, thus shall you say to My servant David, Thus says the Lord of hosts: I took you from the sheepfold, from following the sheep, that you should be prince over My people Israel. [8] And I have been with you wherever you have gone, and I have cut off all your enemies from before you, and I will make your name like the name of the great ones of the earth.

New Living Translation [7] "Now go and say to my servant David, 'This is what the Lord of Heaven's Armies has declared: I took you from tending sheep in the

Reflection

pasture and selected you to be the leader of my people Israel. [8] I have been with you wherever you have gone, and I have destroyed all your enemies before your eyes. Now I will make your name as famous as anyone who has ever lived on the earth!

Contemporary English Version [7]David, this is what I, the LORD All-Powerful, say to you. I brought you in from the fields where you took care of sheep, and I made you the leader of my people. [8]Wherever you went, I helped you and destroyed your enemies right in front of your eyes. I have made you one of the most famous people in the world.

New King James Version [7] Now therefore, thus shall you say to My servant David, 'Thus says the LORD of hosts: "I took you from the sheepfold, from following the sheep, to be ruler over My people Israel. [8] And I have been with you wherever you have gone, and have cut off all your enemies from before you, and have made you a name like the name of the great men who are on the earth.

God promises to take you to a well watered place.

Psalm 66:12

New International Version

[12] You let people ride over our heads;
we went through fire and water,
but you brought us to a place of
abundance.

New American Standard Bible

[12] You made men ride over our heads;
We went through fire and through water,
Yet You brought us out into a place of
abundance.

The Message

[12] Road-tested us inside and out, took us to
hell and back;
Finally he brought us to this well-watered
place.

Amplified Bible

[12] You caused men to ride over our heads [when
we were prostrate]; we went through fire
and through water, but You brought us out
into a broad, moist place [to abundance and
refreshment and the open air].

New Living Translation

[12] Then you put a leader over us.
We went through fire and flood,
but you brought us to a place of great
abundance.

Contemporary English Version

[12] You sent war chariots to crush our skulls. We
traveled through fire and through floods, but
you brought us to a land of plenty.

New King James Version

[12] You have caused men to ride over our heads;
We went through fire and through water;
But You brought us out to rich fulfillment.

Reflection

God promises to lead prisoners to prosperity.

Psalm 68:6

New International Version

⁶ God sets the lonely in families,
  he leads out the prisoners with singing;
  but the rebellious live in a sun-scorched land.

New American Standard Bible

⁶ God makes a home for the lonely;
  He leads out the prisoners into prosperity,
  Only the rebellious dwell in a parched land.

The Message

⁶ God makes homes for the homeless,
  leads prisoners to freedom,
  but leaves rebels to rot in hell.

Amplified Bible

⁶God places the solitary in families and gives the desolate a home in which to dwell; He leads the prisoners out to prosperity; but the rebellious dwell in a parched land.

New Living Translation

⁶ God places the lonely in families;
  he sets the prisoners free and gives them joy.
  But he makes the rebellious live in a sun-scorched land.

Contemporary English Version

⁶You find families for those who are lonely. You set prisoners free and let them prosper, but all who rebel will live in a scorching desert.

New King James Version

⁶ God sets the solitary in families;
  He brings out those who are bound into prosperity;
  But the rebellious dwell in a dry land.

Reflection

God promises to restore you to great honor.

Psalm 71:21

New International Version

²¹ You will increase my honor
and comfort me once more.

New American Standard Bible

²¹ May You increase my greatness
And turn to comfort me.

The Message

²¹ God, you've done it all! Who is quite like
you?
You, who made me stare trouble in the
face,

Amplified Bible

²¹Increase my greatness (my honor) and turn
and comfort me.

New Living Translation

²¹ You will restore me to even greater honor
and comfort me once again.

Contemporary English Version

²¹You will make me truly great
and take my sorrow away.

New King James Version

²¹ You shall increase my greatness,
And comfort me on every side

Reflection

God promises to promote when its time.

Psalm 75:6-7

New International Version

⁶ No one from the east or the west or from the desert can exalt themselves. ⁷ It is God who judges: He brings one down, he exalts another.

New American Standard Bible

⁶ For not from the east, nor from the west, Nor from the desert comes exaltation; ⁷ But God is the Judge; He puts down one and exalts another.

The Message

⁶ He's the One from east to west; from desert to mountains, he's the One. ⁷God rules: he brings this one down to his knees, pulls that one up on her feet.

Amplified Bible

⁶For not from the east nor from the west nor from the south come promotion and lifting up. ⁷But God is the Judge! He puts down one and lifts up another.

New Living Translation

⁶ For no one on earth—from east or west, or even from the wilderness—should raise a defiant fist.⁷ It is God alone who judges;he decides who will rise and who will fall.

Contemporary English Version

⁶ Our LORD and our God, victory doesn't come from the east or the west or from the desert. ⁷You are the one who judges. You can take away power and give it to others.

New King James Version

⁶ For exaltation comes neither from the east Nor from the west nor from the south. ⁷ But God is the Judge: He puts down one, And exalts another.

Reflection

God promises to give you and your children increase.

Psalm 115:14

New International Version

¹⁴ May the LORD cause you to flourish,
  both you and your children.

New American Standard Bible

¹⁴ May the LORD give you increase,
  You and your children.

The Message

¹⁴ Oh, let God enlarge your families—giving growth to you, growth to your children.

Amplified Bible (AM)

¹⁴May the Lord give you increase more and more, you and your children.

New Living Translation

¹⁴ May the Lord richly bless
  both you and your children.

Contemporary English Version

¹⁴I pray that the LORD will let your family
  and your descendants always grow strong.

New King James Version

¹⁴ May the LORD give you increase more and more,
  You and your children.

Reflection

God promises to set you free when you call on Him.

Psalm 118:5

New International Version

⁵ When hard pressed, I cried to the LORD;
    he brought me into a spacious place.

New American Standard Bible

⁵ From my distress I called upon the LORD;
    The LORD answered me and set me in a
large place.

The Message

⁵Pushed to the wall, I called to God;
    from the wide open spaces, he answered.

Amplified Bible

⁵Out of my distress I called upon the Lord;
the Lord answered me and set me free and in
a large place.

New Living Translation

⁵ In my distress I prayed to the Lord,
        and the Lord answered me and set me
free.

Contemporary English Version

⁵When I was really hurting, I prayed to the
    LORD.
        He answered my prayer, and took my
worries away.

New King James Version

⁵ I called on the LORD in distress;
        The LORD answered me and set me in a
broad place.

Reflection

God promises to multiply by the thousands.

Psalm 144:13

New International Version

¹³ Our barns will be filled with every kind of provision. Our sheep will increase by thousands, by tens of thousands in our fields;

New American Standard Bible

¹³ Let our garners be full, furnishing every kind of produce, And our flocks bring forth thousands and ten thousands in our fields;

The Message

¹³ Fill our barns with great harvest, fill our
    fields with huge flocks;
        Protect us from invasion and exile

Amplified Bible

¹³When our garners are full, affording all manner of store, and our sheep bring forth thousands and ten thousands in our pastures;

New Living Translation

¹³ May our barns be filledwith crops of every
    kind.
    May the flocks in our fields multiply by
    the thousands,
        even tens of thousands,

Contemporary English Version

¹³May our barns be filled with all kinds of
    crops.
    May our fields be covered with sheep by
the thousands,

New King James Version

¹³ That our barns may be full,
        Supplying all kinds of produce;
        That our sheep may bring forth thousands
        And ten thousands in our fields;

Reflection

God promises that if you want to be great you must be willing to serve.

Matthew 20:26-28

New International Version

²⁶ Not so with you. Instead, whoever wants to become great among you must be your servant, ²⁷ and whoever wants to be first must be your slave—²⁸ just as the Son of Man did not come to be served, but to serve, and to give his life as a ransom for many."

New American Standard Bible

²⁶ It is not this way among you, but whoever wishes to become great among you shall be your servant, ²⁷ and whoever wishes to be first among you shall be your slave; ²⁸ just as the Son of Man did not come to be served, but to serve, and to give His life a ransom for many."

The Message

²⁴⁻²⁸When the ten others heard about this, they lost their tempers, thoroughly disgusted with the two brothers. So Jesus got them together to settle things down. He said, "You've observed how godless rulers throw their weight around, how quickly a little power goes to their heads. It's not going to be that way with you. Whoever wants to be great must become a servant. Whoever wants to be first among you must be your slave. That is what the Son of Man has done: He came to serve, not be served—and then to give away his life in exchange for the many who are held hostage."

Amplified Bible

²⁶Not so shall it be among you; but whoever wishes to be great among you must be your servant, ²⁷And whoever desires to be first among you must be your slave—²⁸Just as the Son of Man came not to be waited on but to serve, and to give His life as a ransom for many [the price paid to set them free].

Reflection

New Living Translation

²⁶ But among you it will be different. Whoever wants to be a leader among you must be your servant, ²⁷ and whoever wants to be first among you must become your slave. ²⁸ For even the Son of Man came not to be served but to serve others and to give his life as a ransom for many."

Contemporary English Version

²⁶ But don't act like them. If you want to be great, you must be the servant of all the others. ²⁷And if you want to be first, you must be the slave of the rest. ²⁸The Son of Man did not come to be a slave master, but a slave who will give his life to rescue many people.

New King James Version

²⁶ Yet it shall not be so among you; but whoever desires to become great among you, let him be your servant. ²⁷ And whoever desires to be first among you, let him be your slave—²⁸ just as the Son of Man did not come to be served, but to serve, and to give His life a ransom for many."

God promises that His word will endure forever.

Isaiah 40:8

New International Version

⁸ The grass withers and the flowers fall,
  but the word of our God endures
forever."

New American Standard Bible

⁸ The grass withers, the flower fades,
  But the word of our God stands forever.

The Message

⁸ True, the grass withers and the wildflowers
  fade,
  but our God's Word stands firm and
forever."

Amplified Bible

⁸ The grass withers, the flower fades, but the
word of our God will stand forever.

New Living Translation

⁸ The grass withers and the flowers fade,
  but the word of our God stands forever."

Contemporary English Version

⁸ Flowers and grass fade away,
  but what our God has said
  will never change.

New King James Version

⁸ The grass withers, the flower fades,
  But the word of our God stands forever."

Reflection

God promises that His word will burn like a fire.

Jeremiah 23:29

New International Version

[29] "Is not my word like fire," declares the LORD, "and like a hammer that breaks a rock in pieces?

New American Standard Bible

[29] "Is not My word like fire?" declares the LORD, "and like a hammer which shatters a rock?

The Message

[29] Isn't my Message like fire?" God's Decree.
"Isn't it like a sledgehammer busting a rock?

Amplified Bible

[29] Is not My word like fire [that consumes all that cannot endure the test]? says the Lord, and like a hammer that breaks in pieces the rock [of most stubborn resistance]?

New Living Translation

[29] Does not my word burn like fire?" says the Lord. "Is it not like a mighty hammer that smashes a rock to pieces?

Contemporary English Version

[29] My words are a powerful fire; they are a hammer that shatters rocks.

New King James Version

[29] "Is not My word like a fire?" says the
LORD,
"And like a hammer that breaks the rock in pieces?

Reflection

God promises that people do not live by bread alone but by God's word.

Matthew 4:4

New International Version

⁴ Jesus answered, "It is written: 'Man shall not live on bread alone, but on every word that comes from the mouth of God.'"

New American Standard Bible

⁴ But He answered and said, "It is written, 'MAN SHALL NOT LIVE ON BREAD ALONE, BUT ON EVERY WORD THAT PROCEEDS OUT OF THE MOUTH OF GOD.'"

The Message

⁴ Jesus answered by quoting Deuteronomy: "It takes more than bread to stay alive. It takes a steady stream of words from God's mouth."

Amplified Bible

⁴ But He replied, It has been written, Man shall not live and be upheld and sustained by bread alone, but by every word that comes forth from the mouth of God.

New Living Translation

⁴ But Jesus told him, "No! The Scriptures say, 'People do not live by bread alone, but by every word that comes from the mouth of God.'"

Contemporary English Version

⁴ Jesus answered, "The Scriptures say: 'No one can live only on food.

People need every word that God has spoken.'"

New King James Version

⁴ But He answered and said, "It is written, 'Man shall not live by bread alone, but by every word that proceeds from the mouth of God.'

Reflection

God promises that His word will not wear out.

Matthew 24:35

New International Version

³⁵ Heaven and earth will pass away, but my words will never pass away.

New American Standard Bible

³⁵ Heaven and earth will pass away, but My words will not pass away.

The Message

³⁵ Sky and earth will wear out; my words won't wear out.

Amplified Bible

³⁵ Sky and earth will pass away, but My words will not pass away.

New Living Translation

³⁵ Heaven and earth will disappear, but my words will never disappear.

Contemporary English Version

³⁵ The sky and the earth won't last forever, but my words will.

New King James Version

³⁵ Heaven and earth will pass away, but My words will by no means pass away.

Reflection

God promises that the peace of Christ will keep you in tune.

Colossians 3:16

New International Version

¹⁶ Let the message of Christ dwell among you richly as you teach and admonish one another with all wisdom through psalms, hymns, and songs from the Spirit, singing to God with gratitude in your hearts.

New American Standard Bible

¹⁶ Let the word of Christ richly dwell within you, with all wisdom teaching and admonishing one another with psalms and hymns and spiritual songs, singing with thankfulness in your hearts to God.

The Message

¹⁵⁻¹⁷Let the peace of Christ keep you in tune with each other, in step with each other. None of this going off and doing your own thing. And cultivate thankfulness. Let the Word of Christ—the Message—have the run of the house. Give it plenty of room in your lives. Instruct and direct one another using good common sense. And sing, sing your hearts out to God! Let every detail in your lives—words, actions, whatever—be done in the name of the Master, Jesus, thanking God the Father every step of the way.

Amplified Bible

¹⁶Let the word [spoken by] Christ (the Messiah) have its home [in your hearts and minds] and dwell in you in [all its] richness, as you teach and admonish and train one another in all insight and intelligence and wisdom [in spiritual things, and as you sing] psalms and hymns and spiritual songs, making melody to God with [His] grace in your hearts.

Reflection

New Living Translation

[16] Let the message about Christ, in all its richness, fill your lives. Teach and counsel each other with all the wisdom he gives. Sing psalms and hymns and spiritual songs to God with thankful hearts.

Contemporary English Version

[16]Let the message about Christ completely fill your lives, while you use all your wisdom to teach and instruct each other. With thankful hearts, sing psalms, hymns, and spiritual songs to God.

New King James Version

[16] Let the word of Christ dwell in you richly in all wisdom, teaching and admonishing one another in psalms and hymns and spiritual songs, singing with grace in your hearts to the Lord.

God promises in His word that the Lord will provide.

Genesis 22:14

New International Version

¹⁴ So Abraham called that place The LORD Will Provide. And to this day it is said, "On the mountain of the LORD it will be provided."

New American Standard Bible(NASB)

¹⁴ Abraham called the name of that place The LORD Will Provide, as it is said to this day, "In the mount of the LORD it will be provided."

The Message

¹⁴ Abraham named that place God-Yireh (God-Sees-to-It). That's where we get the saying, "On the mountain of God, he sees to it."

Amplified Bible

¹⁴So Abraham called the name of that place The Lord Will Provide. And it is said to this day, On the mount of the Lord it will be provided.

New Living Translation

¹⁴ Abraham named the place Yahweh-Yireh (which means "the Lord will provide"). To this day, people still use that name as a proverb: "On the mountain of the Lord it will be provided."

Contemporary English Version

¹⁴Abraham named that place "The LORD Will Provide." And even now people say, "On the mountain of the LORD it will be provided."

New King James Version

¹⁴ And Abraham called the name of the place, The-LORD-Will-Provide; as it is said to this day, "In the Mount of the LORD it shall be provided."

Reflection

God promises that not one of His promises will ever fail.

Joshua 23:14

New International Version

[14] "Now I am about to go the way of all the earth. You know with all your heart and soul that not one of all the good promises the LORD your God gave you has failed. Every promise has been fulfilled; not one has failed.

New American Standard Bible(NASB)

[14] "Now behold, today I am going the way of all the earth, and you know in all your hearts and in all your souls that not one word of all the good words which the LORD your God spoke concerning you has failed; all have been fulfilled for you, not one of them has failed.

The Message

[14] "As you can see, I'm about to go the way we all end up going. Know this with all your heart, with everything in you, that not one detail has failed of all the good things God, your God, promised you. It has all happened. Nothing's left undone—not so much as a word.

Amplified Bible

[14]And behold, this day I am going the way of all the earth. Know in all your hearts and in all your souls that not one thing has failed of all the good things which the Lord your God promised concerning you. All have come to pass for you; not one thing of them has failed.

New Living Translation

[14] "Soon I will die, going the way of everything on earth. Deep in your hearts you know that every promise of the Lord your God has come true. Not a single one has failed!

Reflection

Contemporary English Version

[14]I will soon die, as everyone must. But deep in your hearts you know that the LORD has kept every promise he ever made to you. Not one of them has been broken.

New King James Version

[14] "Behold, this day I am going the way of all the earth. And you know in all your hearts and in all your souls that not one thing has failed of all the good things which the LORD your God spoke concerning you. All have come to pass for you; not one word of them has failed.

God promises that those who fear the Lord will spend their days in prosperity.

Psalm 25:12-13

New International Version

¹² Who, then, are those who fear the LORD? He will instruct them in the ways they should choose. ¹³ They will spend their days in prosperity, and their descendants will inherit the land.

New American Standard Bible

¹² Who is the man who fears the LORD? He will instruct him in the way he should choose. ¹³ His soul will abide in prosperity, And his descendants will inherit the land.

The Message

¹² My question: What are God-worshipers like? Your answer: Arrows aimed at God's bull's-eye. ¹³ They settle down in a promising place; Their kids inherit a prosperous farm.

Amplified Bible

¹²Who is the man who reverently fears and worships the Lord? Him shall He teach in the way that he should choose. ¹³He himself shall dwell at ease, and his offspring shall inherit the land.

New Living Translation

¹² Who are those who fear the Lord? He will show them the path they should choose. ¹³ They will live in prosperity, and their children will inherit the land.

Contemporary English Version

¹²You will show the right path to all who worship you. ¹³They will have plenty, and then their children will receive the land.

Reflection

New King James Version

¹² Who is the man that fears the LORD?
   Him shall He teach in the way He chooses.
¹³ He himself shall dwell in prosperity,
   And his descendants shall inherit the earth.

RUDOLPH MOSELEY JR.

God promises that God-seekers will lack no good thing.

Psalm 34:10

New International Version

¹⁰ The lions may grow weak and hungry,
but those who seek the LORD lack no good thing.

New American Standard Bible

¹⁰ The young lions do lack and suffer hunger;
But they who seek the LORD shall not be in want of any good thing.

The Message

¹⁰ Young lions on the prowl get hungry,
but God-seekers are full of God.

Amplified Bible

¹⁰The young lions lack food and suffer hunger, but they who seek (inquire of and require) the Lord [by right of their need and on the authority of His Word], none of them shall lack any beneficial thing.

New Living Translation

¹⁰ Even strong young lions sometimes go hungry,
but those who trust in the Lord will lack no good thing.

Contemporary English Version

¹⁰Young lions may go hungry or even starve, but if you trust the LORD, you will never miss out on anything good.

New King James Version

¹⁰ The young lions lack and suffer hunger;
But those who seek the LORD shall not lack any good thing.

Reflection

God promises to give generous gifts to His companions.

Psalm 84:11

New International Version

[11] For the LORD God is a sun and shield; the LORD bestows favor and honor; no good thing does he withhold from those whose walk is blameless.

New American Standard Bible

[11] For the LORD God is a sun and shield; The LORD gives grace and glory; No good thing does He withhold from those who walk uprightly.

The Message

[11]All sunshine and sovereign is God, generous in gifts and glory. He doesn't scrimp with his traveling companions.

Amplified Bible

[11]For the Lord God is a Sun and Shield; the Lord bestows [present] grace and favor and [future] glory (honor, splendor, and heavenly bliss)! No good thing will He withhold from those who walk uprightly.

New Living Translation

[11] For the Lord God is our sun and our shield. He gives us grace and glory. The Lord will withhold no good thing from those who do what is right.

Contemporary English Version

[11]Our LORD and our God, you are like the sun and also like a shield. You treat us with kindness and with honor, never denying any good thing to those who live right.

New King James Version

[11] For the LORD God is a sun and shield; The LORD will give grace and glory; No good thing will He withhold From those who walk uprightly.

Reflection

God promises that wealth and riches will be in the house of those who delight in His word.

Psalm 112:1-3

New International Version

¹Blessed are those who fear the LORD, who find great delight in his commands. ² Their children will be mighty in the land; the generation of the upright will be blessed.³ Wealth and riches are in their houses, and their righteousness endures forever.

New American Standard Bible

¹ Praise the LORD! How blessed is the man who fears the LORD, Who greatly delights in His commandments. ² His descendants will be mighty on earth; The generation of the upright will be blessed. ³ Wealth and riches are in his house, And his righteousness endures forever

The Message

Hallelujah! Blessed man, blessed woman, who fear God, Who cherish and relish his commandments, Their children robust on the earth, And the homes of the upright—how blessed! Their houses brim with wealth And a generosity that never runs dry.

Amplified Bible

¹PRAISE THE Lord! (Hallelujah!) Blessed (happy, fortunate, to be envied) is the man who fears (reveres and worships) the Lord, who delights greatly in His commandments.²His [spiritual] offspring shall be mighty upon earth; the generation of the upright shall be blessed. ³Prosperity and welfare are in his house, and his righteousness endures forever.

New Living Translation

How joyful are those who fear the Lord and delight in obeying his commands.² Their children will be successful everywhere; an entire generation of godly people will be blessed ³ They themselves will be wealthy,

Reflection

Contemporary English Version

¹Shout praises to the LORD! The LORD blesses everyone who worships him and gladly obeys his teachings. ²Their descendants will have great power in the land, because the LORD blesses all who do right. ³They will get rich and prosper and will always be remembered for their fairness and their good deeds will last forever.

New King James Version

¹ Praise the LORD!Blessed is the man who fears the LORD, Who delights greatly in His commandments. ² His descendants will be mighty on earth;The generation of the upright will be blessed. ³ Wealth and riches will be in his house, And his righteousness endures forever.

God promises that you will eat the good of the land.

Isaiah 1:19

New International Version

¹⁹ If you are willing and obedient,
    you will eat the good things of the land;

New American Standard Bible

¹⁹ "(A)If you consent and obey,
    You will (B)eat the best of the land;

The Message

¹⁹ If you'll willingly obey,
    you'll feast like kings.

Amplified Bible

¹⁹If you are willing and obedient, you shall eat
the good of the land;

New Living Translation

¹⁹ If you will only obey me,
    you will have plenty to eat.

Contemporary English Version

¹⁹If you willingly obey me,
    the best crops in the land
      will be yours.

New King James Version

¹⁹ If you are willing and obedient,
    You shall eat the good of the land;

Reflection

God promises provisions for those who seek Him.

Matthew 6:33

New International Version

33 But seek first his kingdom and his righteousness, and all these things will be given to you as well.

New American Standard Bible(NASB)

33 But seek first His kingdom and His righteousness, and all these things will be added to you

The Message

33 Steep your life in God-reality, God-initiative, God-provisions. Don't worry about missing out. You'll find all your everyday human concerns will be met.

Amplified Bible

33But seek (aim at and strive after) first of all His kingdom and His righteousness (His way of doing and being right), and then all these things taken together will be given you besides.

New Living Translation

33 Seek the Kingdom of God[a] above all else, and live righteously, and he will give you everything you need

Contemporary English Version

33But more than anything else, put God's work first and do what he wants. Then the other things will be yours as well.

New King James Version

33 But seek first the kingdom of God and His righteousness, and all these things shall be added to you.

Reflection

God promises to bless the faithful in this life and in the life to come.

Mark 10:29-30

New International Version [29] "Truly I tell you," Jesus replied, "no one who has left home or brothers or sisters or mother or father or children or fields for me and the gospel [30] will fail to receive a hundred times as much in this present age: homes, brothers, sisters, mothers, children and fields—along with persecutions—and in the age to come eternal life.

New American Standard Bible(NASB) [29] Jesus said, "Truly I say to you, there is no one who has left house or brothers or sisters or mother or father or children or farms, for My sake and for the gospel's sake, [30] but that he will receive a hundred times as much now in the present age, houses and brothers and sisters and mothers and children and farms, along with persecutions; and in the age to come, eternal life.

The Message [29-31]Jesus said, "Mark my words, no one who sacrifices house, brothers, sisters, mother, father, children, land—whatever—because of me and the Message will lose out. They'll get it all back, but multiplied many times in homes, brothers, sisters, mothers, children, and land—but also in troubles. And then the bonus of eternal life! This is once again the Great Reversal: Many who are first will end up last, and the last first."

Amplified Bible [29]Jesus said, Truly I tell you, there is no one who has given up and left house or brothers or sisters or mother or father or children or lands for My sake and for the Gospel's [30]Who will not receive a hundred times as much now in this time—houses and brothers and sisters and mothers and children and lands, with persecutions—and in the age to come, eternal life.

Reflection

New Living Translation [29] "Yes," Jesus replied, "and I assure you that everyone who has given up house or brothers or sisters or mother or father or children or property, for my sake and for the Good News, [30] will receive now in return a hundred times as many houses, brothers, sisters, mothers, children, and property—along with persecution. And in the world to come that person will have eternal life.

Contemporary English Version [29] Jesus told him: You can be sure that anyone who gives up home or brothers or sisters or mother or father or children or land for me and for the good news [30] will be rewarded. In this world they will be given a hundred times as many houses and brothers and sisters and mothers and children and pieces of land, though they will also be mistreated. And in the world to come, they will have eternal life.

New King James Version [29] So Jesus answered and said, "Assuredly, I say to you, there is no one who has left house or brothers or sisters or father or mother or wife or children or lands, for My sake and the gospel's, [30] who shall not receive a hundredfold now in this time—houses and brothers and sisters and mothers and children and lands, with persecutions—and in the age to come, eternal life.

God promises health in your body and strength for your spirit.

3 John 1:2

New International Version

² Dear friend, I pray that you may enjoy good health and that all may go well with you, even as your soul is getting along well.

New American Standard Bible (NASB)

² Beloved, I pray that in all respects you may prosper and be in good health, just as your soul prospers.

Amplified Bible

²Beloved, I pray that you may prosper in every way and [that your body] may keep well, even as [I know] your soul keeps well and prospers.

New Living Translation

² Dear friend, I hope all is well with you and that you are as healthy in body as you are strong in spirit.

Contemporary English Version

²dear friend, and I pray that all goes well for you. I hope that you are as strong in body, as I know you are in spirit.

New King James Version

² Beloved, I pray that you may prosper in all things and be in health, just as your soul prospers.

Reflection

Table of Promises

Anger: Psalm 145: 8, Romans 12: 19-21, Proverbs 25: 21-22

Belief: John 3:16, Mark 9:23, Acts 16: 31, John 12:46, John 6:35, Romans 9:33, John 20:29, John 6: 47, John 3:18, John 3:36

Charity: Psalm 41: 1-2, Luke 14: 13,14, Luke 12:33, Ecclesiastes 11:1, Psalm 37:26, Luke 6:38, Proverbs 28:27, 2 Corinthians 9:7

Children: Acts 16: 31, Ephesians 6: 1-3, Isaiah 54: 13, Isaiah 44:3, Psalm 127: 3-5

Comfort: Psalm 46: 1-3, Psalm 23:4, Psalm 138: 7, Psalm 18: 2, Psalm 22:24, Psalm 37:24, Nahum 1:7, Psalm 37:39, Psalm 55:22, John 16:33, Matthew 11:28, Psalm 9:9,

Courage: Psalm 27:14, Isaiah 43:1, 2 Kings 6:16, Psalm 37:3, Isaiah 40:29, Psalm 31:24, Philippians 4:12,13,

Enemies: Isaiah 54:17, Proverbs 16: 7, Job 8:22, Deuteronomy 28:7, Isaiah 54:17, Psalm 27: 5-6, Luke 18: 7, 2 Kings 17:39, Proverbs 3: 25-26, Hebrews 13: 6

Eternal Life: John 6: 47, John 3:16, 1 Corinthians 15:55, John 8:51, Psalm 49:15, Isaiah 25:8, Psalm 37:37, John 3:15, John 11: 25-26, 1 John 5: 13, Romans 8:11, Revelation 21: 4, Romans 6:23, John 14: 2-3, John 10: 27-28, John 6:54,

Faith: Hebrews 11:6, Ephesians 2:8, Hebrews 11: 1, James 1: 5-6, Mark 11:22-23

Faithfulness of God: Deuteronomy 7:9, Deuteronomy 4:31, Numbers 23:19, 2 Timothy 2:13, 2 Peter 3:9, 1 Kings 8:56, Isaiah 25:1, Psalm 9:10, 2 Corinthians 1:20, Isaiah 54:10, Isaiah 46:11

Favor: Psalm 5:12, Psalm 16:8-9, Psalm 30:7, Psalm 44:3, Psalm 56:9, Psalm 68:28, Psalm 71:16, Psalm 89:17, Psalm102:13, Psalm 103: 4-5, Proverbs 4:20-22, Proverbs 16:7, Ezekiel 36:9, Isaiah 45:13, Isaiah 50:4, Isaiah 51:16, Isaiah 58:10, John 10:10, Romans 8:32, 1 Corinthians 1:5, 1 Corinthians 1:30, 2Corinthians 3: 5-6, 2 Corinthians 9:8, 2Corinthians 12:9, 1 John 4:4

Fear: Isaiah 41:13, 2 Timothy 1: 7, Proverbs 3: 25-26, Proverbs 1: 33, Isaiah 14:3, Proverbs 3:24, Hebrews 13:6, Psalm 46:1, Proverbs 29:25, Psalm 91:4-6, Isaiah 43:2, John 14:27, Psalm 23: 4-5, Psalm 27:1-3, Romans 8: 37-39

Food and Clothing: Joel 2:26, Proverbs 13: 25, Psalm 147:14, Psalm 111:5

Forgiveness: Mark 11: 25, 26, Matthew 6: 14, Luke 6:35-38

Fruitfulness: John 15:5, Psalm 92:14, Psalm 1:3

Grace: Psalm 138:8

Guidance: Isaiah 30:21, Psalm 48: 14, Proverbs 16: 9, Psalm 37:23, Isaiah 28: 26, Proverbs 3:6, Proverbs 3:6

Guilt: 1 John 1:9, Isaiah 43:25, Isaiah 55:7, Chronicles 30:9, Psalms 103:12, 1 John 3:20, 2Corinthians 5:17, Hebrews 8:12, Jeremiah 31: 34, 1 John 1:7

Healing: Exodus 15:26, Exodus 23:25, Psalm 103: 2-5, Psalm 105:37, Psalm 107:20, Psalm 118:17, Proverbs 4: 20-22, Isaiah 40: 30-31, Isaiah 53: 4-6, Jeremiah 30:17, Jeremiah33:6, Malachi 4:2, Matthew 8: 2-3, Matthew 8:17, Matthew 9: 35, Matthew 14:36, Mark 16:17-18, Acts 10:38, Romans 8:11, James 5: 15-16, 1 Peter 2:24, 3 John: 2

Help in Troubles: Psalm 37:39, Psalm 146:8, Psalm 37: 24, Psalm 32:7, Psalm 42:11, Psalm 91:10,11, Psalm 31:23, Psalm 138:7, Psalm 34:19, Psalm 18: 2, John 16:33

Holy Spirit: Proverbs 1: 23, John 14: 16-17, John 16:13, Ezekiel 36:27, Galatians 3:14, 1 John 2:27, Romans 8:26-27, Romans 8:15, Romans 14:17

Hope: Psalm 42: 11, Psalm 31:24

Hospitality: Mark 9:41

Humility: Proverbs 15: 33, 1 Peter 5:6

Increase: Exodus 34:24, Joshua 3:5-7, 2Samuel 22:20, 1 Chronicles 4:10, 1 Chronicles 17:7-8, Psalm 66:12, Psalm 68:6, Psalm 71:21, Psalm 75:6-7, Psalm 115:14, Psalm 118:5, Psalm 144:13, Isaiah 54:2-3, Matthew 20:26-28

Joy: Psalm 126: 5-6, John 15: 10-11, Isaiah 51:11, Isaiah 61:10, Nehemiah 8:10

Long Life: Proverbs 3:1,2, Deuteronomy 6:2, Psalm 91:6, Proverbs 10:27, Proverbs 9:11

Love: John 3:16, Psalm 146:8, 1 John 4:10, 1 John 4:19, Deuteronomy 7:13

Meekness: Matthew: 5:5, Isaiah 11:4, Psalm 22:26, Psalm 149:4, 1 Peter 3:4, Psalm 37:11, Proverbs 15:1

Money: Deuteronomy 8:18, Psalm 41:1

Obedience: Deuteronomy 6:18, Philippians 4:9, James 4:7-8, Deuteronomy 6:3, Deuteronomy 7:12, Deuteronomy 29:9, Deuteronomy 5:29, Matthew 5:19, Matthew 7:24-25, Romans 8:28, John 5:24

Patience: Galatians 6:9, Romans 5:3-4

Peace: Philippians 4: 6-7, John 14:27

Prayer: Matthew 7: 7-8, Matthew 21:22, Jeremiah 29:12, Isaiah 65:24, 1John 5:14-15, John 14:13-14, John 15: 7, Matthew 6:6, Proverbs 15:29, Zechariah 13:9, Jeremiah 33:3, Mark 11:24

RUDOLPH MOSELEY JR.

Protection: Proverbs 18:10, Proverbs 3:24, Psalm 21:1, Proverbs 1:33, Psalm 91:9-10, Matthew 5: 11-12

Provision: Genesis 22:14, Joshua 23:14, Psalm 25:12-13, Psalm 34:10, Psalm 84:11, Psalm 112: 1-3, Isaiah 1:19, Matthew 6:33, Mark 10:30, 3 John 2

Repentance: Psalm 34: 18, Psalm 147:3

Righteousness: Proverbs 13:21, Psalm 5:12, 1 Timothy 4:9-10

Salvation: 2 Corinthians 5: 17, 1 John 2: 1-2, 2 Corinthians 5:21

Seeking God: Hosea 10: 12, Hebrews 11: 6, Jeremiah 29:13

Self—Denial: Luke 18: 29, 30

Sickness: Jeremiah: 17:14, Jeremiah 30:17, 1 Peter 2:24, Isaiah 53:5, James 5: 14-16, Exodus 23:25

Sin: 1 John 3:5, Matthew 26:28, Romans 6:14, Isaiah 53: 6, Ezekiel 36: 25-26, Matthew 1:21

Success: Deuteronomy 30:9, Job 22:28, Psalm 1:3, Deuteronomy 28:2-6

Trust: Psalm 46: 1-2, Psalm 37:3-5, Psalm 84:11-12, Proverbs 3:5-6, Matthew 6: 31-32, 1 Peter 5: 7, Psalm 40:4, Psalm 125:1

Victory: Genesis 28:15, Exodus 14: 13-14, Exodus 34:24, Leviticus 26:13, Deuteronomy 28: 13, Deuteronomy 33:27, Joshua 1:9, Joshua 10: 24-25, Psalm 27: 1-2, Psalm 44: 3, Psalm 55:9, Psalm, 56:9, Psalm 60:12, Psalm 66:9, Psalm 118:17, Psalm 138:7, Isaiah 41:10, Isaiah 54:17, Jeremiah 20:11, Jeremiah 39: 17-18, Zephaniah 3: 14-15, Romans 5:17, 1 Corinthians 15: 57-58, 2 Corinthians 2: 14, 2 Thessalonians 3:3, 2 Timothy 4: 17-18

Wisdom: James 1:5 Ecclesiastes 2:26

Word of God: Psalm: 119:130, Proverbs 6:23, Psalm 119:105, Isaiah 40:8, Jeremiah 23:29, Matthew 4:4, Matthew 24:35, Colossians 3:16

Work: Psalm 127: 1, Matthew 11:28

Worry: Philippians 4:19, Psalm 46: 1-2, Jeremiah 17:8, Psalm 9:9-10, Philippians 4:6-7, Psalm 91:15

Worship: Psalm 86:9, John 4: 24

CPSIA information can be obtained at www.ICGtesting.com
Printed in the USA
BVOW070328210313

316047BV00002B/9/P